John Barrow Allen

An elementary Latin grammar

John Barrow Allen

An elementary Latin grammar

ISBN/EAN: 9783337871949

Printed in Europe, USA, Canada, Australia, Japan

Cover: Foto ©Paul-Georg Meister /pixelio.de

More available books at **www.hansebooks.com**

Clarendon Press Series

AN ELEMENTARY

LATIN GRAMMAR

BY

JOHN BARROW ALLEN, M.A.

LATE SCHOLAR OF NEW COLLEGE, OXFORD
AUTHOR OF 'RUDIMENTA LATINA,' 'A FIRST LATIN EXERCISE BOOK'
AND 'A SECOND LATIN EXERCISE BOOK'

Ninety-seventh Thousand

Oxford

AT THE CLARENDON PRESS

M DCCC XCI

[*All rights reserved*]

Oxford

HORACE HART, PRINTER TO THE UNIVERSITY

PREFACE TO THE FIRST EDITION.

This Grammar is intended to give such information as is necessary for starting a learner in Latin. The troublesome nomenclature common to many School Grammars is as far as possible avoided; and a Short Catechism of Syntax takes the place of the usual Latin Rules.

In the treatment of Latin Accidence the beaten tracks pointed out by immemorial usage have been generally adhered to. The principal change is the subdivision of the Perfect into two separate Tenses, conformably to its twofold usage, (*a*) as a Present Past, (*b*) as a Simple Past. This alteration will compel every boy who meets with a Perfect to stop, if only as part of his parsing lesson, and reflect which Tense is meant. It also enables us to group the Tenses in the paradigm under the heads of Primary and Historic, a distinction important for boys to remember.

The principle of teaching by frequent repetition is adhered to throughout. A special aim of the work has been to impart a practical acquaintance with Latin Syntax by means of classified examples rather than a multitude of rules. All or nearly all the possible meanings of each Tense are given once at least with the paradigm of every Verb. To each Conjugation notes are appended explanatory of certain difficulties; among them are included short rules for the translation of the Accusative and Infinitive, and Ablative Absolute.

The Author's best thanks are due to his friends, Henry St. John Reade, Head Master of the Godolphin School, Hammersmith, and Michael Seymour Forster, Head Master of Oswestry Grammar School, who have revised the proof sheets and offered many valuable suggestions. He has also to express his obligations to many of the School Manuals now in use, to which he is indebted for hints on several points of detail. A few rules have been quoted *verbatim*, and acknowledged in their proper place.

Corrections and suggestions of improvements in the work will be thankfully received.

BIRMINGHAM, *June*, 1874.

PREFACE TO THE SECOND EDITION.

THE demand for a Second Edition has furnished an opportunity of making some alterations and additions which were much needed in the Syntax and Appendix. The book is now fitted for use in all Forms below the highest in Classical Schools, and the constant references made to higher authorities will, if attended to, prepare for the transition to Madvig, Roby, the Public Schools Latin Grammar, &c.; whilst for Middle Class Schools, where the standard of reading does not go beyond that of the University Local Examinations, no higher work will be needed.

The Author is indebted for many useful hints to J. Pryce-Jones, Esq., Grove Park School, Wrexham, and the Rev. C. G. Gepp, late Junior Student of Christ Church, Oxford; also, for a masterly and critical examination of the proof sheets, to the Rev. W. F. Moulton, D.D., Head Master of the Wesleyan School, Cambridge.

CAMBRIDGE, *December*, 1877.

CONTENTS.

	PAGE
Alphabet and Parts of Speech.	1
The Noun.	2
Substantives	3
The First Declension	3
The Second Declension	4
The Third Declension	6
The Fourth Declension	8
The Fifth Declension	9
Adjectives	9
Comparison of Adjectives	13
Pronouns	16
The Verb	18
The Verb 'Sum'	20
First Conjugation, Active Voice	26
Second Conjugation, Active Voice	30
Third Conjugation, Active Voice	34
Fourth Conjugation, Active Voice	38
First Conjugation, Passive Voice	42
Second Conjugation, Passive Voice	46
Third Conjugation, Passive Voice	50
Fourth Conjugation, Passive Voice	54
Comparative Table of the Four Conjugations	58
Conjugation of a Deponent Verb	62
Comparative Table of Tenses in Greek, Latin, French, &c.	67
Conjugation of the Anomalous Verbs	68
Interrogative Forms of the Verb	74
Notes on the Conjugations	75
Defective and other Verbs	78
Particles	81
Catechism of Syntax	84
APPENDIX—	
Table of Verbs	105
Rules of Gender	113

CONTENTS.

	PAGE
Notes on the Declensions	122
Numeral Adjectives and Adverbs	133
Table of Relative, Interrogative, and Indefinite Pronouns	137
Terminations of Derived Nouns	138
The Roman Calendar	141
Roman weights and money	143
Abbreviations	144
Explanation of Grammatical Terms	145
Laws of Quantity	149
Parsing Forms	151
Supplementary Rules and Examples	153
Conditional or Hypothetical Sentences	191
Pronunciation of Latin	192

By the same Author.

RUDIMENTA LATINA, containing Accidence and Elementary Exercises, in one volume. Second Edition. Extra fcap. 8vo. *cloth*, 2s.

A FIRST LATIN EXERCISE BOOK. Seventh Edition. Extra fcap. 8vo. *cloth*, 2s. 6d.

A SECOND LATIN EXERCISE BOOK. Second Edition. Extra fcap. 8vo. *cloth*, 3s. 6d.

OXFORD: CLARENDON PRESS.

LATIN GRAMMAR.

ALPHABET AND PARTS OF SPEECH.

§ 1. **Alphabet.** The Latin Alphabet is the same as the English, without W. For the pronunciation, see § 394.

§ 2. **Divisions of Letters.** The letters are divided into
(1) Vowels: a, e, i, o, u, y.
(2) Consonants: the remaining letters.

§ 3. **Diphthongs.** These are, ae (æ), oe (œ), and au[1].

§ 4. **Quantity of Syllables.** Syllables in Latin always have a certain *quantity*,—that is, they are either long, short, or doubtful. The sign - indicates a long, ◡ a short, and ⌣̄ a doubtful syllable.

§ 5. **Parts of Speech.** There are eight Parts of Speech, namely, the Noun-Substantive, Noun-Adjective, Pro-noun, Verb, Ad-verb, Preposition, Conjunction, and Interjection.

NOTE.—These eight Parts of Speech are sometimes put under three heads, namely—(1) The Noun, including Noun-Substantive, Noun-Adjective, and Pronoun; (2) The Verb; (3) The Particle, including Adverb, Preposition, Conjunction, and Interjection.

The Noun-Substantive is the name of any *person* or *thing*, as, magister, *a master*, mensa, *a table.*

The Noun-Adjective expresses the *quality* of a person or thing, as, bonus, *good*, albus, *white.*

---

[1] ei, eu, and ui are found as diphthongs in Interjections, as hei, heu; and in a few other words as neuter, huic, cui, etc.

The Pro-noun is used *instead of* a Substantive or Adjective, as, ille, *he;* meus, *my.*

The Verb expresses an *action*, as, amo, *I love;* or a *condition*, as, amor, *I am loved.*

The Ad-verb is *added to* a Verb or Adjective, and shews *how, when*, or *where*, as **valde** bonus, *very good;* scripsit **heri**, *he wrote yesterday;* **huc** veni, *come hither.*

The Preposition is *put before* Nouns, to shew that they are to be joined to Verbs, or sometimes to Nouns, as, venit **ad** urbem, *he comes to the city;* lupus **inter** oves, *a wolf among sheep.*

The Conjunction *joins together* words or sentences, as, Romŭlus et Remus, *Romulus and Remus.*

The Interjection is an exclamation, as, heu, *alas!*

§ 6. **The Article.** There is no Article, *a, an,* or *the,* in Latin. Thus bellum may mean *war, a war,* or *the war.*

THE NOUN.

§ 7. **Number.** There are two Numbers, the Singular, which speaks of one, as, magister, *a master;* the Plural, which speaks of more than one, as, magistri, *masters.*

§ 8. **Gender.** There are three Genders, (1) the Masculine, as, vir, *a man;* (2) the Feminine, as, mulier, *a woman;* and (3) the Neuter, as, cubile, *a bed.* Nouns which are both Masculine and Feminine are called Common, as, canis, *a dog.* But in Latin names of *things* are not all Neuter (as in English) many being Masculine, as, murus, *a wall,* and many Feminine, as, mensa, *a table.* (For the General and Special Rules of Gender, see pp. 118–121.)

§ 9. **Cases.** There are six Cases, the Nominative, Vocative, Accusative, Genitive, Dative, and Ablative. In English these Cases are distinguished by means of prepositions, as,

Genitive, *of* a man, Dative, *to* a man, Ablative, *by*, *with*, or *from* a man. But in Latin they are distinguished *by altering the last syllable*, as will be explained directly under *Stem* and *Flexion*.

§ 10. **Oblique Cases.** The Accusative, Genitive, Dative, and Ablative are called Oblique Cases.

§ 11. **Stem.** The Stem is *that part of a Noun which remains unaltered* in all the Cases and in both Numbers; as, **mūr** in mūr-us, *a wall;* mur-o, *to a wall;* mur-i, *walls;* **vall** in vall-is, *a valley;* vall-i, *to a valley;* vall-es, *valleys*.

§ 12. **Flexion.** Flexions (also called Inflexions or Terminations) are *the Syllables added to the Stem* for the purpose of distinguishing the different Cases and Numbers.

NOTE.—This will be best understood by looking at mens-a or any other Noun in the declensions that immediately follow.

§ 13. **Declension.** Declensions are *the different ways in which Nouns are declined*, that is, the different ways in which their Cases and Numbers are formed by means of adding different Flexions to the Stem.

SUBSTANTIVES.

§ 14. **The five Declensions.** Of Substantives there are five Declensions, which are known by the endings of their Genitive Case Singular. The 1st Declension has Gen. Sing. in **-ae**; the 2nd in **-i**; the 3rd in **-ĭs**; the 4th in **-ūs**; the 5th in **-ei**.

§ 15.   THE FIRST DECLENSION.

Nominative. The Nominative Case ends in -ă.

Gender. Feminine; except a few names of men, as, Publicola, *Publicola*, or designations of men, as, poeta, *a poet*, which are masculine.

	SINGULAR.	PLURAL.
Nom.	Mensă, *a table.*	Mens-ae, *tables.*
Voc.	Mens-ă, *O table.*	Mens-ae, *O tables.*
Acc.	Mens-am, *a table.*	Mens-ās, *tables.*
Gen.	Mens-ae, *of a table.*	Mens-arum, *of tables.*
Dat.	Mens-ae, *to* or *for a table.*	Mens-īs, *to* or *for tables.*
Abl.	Mens-ā, *by, with,* or *from a table.*	Mens-īs, *by, with,* or *from tables.*

§ 16.   THE SECOND DECLENSION.

Nominative.   The Nominative ends in -**ŭs, -ĕr,** and -**um.**
Gender.   -us and -er generally Masculine, -um Neuter.

	SINGULAR.	PLURAL.
Nom.	Mūrŭs, *a wall.*	Mur-i, *walls.*
Voc.	Mur-ĕ, *O wall.*	Mur-i, *O walls.*
Acc.	Mur-um, *a wall.*	Mur-ōs, *walls.*
Gen.	Mur-i, *of a wall.*	Mur-orum, *of walls.*
Dat.	Mur-o, *to* or *for a wall.*	Mur-īs, *to* or *for walls.*
Abl.	Mur-o, *by, with,* or *from a wall.*	Mur-īs, *by, with,* or *from walls.*

	SINGULAR.	PLURAL.
Nom.	Măgistĕr, *a master.*	Magistr-i, *masters.*
Voc.	Magistĕr, *O master.*	Magistr-i, *O masters*
Acc.	Magistr-um, *a master.*	Magistr-os, *masters.*
Gen.	Magistr-i, *a master's,* or *of a master.*	Magistr-orum, *of masters.*
Dat.	Magistr-o, *to* or *for a master.*	Magistr-īs, *to* or *for masters.*
Abl.	Magistr-o, *by, with,* or *from a master.*	Magistr-īs, *by, with,* or *from masters.*

Note. The Ablative of Nouns denoting a *living thing,* as, magister, puer, judex, etc., usually requires a Preposition, as, **a (ab),** *by, from,* **cum,** *with,* etc.

Some Nouns in **-er** preserve the **e** before **-r** through all the cases, instead of dropping it, as, puer, *a boy*.

	SINGULAR.	PLURAL.
Nom.	Puĕr, *a boy*.	Puer-i, *boys*.
Voc.	Puĕr, *O boy*.	Puer-i, *O boys*.
Acc.	Puer-um, *a boy*.	Puer-os, *boys*.
Gen.	Puer-i, *a boy's*, or *of a boy*.	Puer-orum, *of boys*.
Dat.	Puer-o, *to* or *for a boy*.	Puer-īs, *to* or *for boys*.
Abl.	Puer-o[1], *by*, *with*, or *from a boy*.	Puer-īs[1], *by*, *with*, or *from boys*.

Like 'puer' are declined,—gener, socer, vesper, Liber, and compounds of gero, *I carry*, and fero, *I bear*, as, armiger[2].

	SINGULAR.	PLURAL.
N.V.A.	Bellum, *war*, or *O war*.	Bell-ă, *wars*, or *O wars*.
Gen.	Bell-i, *of war*.	Bell-orum, *of wars*.
Dat.	Bell-o, *to* or *for war*.	Bell-īs, *to* or *for wars*.
Abl.	Bell-o, *by*, *with*, or *from war*.	Bell-īs, *by*, *with*, or *from wars*.

Note on Neuter Nouns. The Nominative, Accusative, and Vocative Cases of all Neuter Nouns are the same in each number, and in the Plural they always end in **-ă**.

Note on the Genitive of the Second Declension. Nouns in **-ius, -ium** often contract **-ii** into **-i** in the Genitive, as, filius, *a son*, Gen. filii *or* fili; ingenium, *ability*, Gen. ingenii, *or* ingĕni.

Note on the Vocative of the Second Declension. Filius, *a son*, and names of men ending in **-ius**, make **-i** in the Vocative; as, filius, Voc. fili, *O son;* Virgilius, *Virgil*, Voc. Virgili, *O Virgil*. Deus, *God*, has Voc. Deus (not Dee), *O God*.

---

[1] A Preposition must be used with the Latin word. See § 16, *Note*.
[2] *Son-in-law, father-in-law, evening, Bacchus, armour-bearer.*

§ 17. THE THIRD DECLENSION.

Nominative and Gender. The Nominative ends variously. The Gender is also various. (For terminations of the Nominative, and rules of Gender, see pp. 119-121.)

Divisions. Nouns of this Declension have two divisions, namely, (1) Nouns which have -um in the Genitive Plural; (2) Nouns which have -ium in the Genitive Plural.

Nouns *increasing* (i. e. having more Syllables in the Genitive than in the Nominative) make -um in the Gen. Pl.; Nouns *not increasing* make -ium. For the exceptions see p. 126.

Nouns in -um.

1. *Masculine* or *Feminine.*

	SINGULAR.	PLURAL.
N.V.	Jūdex, *a judge,* or *O judge.*	Judic-ēs, *judges,* or *O judges.*
Acc.	Judĭc-em, *a judge.*	Judic-ēs, *judges.*
Gen.	Judic-ĭs, *of a judge.*	Judic-um, *of judges.*
Dat.	Judic-i, *to* or *for a judge.*	Judic-ĭbŭs, *to* or *for judges.*
Abl.	Judic-ĕ[1], *by, with,* or *from a judge.*	Judic-ĭbŭs[1], *by, with,* or *from judges.*

	SINGULAR.			
	Law.	*Lion.*	*Flower.*	*Soldier.*
N.V.	Lex.	Leo.	Flos.	Milĕs.
Acc.	Lēg-em.	Leōn-em.	Flōr-em.	Milĭt-em.
Gen.	„ -ĭs.	„ -ĭs.	„ -ĭs.	„ -ĭs.
Dat.	„ -i.	„ -i.	„ -i.	„ -i.
Abl.	„ -ĕ.	„ -ĕ.	„ -ĕ.	„ -ĕ.
	PLURAL.			
N.V.A.	Leg-ēs.	Leōn-ēs.	Flor-ēs.	Milit-ēs.
Gen.	„ -um.	„ -um.	„ -um.	„ -um.
Dat. Abl.	„ -ĭbŭs.	„ -ĭbŭs.	„ -ĭbŭs.	„ -ĭbŭs.

[1] A Preposition must be used with the Latin word. See § 16, *Note.*

2. *Neuter.*

	SINGULAR.	PLURAL.
N.A.V.	Ŏpŭs, *a work*, or *O work*.	Oper-ă, *works*, or *O works*.
Gen.	Opĕr-ĭs, *of a work*.	Oper-um, *of works*.
Dat.	Oper-i, *to* or *for a work*.	Oper-ĭbŭs, *to* or *for works*.
Abl.	Oper-ĕ, *by, with*, or *from a work*.	Oper-ĭbŭs, *by, with*, or *from works*.

SINGULAR.

	Shore.	Song.	Head.	Journey.
N.V.A.	Lītŭs	Carmĕn.	Căpŭt.	Ĭtĕr.
Gen.	Lĭtŏr-ĭs.	Carmĭn-ĭs.	Capĭt-ĭs.	Itinĕr-ĭs.
Dat.	„ -i.	„ -i.	„ -i.	„ -i.
Abl.	„ -ĕ.	„ -ĕ.	„ -ĕ.	„ -ĕ.

PLURAL.

N.V.A.	Lĭtŏr-ă.	Carmĭn-ă.	Capĭt-ă.	Itinĕr-ă.
Gen.	„ -um.	„ -um.	„ -um.	„ -um.
Dat. Abl.	„ -ĭbŭs.	„ -ĭbŭs.	„ -ĭbŭs.	„ -ĭbŭs.

Nouns in -ium.

1. *Masculine* or *Feminine*.

	SINGULAR.	PLURAL.
N.V.	Vallĭs, *a valley*, or *O valley*.	Vall-ēs, *valleys*, or *O valleys*.
Acc.	Vall-em, *a valley*.	Vall-ēs, or -ĭs, *valleys*.
Gen.	Vall-ĭs, *of a valley*.	Vall-ium, *of valleys*.
Dat.	Vall-i, *to* or *for a valley*.	Vall-ĭbŭs, *to* or *for valleys*.
Abl.	Vall-ĕ, *by, with*, or *from a valley*.	Vall-ĭbŭs, *by, with*, or *from valleys*.

SINGULAR.	PLURAL.
N.V. Nūbēs, *a cloud*, or *O cloud*.	Nub-ēs, *clouds*, or *O clouds*.
Acc. Nub-em, *a cloud*.	Nub-ēs, or -īs, *clouds*.
Gen. Nub-ĭs, *of a cloud*.	Nub-ium, *of clouds*.
Dat. Nub-i, *to* or *for a cloud*.	Nub-ĭbŭs, *to* or *for clouds*.
Abl. Nub-ĕ, *by*, *with*, or *from a cloud*.	Nub-ĭbŭs, *by*, *with*, or *from clouds*.

2. *Neuter.*

SINGULAR.	PLURAL.
N.A.V. Mărĕ, *the sea*, or *O sea*.	Mar-iă, *seas*, or *O seas*.
Gen. Mar-ĭs, *of the sea*.	Mar-ium, *of seas*.
Dat. Mar-i, *to* or *for the sea*.	Mar-ĭbŭs, *to* or *for seas*.
Abl. Mar-i, *by*, *with*, or *from the sea*.	Mar-ĭbŭs, *by*, *with*, or *from seas*.

SINGULAR.	PLURAL.
N.A.V. Cŭbīlĕ, *a bed*, or *O bed*.	Cubil-iă, *beds*, or *O beds*.
Gen. Cubil-ĭs, *of a bed*.	Cubil-ium, *of beds*.
Dat. Cubil-i, *to* or *for a bed*.	Cubil-ĭbŭs, *to* or *for beds*.
Abl. Cubil-i, *by*, *with*, or *from a bed*.	Cubil-ĭbŭs, *by*, *with*, or *from beds*.

§ 18. THE FOURTH DECLENSION.

Nominative. The Nominative ends in -ŭs and -u.
Gender. -us generally Masculine, -u Neuter.

SINGULAR.	PLURAL.
N.V. Grădŭs, *a step*, or *O step*.	Grad-ūs, *steps*, or *O steps*.
Acc. Grad-um, *a step*.	Grad-ūs, *steps*.
Gen. Grad-ūs, *of a step*.	Grad-uum, *of steps*.
Dat. Grad-ui or -u, *to* or *for a step*.	Grad-ĭbŭs, *to* or *for steps*.
Abl. Grad-u, *by*, *with*, or *from a step*.	Grad-ĭbŭs, *by*, *with*, or *from steps*.

SINGULAR.	PLURAL.
N.A. Gĕnu, *a knee.*	Gen-uă, *knees.*
Voc. Genu, *O knee.*	Gen-uă, *O knees.*
Gen. Gen-ūs, *of a knee.*	Gen-uum, *of knees.*
D.A. Gen-u, *to, for, by, with, or from a knee.*	Gen-ĭbŭs, *to, for, by, with, or from knees.*

Note. The Dat. and Abl. Pl. of the Fourth Declension are sometimes written **-ŭbus** instead of **-ibus**, as, genŭbus.

§ 19. THE FIFTH DECLENSION.

Nominative. The Nominative ends in **-es**.

Gender. Feminine, except dies, *a day*, which is Common in the Singular, Masculine in the Plural.

SINGULAR.	PLURAL.
N.V. Diēs, *a day*, or *O day.*	Di-ēs, *days*, or *O days.*
Acc. Di-em, *a day.*	Di-ēs, *days.*
Gen. Di-ēi, *of a day.*	Di-ērum, *of days.*
Dat. Di-ei, *to* or *for a day.*	Di-ēbŭs, *to* or *for days.*
Abl. Di-ē, *by, with*, or *from a day.*	Di-ēbŭs, *by, &c., days.*

§ 20. ADJECTIVES.

Adjectives are divided into two classes, the First Class having flexions like those of the First and Second Declensions, and the Second Class like those of the Third Declension, of Nouns Substantive.

§ 21. **Adjectives of the First Class.** Adjectives of the First Class have three terminations to each Case, denoting the Masculine, Feminine, and Neuter Gender, as, bonus, bona, bonum, *good;* niger, nigra, nigrum, *black.* The Masculine and Neuter flexions are like those of the Second Declension of Substantives, the Feminine like those of the First.

	SINGULAR.			PLURAL.		
	M.	F.	N.	M.	F.	N.
Nom.	Bŏnŭs,	-ă,	-um.	Bon-i,	-ae,	-ă.
Voc.	Bon-ĕ,	-ă,	-um.			
Acc.	Bon-um,	-am,	-um.	Bon-os,	-as,	-ă.
Gen.	Bon-i,	-ae,	-i.	Bon-orum,	-arum,	-orum.
Dat.	Bon-o,	-ae,	-o.	Bon-īs (of all Genders).		
Abl.	Bon-o,	-ā,	-o.			

Note. Adjectives cannot stand alone but must always belong to some Substantive, as, bonus rex, *a good king*. When the Substantive is omitted, the word *man* must be understood with Masculine Adjectives, *woman* with Feminines, and *thing* with Neuters; as, boni, *good men;* bonă, *good things, goods*.

	SINGULAR.			PLURAL.		
	M.	F.	N.	M.	F.	N.
N.V.	Nĭgĕr,	nigr-ă,	nigr-um.	Nigr-i,	-ae,	-ă.
Acc.	Nigr-um,	-am,	-um.	Nigr-os,	-as,	-ă.
Gen.	Nigr-i,	-ae,	-i.	Nigr-orum,	-arum,	-orum.
Dat.	Nigr-o,	-ae,	-o.	Nigr-īs (of all Genders).		
Abl.	Nigr-o,	-ā,	-o.			

Note. Some Adjectives in **-er** preserve the **e** throughout, like puer, as tener, tenera, tenerum, *tender*.

	SINGULAR.			PLURAL.		
	M.	F.	N.	M.	F.	N.
N.V.	Tenĕr,	-ă,	-um.	Tener-i,	-ae,	-ă.
Acc.	Tener-um,	-am,	-um.	Tener-os,	-as,	-ă.
Gen.	Tener-i,	-ae,	-i.	Tener-orum,	-arum,	-orum.
Dat.	Tener-o,	-ae,	-o.	Tener-īs (of all Genders).		
Abl.	Tener-o,	-ā,	-o.			

Like 'tener' are declined—lacer, liber, asper, miser; compounds of gero and fero, as corniger, frugifer; and sometimes dexter[1].

---

[1] *Torn, free, rough, miserable; horn-bearing, fruit-bearing; on the right hand.*

§ 22. Adjectives of the Second Class. Adjectives of the Second Class are called Adjectives of Two Terminations, and have flexions like those of the 3rd Decl. of Substantives: as, tristis, *gloomy;* melior, *better;* felix, *happy;* ingens, *vast.*

	SINGULAR.		PLURAL.	
	M. F.	N.	M. F.	N.
N.V.	Tristĭs,	tristĕ. ⎫	Trist-ēs,	trist-ĭă.
Acc.	Trist-em,	tristĕ. ⎭		
Gen.	Trist-ĭs.		Trist-ium.	
Dat.	Trist-i.	⎫	Trist-ĭbus.	
Abl.	Trist-i.	⎭		
N.V.	Meliŏr,	meliŭs. ⎫	Melior-ēs,	melior-ă.
Acc.	Melior-em,	meliŭs. ⎭		
Gen.	Melior-ĭs.		Melior-um.	
Dat.	Melior-i.	⎫	Melior-ĭbus.	
Abl.	Melior-ĕ.	⎭		
N.V.	Felix.	⎫	Felic-ēs,	felic-ĭă.
Acc.	Felīc-em,	felix. ⎭		
Gen.	Felic-ĭs.		Felic-ium.	
Dat.	Felic-i.	⎫	Felic-ĭbus.	
Abl.	Felic-i (*rarely* -ĕ). ⎭			
N.V.	Ingens.	⎫	Ingent-ēs,	ingent-ĭă.
Acc.	Ingent-em,	ingens. ⎭		
Gen.	Ingent-ĭs.		Ingent-ium.	
Dat.	Ingent-i.	⎫	Ingent-ĭbus.	
Abl.	Ingent-ĕ (*or* -i). ⎭			

Some Adjectives in **-er** belong to this class, but have a Feminine form in the Nominative Singular, as, ācer, *keen.*

	M. F.	N.	M. F.	N.
N.V.	Acĕr, acr-ĭs,	acr-ĕ.	Acr-ēs,	acr-ĭă.
Acc.	Acr-em,	acr-e.	Acr-ōs,	acr-ĭă.
Gen.	Acr-ĭs.		Acr-ium.	
D.A.	Acr-i.		Acr-ĭbus.	

Like 'acer' are declined,—alăcer, celĕber, equester, pedester, volŭcer, salūber, celer, and a few others[1]. Celer keeps the e throughout, as, Sing. N.V. Celer, celĕris, celĕre.

§ 23. **Numeral and Quasi-Numeral Adjectives.** These for the most part make Gen. Sing. in -ius, and the Dat. in -i; as, ūnus, *one ;* ălius, *another ;* ŭter, *which of two.*

	SINGULAR.			PLURAL.		
	M.	F.	N.	M.	F.	N.
Nom.	Unŭs,	-ă,	-um.	Un-i,	-ae,	-ă.
Acc.	Un-um	-am,	-um.	Un-os,	-as,	-ă.
Gen.	Un-ĭus (of all Genders).			Un-orum,	-arum,	-orum.
Dat.	Un-i (of all Genders).			Un-īs (of all Genders).		
Abl.	Un-o,	-a,	-o.			

Nom.	Aliŭs,	-ă,	-ŭd.	Ali-i,	-ae,	-ă.
Acc.	Ali-um,	-am,	-ud.	Ali-os,	-as,	-ă.
Gen.	Alī-us (of all Genders).			Ali-orum,	-arum,	-orum.
Dat.	Alĭ-i (of all Genders).			Ali-īs (of all Genders).		
Abl.	Ali-o,	-a,	-o.			

Nom.	Utĕr,	utr-ă,	utr-um.	Utr-i,	-ae,	-ă.
Acc.	Utr-um,	-am,	-um.	Utr-os,	-as,	-ă.
Gen.	Utr-ĭus (of all Genders).			Utr-orum,	-arum,	-orum.
Dat.	Utr-i (of all Genders).			Utr-īs (of all Genders).		
Abl.	Utr-o,	-a,	-o.			

The Adjectives which make -ius in Gen. Sing. and -i in Dat. are:

Unus, solus, totus, ullus,
Uter, alter, neuter, nullus[2];

with alius, *another*, and compounds of uter, as uterque, *each of two*, the suffix -que being added to each of the cases, as, Sing. Nom. uterque, utrăque, utrumque. Those in -us are

---

[1] *Brisk, celebrated, equestrian, pedestrian, winged, healthful, swift.*

[2] *One, alone* or *the only, the whole, any at all; which of two, the other* or *one of two, neither, none.*

declined like unus, those in -er like uter. But alter keeps the e throughout, as Sing. N. alter, altĕra, altĕrum.

Unus is only used in the Plural when it agrees with a Noun which has no Singular, or which has a different meaning in the Plural from the Singular, as, una castra, *one camp*, unae litterae, *one epistle*.

The Numerals duo, *two*, and tres, *three*, are thus declined:

	PLURAL.			PLURAL.	
M.	F.	N.		M.F.	N.
Nom. Duŏ,	duae,	duŏ.		Trēs,	triă.
Acc. Du-os or duŏ,	du-as,	duŏ.		Trēs,	triă.
Gen. Du-orum,	du-arum,	du-orum.		Tr-ium.	
D.Ab. Du-ōbus,	du-ābus,	du-ōbus.		Trĭ-bus.	

Ambo, *both*, is declined like duo.

The other Cardinal Numbers, (see p. 133) from quattuor, *four*, to centum, *a hundred*, are indeclinable.

§ 24. COMPARISON OF ADJECTIVES.

Adjectives have three degrees of Comparison, the Positive, Comparative, and Superlative.

§ 25. **Rule for Comparison of Adjectives.** The Comparative is formed from the Positive by changing -i or -is of the Genitive into -ior.

The Superlative is formed from the Positive by changing -i or -is of the Genitive into -issĭmus [1], as,

Positive.	Comparative.	Superlative.
Durus, *hard*, G. duri,	durior, *harder*,	durissimus, *hardest*, or *very hard*.
Brevis, *short*, G. brevis,	brevior, *shorter*,	brevissimus, *shortest*, or *very short*.
Audax, *bold*, G. audacis,	audacior, *bolder*,	audacissimus, *boldest*, or *very bold*.

[1] Often written -issumus.

§ 26. **Exceptions.**

(*a*) *Adjectives in* **-er.** Adjectives in **-er** form their Comparatives according to the rule, but form their Superlatives from the *Nominative* Masculine Singular of the Positive by adding **-rĭmus**, as, pulcher, *beautiful*, Gen. pulchri, Comparative pulchrior, *more beautiful*, Superlative pulcherrimus, *most beautiful* or *very beautiful*.

(*b*) *Adjectives in* -**ilis**. Six Adjectives in **-ilis**, namely—

facilis, *easy*,   similis, *like*,   gracilis, *slender*,
difficilis, *difficult*,   dissimilis, *unlike*,   humilis, *lowly*,

form their Superlative by changing **-is** of the Genitive into **-lĭmus**, as, facilis, *easy*, facillimus. Other Adjectives in -ilis have commonly no Superlative.

(*c*) **-us** *preceded by a Vowel*. If a vowel comes before **-us** in the Nominative, the comparison is generally made by the Adverbs magis, *more*, and maxime, *most*, as, idoneus, *useful*, magis idoneus, *more useful*, maxime idoneus, *most useful* or *very useful*. Except when **qu** precedes, as antiquus, *ancient*, antiquior, antiquissimus.

(*d*) **-dĭcus, -fĭcus, -vŏlus.** Adjectives in **-dicus, -ficus,** and **-volus**, make **-entior, -entissimus** in the Comparative and Superlative, as, malevŏl-**us**, *spiteful*, malevol-**entior**, malevol-**entissimus**.

§ 27. **Irregular Comparison.** Many Adjectives are compared irregularly, as:

Positive.	Comparative.	Superlative.
Bonus, *good*,	melior,	optimus.
Malus, *bad*,	pejor,	pessimus.
Magnus, *great*,	major,	maximus.
Parvus, *small*,	minor,	minimus.
Multus, *much*,	plus,	plurimus.
Nequam, *worthless*,	nequior,	nequissimus.

Other irregular comparisons worthy of notice are:

Positive.	Comparative.	Superlative.
Senex, *old*,	senior,	[natu maximus].
Juvĕnis, *young*,	junior,	[natu minimus].
Dexter, *on the right*,	dexterior,	dextĭmus.
Sinister, *on the left*,	sinisterior,	sinistĭmus.
Sacer, *sacred*,	...	sacerrimus.
Surdus, *deaf*,	surdior	...

Four Adjectives derived from Prepositions have a double Superlative:

Preposition.	Positive Adjective.	Comparative.	Superlative.
Extra, *outside*,	extĕrus, *outward*,	exterior,	extrēmus *and* extĭmus.
Infra, *beneath*,	infĕrus, *low*,	inferior,	infĭmus *and* īmus.
Supra, *above*,	supĕrus, *high*,	superior,	suprēmus *and* summus.
Post, *after*,	postĕrus, *next after*,	posterior,	postrēmus *and* postŭmus.

Six Adjectives derived from Prepositions have no Positive:

Preposition.	Comparative Adj.	Superlative.
Citra, *on this side*,	citĕrior,	citimus.
De, *down from*,	detĕrior (*less good*),	deterrimus.
Intra, *within*,	intĕrior,	intimus.
Prae, *before*,	prior (*former*),	prīmus (*first*).
Prope, *near*,	propior,	proximus.
Ultra, *beyond*,	ultĕrior,	ultimus (*last*).

§ 28. **Comparison of Adverbs.** Adverbs derived from Adjectives usually make **-ius** in the Comparative, and **-issime** in the Superlative, as:

Digne, *worthily*,	dignius,	dignissime.
Gravĭter, *heavily*,	gravius,	gravissime.
Audacter, *boldly*,	audacius,	audacissime.

§ 29. **PRONOUNS.**

Pronouns are (1) Personal, (2) Reflexive, (3) Possessive, (4) Demonstrative, (5) Definitive, (6) Relative, (7) Interrogative, and (8) Indefinite. Of these the Personal and Reflexive are Substantival Pronouns, the others Adjectival.

§ 30. **Personal Pronouns.** The Personal Pronouns are ĕgó, *I*, and tū, *thou or you*, which are thus declined:

	SINGULAR.	PLURAL.
Nom.	Ego, *I*.	Nos, *we*.
Acc.	Mē, *me*.	Nos, *us*.
Gen.	Mei, *of me*.	Nostrum *or* Nostri, *of us*.
Dat.	Mĭhĭ, *to* or *for me*.	Nōbīs, *to* or *for us*.
Abl.	Mē[1], *by, with,* or *from me*.	Nōbīs[1], *by, with,* or *from us*.
N.V.	Tu, *thou or you*.	Vos, *ye or you*.
Acc.	Tē, *thee or you*.	Vos, *you*.
Gen.	Tui, *of thee or you*.	Vestrum *or* Vestri, *of you*.
Dat.	Tĭbĭ, *to* or *for thee or you*.	Vōbīs, *to* or *for you*.
Abl.	Tē[1], *by, with,* or *from thee or you*.	Vōbīs[1], *by, with,* or *from you*.

Note. **Ille, illa, illud,** and **is, ea, id,** are often used as Personal Pronouns, and translated *he, she, it.*

§ 31. **Reflexive Pronoun.** The Reflexive Pronoun is **se,** *himself, herself, itself,* or *themselves.*

Nom. (wanting).
Acc. Sē or sēsē, *himself, herself, itself,* or *themselves.*
Gen. Sui, *of himself, herself, itself, themselves.*
Dat. Sĭbĭ, *to* or *for himself, herself, itself, themselves.*
Abl. Sē[1] *or* sēsē, *by, with,* or *from himself,* etc.

§ 32. **Possessive Pronouns.** The Possessive Pronouns are **meus,** *my,* **tuus,** *thy,* **suus,** *his own, her own, its own,* or *their own,* and **cujus,** *whose,* which are declined like

---

[1] A Preposition must be used. See § 16, *Note*; and § 222.

bonus; **noster,** *our,* and **vester,** *your,* which are declined like pulcher.

Note. **Meus** has **mi** in the Vocative Singular Masculine. **Tuus** and **suus** have no Vocative.

§ 33. **Demonstrative Pronouns.** The Demonstrative Pronouns are **hic,** *this,* **is,** *that,* **ille,** *that,* **iste,** *that.*

	SINGULAR.			PLURAL.		
	M.	F.	N.	M.	F.	N.
Nom.	Hic,	haec,	hoc.	Hi,	hae,	haec.
Acc.	Hunc,	hanc,	hoc.	Hos,	has,	haec.
Gen.	Hujus (of all Genders).			Horum,	harum,	horum.
Dat.	Huic (of all Genders).			His (of all Genders).		
Abl.	Hoc,	hac,	hoc.			
Nom.	Is,	ea,	id.	Ii (ei),	eae,	ea.
Acc.	Eum,	eam,	id.	Eos,	eas,	ea.
Gen.	Ejus (of all Genders).			Eorum,	earum,	eorum.
Dat.	Ei (of all Genders).			Iis *or* eis (of all Genders).		
Abl.	Eo,	eā,	eo.			
Nom.	Ille,	illa,	illud.	Illi,	illae,	illa.
Acc.	Illum,	illam,	illud.	Illos,	illas,	illa.
Gen.	Illīus (of all Genders).			Illorum,	illarum,	illorum.
Dat.	Illi (of all Genders).			Illis (of all Genders).		
Abl.	Illo,	illā,	illo.			

Iste is declined like **ille.**

Note. **Hic** means *this near me,* or *this of mine,* **iste,** *that near you,* or *that of yours,* and **ille,** *that yonder* or *that other.*

§ 34. **Definitive Pronouns.** The Definitive Pronouns are **idem,** *the same,* and **ipse,** *self.*

	SINGULAR.			PLURAL.		
	M.	F.	N.	M.	F.	N.
N.	Īdem,	eădem,	ĭdem.	Iīdem,	eaedem,	eădem.
A.	Eundem,	eandem,	ĭdem.	Eosdem,	easdem,	eadem.
G.	Ejusdem (of all Genders).			Eorundem, earundem, eorundem.		
D.	Eīdem (of all Genders).			Eīsdem *or* Iīsdem (of all Genders).		
A.	Eodem,	eādem,	eodem.			

c

Ipse is declined like **ille**, except that it makes **ipsum** in the Neuter Nom. and Acc.

§ 35. **Relative Pronoun.** The Relative Pronoun is **qui**, *who* or *which*.

	SINGULAR.			PLURAL.		
	M.	F.	N.	M.	F.	N.
Nom.	Qui,	quae,	quod.	Qui,	quae,	quae.
Acc.	Quem,	quam,	quod.	Quos,	quas,	quae.
Gen.	Cujus (of all Genders).			Quorum,	quarum,	quorum.
Dat.	Cui (of all Genders).			Quibus *or* queis *or* quîs (of all Genders).		
Abl.	Quo, qua, quo. / Qui, qui, qui.					

§ 36. **Interrogative Pronoun.** The Interrogative Pronoun is Nom. **quis, (quis), quid,** *who?* or *what?* declined in the other cases like **qui**, except that it makes **quid** instead of **quod** in the Neuter. If it agrees with a Substantive the form is **qui, quae, quod,** declined exactly like **qui**.

§ 37. **Indefinite Pronoun.** The Indefinite Pronoun is Nom. **quis, (qua), quid,** *any,* declined in the other cases like **qui**, except that it makes **quid** instead of **quod** in the Neuter Singular, and **quă** or **quae** in the Neuter Plural. If it agrees with a Substantive the form is **qui, quae** (or **quă**), **quod,** declined exactly like the Relative **qui**, except Neuter Plural **quă** or **quae**. See also § 166.

THE VERB.

§ 38. **Voice.** Verbs have two Voices, the Active, as, amo, *I love;* the Passive, as, amor, *I am loved.*

§ 39. **Transitive and Intransitive Verbs.** Transitive Verbs are those in which the action passes on directly to some person or thing, which is called the Object, as, amo te, *I love thee.* Intransitive or Neuter Verbs are those in which the action does not pass on directly to an Object, as, sto, *I stand.* Intransitive Verbs have no Passive Voice, except in what is called the Impersonal Passive Construction, as, statur, *it is stood*, or *a stand is made*.

§ 40. **Deponents.** Deponent Verbs are Passive in form but lay aside (depono) the Passive meaning, as, hortor, *I exhort*.

§ 41. **Moods.** There are four Moods, the Indicative, Subjunctive, Imperative, and Infinitive. The first three constitute the Verb Finite, the last one the Verb Infinite.

§ 42. **Tenses.** There are Seven Tenses, four Primary, namely, the Present, Future Simple, Perfect, Future Perfect; and three Historic, namely, the Imperfect, Aorist, and Pluperfect. (For a Synopsis of Tense meanings, and comparison of the forms in Greek, French, &c., see p. 67.)

§ 43. **Number and Person.** There are in each Tense two Numbers, Singular and Plural, and in each Number three Persons, First, Second, and Third.

§ 44. **Conjugation.** Verbs have four different kinds of Flexion, which are called the Four Conjugations.

The First takes -**āre** in the Infin. Mood, as, amāre, *to love*.
The Second takes -**ēre** in the Infin. Mood, as, monēre, *to advise*.
The Third takes -**ĕre** in the Infin. Mood, as, regĕre, *to rule*.
The Fourth takes -**īre** in the Infin. Mood, as, audīre, *to hear*.

§ 45. **Principal Parts of the Verb.** The parts of the Verb from which all the other Tenses may be formed are the Present, Perfect, and Supine in **-um**. These, together with the Infinitive Mood, are to be named when the principal parts of a Verb are required, e.g.:

	Pres. Indic.	Infinitive.	Perfect Indic.	Supine.
1st Conj.	Amo,	amāre,	amāvi,	amātum.
2nd Conj.	Moneo,	monēre,	monui,	monĭtum.
3rd Conj.	Rego,	regĕre,	rexi,	rectum.
4th Conj.	Audio,	audīre,	audīvi,	audītum.

§ 46. **The Verb Sum, Esse, Fui,** *to be.* Before other Verbs are conjugated it is necessary to learn the Auxiliary Verb **sum, esse, fui,** *to be.*

§ 47. INDICATIVE MOOD.

Primary Tenses.

Present Tense.	S. sum, *I am.* ĕs, *Thou art.* est, *He is.* [See also § 61.] P. sŭmus, *We are.* estis, *Ye are.* sunt, *They are.*
Future-Simple Tense.	S. ĕro, *I shall be.* eris, *Thou wilt be.* erit, *He will be.* P. erĭmus, *We shall be.* erĭtis, *Ye will be.* erunt, *They will be.*
Perfect Tense.	S. fŭi, *I have been.* fuisti, *Thou hast been.* fuit, *He has been.* P. fuĭmus, *We have been.* fuistis, *Ye have been.* fuērunt *or* fuēre, *They have been.*
Future-Perfect Tense.	S. fŭĕro, *I shall have been.* fueris, *Thou wilt have been.* fuerit, *He will have been.* P. fuerĭmus, *We shall have been.* fuerĭtis, *Ye will have been.* fuerint, *They will have been.*

INDICATIVE MOOD (*continued*).
Historic Tenses.

IMPERFECT TENSE.	S. ĕram, *I was.* eras, *Thou wast.* erat, *He was.* P. erāmus, *We were.* eratis, *Ye were.* erant, *They were.*
AORIST TENSE.	S. fui, *I was.* fuisti, *Thou wast.* fuit, *He was.* P. fuĭmus, *We were.* fuistis, *Ye were.* fuērunt *or* fuēre, *They were.*
PLUPERFECT TENSE.	S. fŭĕram, *I had been.* fueras, *Thou hadst been.* fuerat, *He had been.* P. fuerāmus, *We had been.* fueratis, *Ye had been.* fuerant, *They had been.*

Note. The Pronoun *you* may be used to translate both the Second Person Singular, and the Second Person Plural.

SUBJUNCTIVE or CONJUNCTIVE MOOD.

Primary Tenses.

Present Tense.	S. sim, *I may be*, or *may I be*. sis, *Thou mayst be*, or *mayst thou be*. sit, *He may be*, or *may he be*. P. sīmus, *We may be*, or *may we be*. sitis, *Ye may be*, or *may ye be*. sint, *They may be*, or *may they be*.	But often translated as a Present Indicative.
Future-Simple Tense.	The Future Simple in this mood is formed by combining the Future Participle with *sim* or *essem*, as *futurus sim* or *essem*[1]. (The form *futurus essem* belongs to the Historic Tenses.) The Tense is thus declined— S. futurus sim *or* essem.[2] futurus sis *or* esses. futurus sit *or* esset. P. futuri simus *or* essēmus. futuri sitis *or* essetis. futuri sint *or* essent.	
Perfect Tense.	S. fŭĕrim, *I may have been*. fueris, *Thou mayst have been*. fuerit, *He may have been*. P. fuerĭmus, *We may have been*. fueritis, *Ye may have been*. fuerint, *They may have been*.	But often translated as a Perfect or Aorist Indicative.

---

[1] Or, more properly, futur-us, -ă, -um sim or essem. See § 61.

[2] No English translation which will be of any use to the learner can be given for this Tense. Where it occurs in Latin it is translated either by a Simple Future Indicative, as, incertum est an in urbe futurus sit, *it is uncertain whether he will be in the city*, or by *would*, as, incertum erat an in urbe futurus esset, *it was uncertain whether he would be in the city*.

SUBJUNCTIVE MOOD (*continued*).
Historic Tenses.

Imperfect Tense.	S. essem,[1] *I should* or *might be.* esses, *Thou wouldst* or *mightst be.* esset, *He would* or *might be.* P. essēmus, *We should* or *might be.* essētis, *Ye would* or *might be.* essent, *They would* or *might be.*	But often translated as an Imperfect or Aorist Indicative.
Aorist Tense.	Rendered variously by *fuerim, essem,* and *fuissem.* See §§ 205, 206.	
Pluperfect Tense.	S. fŭissem, *I should* or *might* fuisses, *Thou wouldst* or *mightst* fuisset, *He would* or *might* P. fuissēmus, *We should* or *might* fuissētis, *Ye would* or *might* fuissent, *They would* or *might* } *have been.*	But often translated as a Pluperfect Indicative.

---

[1] Another form of the Imperfect is fŏrem, fores, foret, foremus, foretis, forent.

IMPERATIVE MOOD.

Present Tense.	*Sing.* 2 Pers. es, *be thou*, esto, *thou must be.* 3 Pers. esto, *he must be.* *Plur.* 2 Pers. este, *be ye*, estōte, *ye must be.* 3 Pers. sunto, *they must be.*

Note 1. The forms esto, esto, estote, sunto, are sometimes reckoned as Future Imperatives.

Note 2. The Present Subjunctive is often used in a Present Imperative sense, as, sim, *let me be,* sis, *be thou,* sit, *let him be,* &c.

VERB INFINITE.

Infinitive Mood.	Present and Imperfect,	esse, *to be.*
	Perfect and Pluperfect,	fŭisse, *to have been.*
	Future,	fŏre *or* fŭtūrus esse, *to be about to be.*
Participle.	Future,	fŭtūrus, *about to be.*

§ 47.] THE AUXILIARY VERB 'SUM.' 25

Compounds of **Sum.** Like sum are declined its compounds,

absum, *I am absent.*
adsum, *I am present.*
desum, *I am wanting.*
insum, *I am in.*
intersum, *I am present.*

obsum, *I am in the way.*
praesum, *I am set over.*
prosum, *I am of use.*
subsum, *I am under.*
supersum, *I am surviving.*

Subsum wants the Perfect, and tenses derived from it. Prosum inserts *d* before *e*, as Ind. Pres. prosum, pro*d*es, pro*d*est, pros*ŭ*mus, pro*d*estis, prosunt. Possum [for potis sum], *to be able*, will be fully conjugated hereafter (see p. 68). Absum and praesum alone have Present Participles, absens and praesens.

EXAMPLES.

INDICATIVE MOOD.

	Present.	*Perfect.*	*Imperfect.*
S.	ab-sum.	de-fui.	in-ĕram.
	ab-es.	de-fuisti.	in-eras.
	ab-est.	de-fuit.	in-erat.
P.	ab-sŭmus.	de-fuimus.	in-erāmus.
	ab-estis.	de-fuistis.	in-eratis.
	ab-sunt.	de-fuēr-unt, *or* -ēre.	in-erant.

SUBJUNCTIVE MOOD.

S.	ob-sim.	prae-fuerim.	pro*d*-essem.
	ob-sis.	prae-fueris.	pro*d*-esses.
	ob-sit.	prae-fuerit.	pro*d*-esset.
P.	ob-sīmus.	prae-fuerimus.	pro*d*-essēmus.
	ob-sitis.	prae-fuerĭtis.	pro*d*-essetis.
	ob-sint.	prae-fuerint.	pro*d*-essent.

§ 48. First Conjugation. Active Voice.

INDICATIVE MOOD.

Primary Tenses.

Present Tense.	S. ăm-o, *I love, am loving,* or *do love.* am-as, *Thou lovest, art loving,* or *dost love.* am-at, *He loves, is loving,* or *does love.* P. am-āmus, *We love, are loving,* or *do love.* am-atis, *Ye love, are loving,* or *do love.* am-ant, *They love, are loving,* or *do love.*
Future-Simple Tense.	S. am-ābo, *I shall love.* am-abis, *Thou wilt love.* am-abit, *He will love.* P. am-abĭmus, *We shall love.* am-abĭtis, *Ye will love.* am-abunt, *They will love.*
Perfect Tense.	S. amāv-i, *I have loved.* amav-isti, *Thou hast loved.* amav-it, *He has loved.* P. amav-ĭmus, *We have loved.* amav-istis, *Ye have loved.* amav-ērunt *or* -ēre, *They have loved.*
Future-Perfect Tense.	S. amāv-ĕro, *I shall have loved.* amav-eris, *Thou wilt have loved.* amav-erit, *He will have loved.* P. amav-erĭmus, *We shall have loved.* amav-erĭtis, *Ye will have loved.* amav-erint, *They will have loved.*

INDICATIVE MOOD (*continued*).
Historic Tenses.

Imperfect Tense.	S. am-ābam, *I was loving*, or *I loved*.[1] am-abas, *Thou wast loving*, or *thou lovedst*. am-abat, *He was loving*, or *he loved*. P. am-abāmus, *We were loving*, etc. am-abatis, *Ye were loving*. am-abant, *They were loving*.
Aorist Tense.	S. amāv-i, *I loved*, or *did love*. amav-isti, *Thou lovedst*, or *didst love*. amav-it, *He loved*, or *did love*. P. amav-ĭmus, *We loved*, etc. amav-istis, *Ye loved*. amav-ērunt *or* -ēre, *They loved*.
Pluperfect Tense.	S. amāv-ĕram, *I had loved*. amav-eras, *Thou hadst loved*. amav-erat, *He had loved*. P. amav-erāmus, *We had loved*. amav-eratis, *Ye had loved*. amav-erant, *They had loved*.

[1] See also § 64.

SUBJUNCTIVE or CONJUNCTIVE MOOD.
Primary Tenses.

Present Tense.	S. am-em, *I may love,* or *may I love.* am-es, *Thou mayst love,* etc. am-et, *He may love.* P. am-ēmus, *We may love.* am-etis, *Ye may love.* am-ent, *They may love.*	But often translated as a Present Indicative.
Perfect Tense.	S. amav-ĕrim, *I may* amav-eris, *Thou mayst* amav-erit, *He may* P. amav-erĭmus, *We may* amav-erĭtis, *Ye may* amav-erint, *They may* *have loved.*	But often translated as a Perfect or Aorist Indicative.

Historic Tenses.

Imperfect Tense.	S. am-ārem, *I should* or *might love.* am-ares, *Thou wouldst love,* etc. am-aret, *He would love.* P. am-arēmus, *We should love.* am-aretis, *Ye would love.* am-arent, *They would love.*	But often translated as an Imperfect or Aorist Indicative.
Pluperfect Tense.	S. amav-issem, *I* amav-isses, *Thou* amav-isset, *He* P. amav-issēmus, *We* amav-issetis, *Ye* amav-issent, *They* *should or might have loved.*	But often translated as a Pluperfect Indicative.

Future Simple Tense. The Future Simple in this Mood is formed by combining the Future Participle with *sim* or *essem*, as *amaturus sim* or *essem*. The form with *sim* belongs to the Primary Tenses, the form with *essem* to the Historic.

Aorist Tense. The Aorist Subjunctive is rendered variously by *amaverim, amarem,* and *amavissem.* See §§ 205, 206.

IMPERATIVE MOOD.

PRESENT TENSE.	S.	2 Pers.	am-ā, *love thou,*	am-āto, *thou must love.*
		3 Pers.		am-āto, *he must love.*
	P.	2 Pers.	am-āte, *love ye,*	am-ātōte, *ye must love*
		3 Pers.		am-anto, *they must love.*

Note 1. The forms amato, amato, amatote, amanto are sometimes reckoned as Future Imperatives.

Note 2. The Present Subjunctive is often used in a Present Imperative sense, as, amem, *let me love,* ames, *love thou,* amet, *let him love,* &c.

VERB INFINITE.

Infinitive Mood.	{	PRESENT AND IMPERFECT,	ăm-āre, *to love* (or *loving,* in the sense of 'the act of loving.')
		PERFECT AND PLUPERFECT,	amāv-isse, *to have loved.*
		FUTURE,	amātūrus esse, *to be about to love.*
Gerunds.	{	ACCUSATIVE,	am-andum, *loving.*
		GENITIVE,	am-andi, *of loving.*
		DAT. ABL.,	am-ando, *for* or *by loving.*
Supines.	{	in -um	am-ātum, *in order to love.*
		in -u	am-ātu, *in loving.*
Participles.	{	PRESENT,	am-ans, *loving* (declined like ingens).
		PERFECT,	(wanting, see § 302.)
		FUTURE,	am-ātūrus, *about to love.*

§ 49. Second Conjugation. Active Voice.

INDICATIVE MOOD.

Primary Tenses.

Present Tense.	S.	mŏn-eo, *I advise, am advising*, or *do advise.* mon-es, *Thou advisest, art advising*, or *dost advise.* mon-et, *He advises*, etc.
	P.	mon-ēmus, *We advise.* mon-etis, *Ye advise.* mon-ent, *They advise.*
Future-Simple Tense.	S.	mon-ēbo, *I shall advise.* mon-ebis, *Thou wilt advise.* mon-ebit, *He will advise.*
	P.	mon-ebĭmus, *We shall advise.* mon-ebitis, *Ye will advise.* mon-ebunt, *They will advise.*
Perfect Tense.	S.	monŭ-i, *I have advised.* monu-isti, *Thou hast advised.* monu-it, *He has advised.*
	P.	monu-ĭmus, *We have advised.* monu-istis, *Ye have advised.* monu-ērunt *or* -ēre, *They have advised.*
Future-Perfect Tense.	S.	monŭ-ĕro, *I shall have advised.* monu-eris, *Thou wilt have advised.* monu-erit, *He will have advised.*
	P.	monu-erĭmus, *We shall have advised.* monu-erĭtis, *Ye will have advised.* monu-erint, *They will have advised.*

INDICATIVE MOOD (*continued*).

Historic Tenses.

Imperfect Tense.	*S.* mon-ēbam, *I was advising* or *I advised.* mon-ebas, *Thou wast advising,* etc. mon-ebat, *He was advising.* *P.* mon-ebāmus, *We were advising.* mon-ebatis, *Ye were advising.* mon-ebant, *They were advising.*
Aorist Tense.	*S.* monŭ-i, *I advised* or *did advise.* monu-isti, *Thou advisedst,* etc. monu-it, *He advised.* *P.* monu-ĭmus, *We advised.* monu-istis, *Ye advised.* monu-ērunt *or* -ēre, *They advised.*
Pluperfect Tense.	*S.* monŭ-ĕram, *I had advised.* monu-eras, *Thou hadst advised.* monu-erat, *He had advised.* *P.* monu-erāmus, *We had advised.* monu-eratis, *Ye had advised.* monu-erant, *They had advised.*

SUBJUNCTIVE or CONJUNCTIVE MOOD.
Primary Tenses.

Present Tense.	S. mon-ĕam, *I may advise* or *may I advise.* mon-eas, *Thou mayst advise,* etc. mon-eat, *He may advise.* P. mon-eāmus, *We may advise.* mon-eatis, *Ye may advise.* mon-eant, *They may advise.*
Perfect Tense.	S. monŭ-ĕrim, *I may have advised.* monu-eris, *Thou mayst have advised.* monu-erit, *He may have advised.* P. monu-erĭmus, *We may have advised.* monu-erĭtis, *Ye may have advised.* monu-erint, *They may have advised.*

Historic Tenses.

Imperfect Tense.	S. mon-ērem, *I should* or *might advise.* mon-eres, *Thou wouldst advise,* etc. mon-eret, *He would advise.* P. mon-erēmus, *We should advise.* mon-eretis, *Ye would advise.* mon-erent, *They would advise.*
Pluperfect Tense.	S. monŭ-issem, *I should* or *might have advised.* monu-isses, *Thou wouldst have advised,* etc. monu-isset, *He would have advised.* P. monu-issēmus, *We should have advised.* monu-issetis, *Ye would have advised.* monu-issent, *They would have advised.*

Future Simple Tense. The Future Simple in this Mood is formed by combining the Future Participle with *sim* or *essem,* as *moniturus sim* or *essem.* The form with *sim* belongs to the Primary Tenses, the form with *essem* to the Historic.

Aorist Tense. The Aorist Subjunctive is rendered variously by *monuerim, monērem,* and *monuissem.* See §§ 205, 206.

IMPERATIVE MOOD.

Present Tense.

S. 2 Pers. mon-ē, *advise thou*, mon-ēto, *thou must advise*.
3 Pers. mon-ēto, *he must advise*.
P. 2 Pers. mon-ēte, *advise ye*, mon-ētōte, *ye must advise*.
3 Pers. mon-ento, *they must advise*.

Note 1. The forms moneto, moneto, monetote, monento are sometimes reckoned as Future Imperatives.

Note 2. The Present Subjunctive is often used in a Present Imperative sense, as, moneam, *let me advise*, moneas, *advise thou*, moneat, *let him advise*, etc.

VERB INFINITE.

Infinitive Mood.	Present and Imperfect,	mon-ēre, *to advise* (or *advising* in the sense of 'the act of advising').
	Perfect and Pluperfect,	monŭ-isse, *to have advised*.
	Future,	mon-ĭtūrus esse, *to be about to advise*.
Gerunds.	Accusative,	mon-endum, *advising*.
	Genitive,	mon-endi, *of advising*.
	Dat. Abl.,	mon-endo, *for* or *by advising*.
Supines.	in -um	mon-ĭtum, *in order to advise*.
	in -u	mon-ĭtu, *in advising*.
Participles.	Present,	mon-ens, *advising* (declined like ingens).
	Perfect,	(wanting, see § 302).
	Future,	mon-ĭtūrus, *about to advise*.

§ 50. Third Conjugation. Active Voice.

INDICATIVE MOOD.

Primary Tenses.

Present Tense.	S. rĕg-o, *I rule, am ruling,* or *do rule.* reg-is, *Thou rulest, art ruling,* or *dost rule.* reg-it, *He rules, is ruling,* or *does rule.* P. reg-ĭmus, *We rule, are ruling,* or *do rule.* reg-itis, *Ye rule, are ruling,* or *do rule.* reg-unt, *They rule, are ruling,* or *do rule.*
Future-Simple Tense.	S. reg-am, *I shall rule.* reg-es, *Thou wilt rule.* reg-et, *He will rule.* P. reg-ēmus, *We shall rule.* reg-etis, *Ye will rule.* reg-ent, *They will rule.*
Perfect Tense.	S. rex-i, *I have ruled.* rex-isti, *Thou hast ruled.* rex-it, *He has ruled.* P. rex-ĭmus, *We have ruled.* rex-istis, *Ye have ruled.* rex-ērunt *or* -ēre, *They have ruled.*
Future-Perfect Tense.	S. rex-ĕro, *I shall have ruled.* rex-eris, *Thou wilt have ruled.* rex-erit, *He will have ruled.* P. rex-erĭmus, *We shall have ruled.* rex-erĭtis, *Ye will have ruled.* rex-erint, *They will have ruled.*

INDICATIVE MOOD (*continued*).
Historic Tenses.

Imperfect Tense.	S. reg-ēbam, *I was ruling*, or *I ruled*. reg-ebas, *Thou wast ruling*, etc. reg-ebat, *He was ruling*. P. reg-ebāmus, *We were ruling*. reg-ebatis, *Ye were ruling*. reg-ebant, *They were ruling*.
Aorist Tense.	S. rex-i, *I ruled* or *did rule*. rex-isti, *Thou ruledst*, etc. rex-it, *He ruled*. P. rex-ĭmus, *We ruled*. rex-istis, *Ye ruled*. rex-ērunt *or* -ēre, *They ruled*.
Pluperfect Tense.	S. rex-ĕram, *I had ruled*. rex-eras, *Thou hadst ruled*. rex-erat, *He had ruled*. P. rex-erāmus, *We had ruled*. rex-eratis, *Ye had ruled*. rex-erant, *They had ruled*.

Note on verbs in -io. Certain Verbs of the Third Conjugation end in -io in the First Person Present Indicative, as capio, *I take*, facio, *I make*, fugio, *I fly*, etc. These retain the i except before i, final e, and short er, as Pres. Indic. fugi-o, fug-is, fug-it, fug-ĭmus, fug-ĭtis, fugi-unt; Future Indic. fugi-am; Pres. Imperative, fug-e; Imperf. Subj. fugĕrem; Present Infinitive, fug-ĕre.

SUBJUNCTIVE or CONJUNCTIVE MOOD.
Primary Tenses.

Present Tense.	S. reg-am, *I may rule,* or *may I rule.* reg-as, *Thou mayst rule,* or *mayst thou rule.* reg-at, *He may rule,* or *may he rule.* P. reg-āmus, *We may rule,* or *may we rule* reg-atis, *Ye may rule,* or *may ye rule.* reg-ant, *They may rule,* or *may they rule.*
Perfect Tense.	S. rex-ĕrim, *I may have ruled.* rex-eris, *Thou mayst have ruled.* rex-erit, *He may have ruled.* P. rex-erĭmus, *We may have ruled.* rex-erĭtis, *Ye may have ruled.* rex-erint, *They may have ruled.*

Historic Tenses.

Imperfect Tense.	S. reg-ĕrem, *I should* or *might rule.* reg-eres, *Thou wouldst rule,* etc. reg-eret, *He would rule.* P. reg-erēmus, *We should rule.* reg-eretis, *Ye would rule.* reg-erent, *They would rule.*
Pluperfect Tense.	S. rex-issem, *I should* or *might have ruled.* rex-isses, *Thou wouldst have ruled,* etc. rex-isset, *He would have ruled.* P. rex-issēmus, *We should have ruled.* rex-issetis, *Ye would have ruled.* rex-issent, *They would have ruled.*

Future Simple Tense. The Future Simple in this Mood is formed by combining the Future Participle with *sim* or *essem*, as *recturus sim* or *essem*. The form with *sim* belongs to the Primary Tenses, the form with *essem* to the Historic.

Aorist Tense. The Aorist Subjunctive is rendered variously by *rexĕrim, regĕrem,* and *rexissem.* See §§ 205, 206.

IMPERATIVE MOOD.

Present Tense.	S. 2 Pers. reg-ĕ, *rule thou*, reg-ĭto, *thou must rule.* 3 Pers. reg-ĭto, *he must rule.* P. 2 Pers. reg-ĭte, *rule ye*, reg-ĭtōte, *ye must rule.* 3 Pers. reg-unto, *they must rule.*

Note 1. The forms regito, regito, regitote, regunto are sometimes reckoned as Future Imperatives.

Note 2. The Present Subjunctive is often used in a Present Imperative sense, as regam, *let me rule*, regas, *rule thou*, regat, *let him rule*, etc.

VERB INFINITE.

Infinitive Mood.	Present and Imperfect,	reg-ĕre, *to rule* (or *ruling*, in the sense of 'the act of ruling').
	Perfect and Pluperfect,	rex-isse, *to have ruled.*
	Future,	rect-ūrus esse, *to be about to rule.*
Gerunds.	Accusative,	reg-endum, *ruling.*
	Genitive,	reg-endi, *of ruling.*
	Dat. Abl.	reg-endo, *for* or *by ruling.*
Supines.	in -um	rect-um, *in order to rule.*
	in -u	rect-u, *in ruling.*
Participles.	Present,	reg-ens, *ruling* (declined like ingens).
	Perfect,	(wanting, see § 302.)
	Future,	rect-ūrus, *about to rule.*

§ 51. Fourth Conjugation. Active Voice.

INDICATIVE MOOD.
Primary Tenses.

Present Tense.	S. aud-ĭo, *I hear, am hearing,* or *do hear.* aud-is, *Thou hearest, art hearing,* or *dost* [*hear.* aud-it, *He hears,* etc. P. aud-īmus, *We hear.* aud-itis, *Ye hear.* aud-iunt, *They hear.*
Future-Simple Tense.	S. aud-ĭam, *I shall hear.* aud-ies, *Thou will hear.* aud-iet, *He will hear.* P. aud-iēmus, *We shall hear.* aud-ietis, *Ye will hear.* aud-ient, *They will hear.*
Perfect Tense.	S. audīv-i, *I have heard.* audiv-isti, *Thou hast heard.* audiv-it, *He has heard.* P. audiv-ĭmus, *We have heard.* audiv-istis, *Ye have heard.* audiv-ērunt *or* -ēre, *They have heard.*
Future-Perfect Tense.	S. audīv-ĕro, *I shall have heard.* audiv-eris, *Thou will have heard.* audiv-erit, *He will have heard.* P. audiv-erĭmus, *We shall have heard.* audiv-erĭtis, *Ye will have heard.* audiv-erint, *They will have heard.*

INDICATIVE MOOD (*continued*).
Historic Tenses.

Imperfect Tense.	S. aud-iēbam, *I was hearing,* or *I heard.* aud-iebas, *Thou wast hearing,* etc. aud-iebat, *He was hearing.* P. aud-iebāmus, *We were hearing.* aud-iebatis, *Ye were hearing.* aud-iebant, *They were hearing.*
Aorist Tense.	S. audīv-i, *I heard* or *did hear.* audiv-isti, *Thou heardest,* etc. audiv-it, *He heard.* P. audiv-ĭmus, *We heard.* audiv-istis, *Ye heard.* audiv-ērunt *or* -ēre, *They heard.*
Pluperfect Tense.	S. audīv-ĕram, *I had heard.* audiv-eras, *Thou hadst heard.* audiv-erat, *He had heard.* P. audiv-erāmus, *We had heard.* audiv-eratis, *Ye had heard.* audiv-erant, *They had heard.*

	SUBJUNCTIVE or CONJUNCTIVE MOOD. Primary Tenses.
Present Tense.	S. aud-iam, *I may hear*, or *may I hear*. aud-ias, *Thou mayst hear*, or *mayst thou hear*. aud-iat, *He may hear*, or *may he hear*. P. aud-iāmus, *We may hear*, or *may we hear*. aud-iatis, *Ye may hear*, or *may ye hear*. aud-iant, *They may hear*, or *may they hear*.
Perfect Tense.	S. audīv-ĕrim, *I may have heard*. audiv-eris, *Thou mayst have heard*. audiv-erit, *He may have heard*. P. audiv-erĭmus, *We may have heard*. audiv-erĭtis, *Ye may have heard*. audiv-erint, *They may have heard*.
	Historic Tenses.
Imperfect Tense.	S. aud-īrem, *I should* or *might hear*. aud-ires, *Thou shouldst hear*, etc. aud-iret, *He would hear*. P. aud-irēmus, *We should hear*. aud-iretis, *Ye would hear*. aud-irent, *They would hear*.
Pluperfect Tense.	S. audiv-issem, *I should* or *might have heard*. audiv-isses, *Thou wouldst have heard*, etc. audiv-isset, *He would have heard*. P. audiv-issēmus, *We should have heard*. audiv-issetis, *Ye would have heard*. audiv-issent, *They would have heard*.

Future Simple Tense. The Future Simple in this Mood is formed by combining the Future Participle with *sim* or *essem*, as *auditurus sim* or *essem*. The form with *sim* belongs to the Primary Tenses, the form with *essem* to the Historic.

Aorist Tense. The Aorist Subjunctive is rendered variously by *audivĕrim, audirem,* and *audivissem.* See §§ 205, 206.

IMPERATIVE MOOD.

Present Tense.

S.	2 Pers. aud-i, *hear thou*,	aud-īto, *thou must hear*.
	3 Pers.	aud-īto, *he must hear*.
P.	2 Pers. aud-īte, *hear ye*,	aud-ītōte, *ye must hear*.
	3 Pers.	aud-iunto, *they must hear*.

Note 1. The forms audito, audito, auditote, audiunto are sometimes reckoned as Future Imperatives.

Note 2. The Present Subjunctive is often used in a Present Imperative sense, as, audiam, *let me hear*, audias, *hear thou*, audiat, *let him hear*, etc.

VERB INFINITE.

Infinitive Mood.
- Present and Imperfect, aud-īre, *to hear* (or *hearing* in the sense of 'the act of hearing').
- Perfect and Pluperfect, audīv-isse, *to have heard*.
- Future, audītūrus esse, *to be about to hear*.

Gerunds.
- Accusative, aud-iendum, *hearing*.
- Genitive, aud-iendi, *of hearing*.
- Dat. Abl., aud-iendo, *for* or *by hearing*.

Supines.
- in -um, aud-ītum, *in order to hear*.
- in -u, aud-ītu, *in hearing*.

Participles.
- Present, aud-iens, *hearing* (declined like ingens).
- Perfect, (wanting, see § 302.)
- Future, aud-ītūrus, *about to hear*.

§ 52. First Conjugation. Passive Voice.

INDICATIVE MOOD.
Primary Tenses.

Present Tense.
S. am-or, *I am loved* or *am being loved.*
am-āris *or* -ārĕ, *Thou art loved,* etc.
am-atur, *He is loved.*
P. am-amur, *We are loved.*
am-amĭni, *Ye are loved.*
am-antur, *They are loved.*

Future-Simple Tense.
S. am-ābor, *I shall be loved.*
am-abĕris *or* -abĕre, *Thou will be loved.*
am-abĭtur, *He will be loved.*
P. am-abĭmur, *We shall be loved.*
am-abĭmĭni, *Ye will be loved.*
am-abuntur, *They will be loved.*

Perfect Tense.
S. am-ātus sum[1], *I have been loved.*
am-atus es, *Thou hast been loved.*
am-atus est, *He has been loved.*
P. am-ati sŭmus, *We have been loved.*
am-ati estis, *Ye have been loved.*
am-ati sunt, *They have been loved.*

Future-Perfect Tense.
S. am-atus ĕro[2], *I shall have been loved.*
am-atus eris, *Thou will have been loved.*
am-atus erit, *He will have been loved.*
P. am-ati erĭmus, *We shall have been loved.*
am-ati erĭtis, *Ye will have been loved.*
am-ati erunt, *They will have been loved.*

---

[1] *or* fui, etc.   [2] *or* fuĕro, etc.

INDICATIVE MOOD (*continued*).
Historic Tenses.

Imperfect Tense.	*S.* am-ābar, *I was being loved,* or *I was loved.* am-abāris *or* -abāre, *Thou wast being loved,* am-abatur, *He was being loved.* [etc. *P.* am-abamur, *We were being loved.* am-abamĭni, *Ye were being loved.* am-abantur, *They were being loved.*
Aorist Tense.	*S.* am-atus sum[1], *I was loved.* am-atus es, *Thou wast loved.* am-atus est, *He was loved.* *P.* am-ati sŭmus, *We were loved.* am-ati estis, *Ye were loved.* am-ati sunt, *They were loved.*
Pluperfect Tense.	*S.* am-atus ĕram[2], *I had been loved.* am-atus eras, *Thou hadst been loved.* am-atus erat, *He had been loved.* *P.* am-ati erāmus, *We had been loved.* am-ati eratis, *Ye had been loved.* am-ati erant, *They had been loved.*

[1] *or* fui, etc.   [2] *or* fuĕram, etc.

SUBJUNCTIVE or CONJUNCTIVE MOOD.
Primary Tenses.

PRESENT TENSE.	S. am-er, *I may be loved*, or *may I be loved.* am-ēris *or* -ēre, *Thou mayst be loved*, etc. am-etur, *He may be loved.* P. am-emur, *We may be loved.* am-emini, *Ye may be loved.* am-entur, *They may be loved.*
PERFECT TENSE.	S. amatus sim [1], *I may have been loved.* amatus sis, *Thou mayst have been loved.* amatus sit, *He may have been loved.* P. amati sīmus, *We may have been loved.* amati sitis, *Ye may have been loved.* amati sint, *They may have been loved.*

Historic Tenses.

IMPERFECT TENSE.	S. am-ārer, *I should* or *might be loved.* am-arēris *or* -arēre, *Thou wouldst be loved,* am-aretur, *He would be loved.* [etc. P. am-aremur, *We should be loved.* am-aremini, *Ye would be loved.* am-arentur, *They would be loved.*
PLUPERFECT TENSE.	S. amatus essem [2], *I should* or *might have been loved.* amatus esses, *Thou wouldst have been loved.* amatus esset, *He would have been loved.* P. amati essēmus, *We should have been loved.* amati essetis, *Ye would have been loved.* amati essent, *They would have been loved.*

Future-Simple Tense. Wanting: see § 296.
Aorist Tense. Rendered variously by *amatus sim, amarer,* and *amatus essem.* See §§ 205, 206.

[1] or fuěrim, etc.   [2] or fuissem, etc.

IMPERATIVE MOOD.

Present Tense.

S. 2 Pers. am-āre, *be thou loved*, am-ātor, *thou must be loved.*
3 Pers. am-ātor, *he must be loved.*
P. 2 Pers. am-āmĭni, *be ye loved.*
3 Pers. am-antor, *they must be loved.*

Note 1. The forms amator, amator, amantor are sometimes reckoned as Future Imperatives.

Note 2. The Present Subjunctive is often used in a Present Imperative sense, as amer, *let me be loved*, ameris, *be thou loved*, ametur, *let him be loved*, etc.

VERB INFINITE.

Infinitive Mood.

Present and Imperfect,	am-āri,	*to be loved.*
Perfect and Pluperfect,	amātus esse *or* fuisse,	*to have been loved.*
Future,	amātum īri,	*to be about to be loved.*

Participles.

Present, (wanting). The meaning '*whilst being loved*' may be rendered by *dum* with Present Indicative, as, dum amatur.
Perfect, amātus, *loved, being loved*, or *having been loved.*
Future, (wanting.)
Gerundive, am-andus, *that must be loved.*

§ 53. SECOND CONJUGATION. PASSIVE VOICE.

INDICATIVE MOOD.
Primary Tenses.

PRESENT TENSE.	S. mŏn-ĕor, *I am advised,* or *am being ad-* mon-ēris *or* -ēre, *Thou art advised.* [*vised.* mon-etur, *He is advised.* P. mon-emur, *We are advised.* mon-emĭni, *Ye are advised.* mon-entur, *They are advised.*
FUTURE- SIMPLE TENSE.	S. mon-ēbor, *I shall be advised.* [*vised.* mon-ēbĕris *or* -ēbĕre, *Thou wilt be ad-* mon-ebitur, *He will be advised.* P. mon-ēbĭmur, *We shall be advised.* mon-ebimini, *Ye will be advised.* mon-ebuntur, *They will be advised.*
PERFECT TENSE.	S. monĭtus sum [1], *I have been advised.* monitus es, *Thou hast been advised.* monitus est, *He has been advised.* P. moniti sŭmus, *We have been advised.* moniti estis, *Ye have been advised.* moniti sunt, *They have been advised.*
FUTURE- PERFECT TENSE.	S. monitus ĕro [2], *I shall have been advised.* monitus eris, *Thou wilt have been advised.* monitus erit, *He will have been advised.* P. moniti erimus, *We shall have been advised.* moniti eritis, *Ye will have been advised.* moniti erunt, *They will have been advised.*

[1] or fui. etc.   [2] or fuĕro, etc.

INDICATIVE MOOD (*continued*).
Historic Tenses.

Imperfect Tense.	S. mon-ēbar, *I was being advised*, or *I was advised*. [*advised*. mon-ebāris *or* -ebare, *Thou wast being* mon-ebatur, *He was being advised*. P. mon-ebamur, *We were being advised*. mon-ebamini, *Ye were being advised*. mon-ebantur, *They were being advised*.
Aorist Tense.	S. monitus sum [1], *I was advised*. monitus es, *Thou wast advised*. monitus est, *He was advised*. P. moniti sŭmus, *We were advised*. moniti estis, *Ye were advised*. moniti sunt, *They were advised*.
Pluperfect Tense.	S. monitus eram [2], *I had been advised*. monitus eras, *Thou hadst been advised*. monitus erat, *He had been advised*. P. moniti erāmus, *We had been advised*. moniti eratis, *Ye had been advised*. moniti erant, *They had been advised*.

[1] *or* fui, etc.   [2] *or* fueram, etc.

SUBJUNCTIVE or CONJUNCTIVE MOOD.
Primary Tenses.

Present Tense.	*S.* mon-ĕar, *I may be advised,* or *may I be advised.* mon-ĕāris *or* -ĕāre, *Thou mayst be advised,* mon-eatur, *He may be advised.* [etc. *P.* mon-eamur, *We may be advised.* mon-eamini, *Ye may be advised.* mon-eantur, *They may be advised.*
Perfect Tense.	*S.* monitus sim [1], *I may have been advised.* monitus sis, *Thou mayst have been advised.* monitus sit, *He may have been advised.* *P.* moniti sīmus, *We may have been advised.* moniti sitis, *Ye may have been advised.* moniti sint, *They may have been advised.*

Historic Tenses.

Imperfect Tense.	*S.* mon-ērer, *I should* or *might be advised.* mon-erēris *or* -erēre, *Thou wouldst be advised,* etc. mon-eretur, *He would be advised.* *P.* mon-erēmur, *We should be advised.* mon-eremini, *Ye would be advised.* mon-erentur, *They would be advised.*
Pluperfect Tense.	*S.* monitus essem [2], *I should have been advised.* monitus esses, *Thou wouldst have been advised.* monitus esset, *He would have been advised.* *P.* moniti essemus, *We should have been advised.* moniti essetis, *Ye would have been advised.* moniti essent, *They would have been advised.*

Future-Simple Tense. Wanting: see § 296.

Aorist Tense. Rendered variously by *monitus sim, monērer,* and *monitus essem.* See §§ 205, 206.

[1] or fuerim, etc.   [2] or fuissem, etc.

IMPERATIVE MOOD.

Present Tense.	*Sing.* 2 Pers.	mon-ēre, *be thou advised*, mon-ētor, *thou must be advised.*
	3 Pers.	mon-ētor, *he must be advised.*
	Plur. 2 Pers.	mon-ēmĭni, *be ye advised.*
	3 Pers.	mon-entor, *they must be advised.*

Note 1. The forms monetor, monetor, monentor are sometimes reckoned as Future Imperatives.

Note 2. The Present Subjunctive is often used in a Present Imperative sense, as monear, *let me be advised*, moneaɩis, *be thou advised*, moneatur, *let him be advised*, etc.

VERB INFINITE.

Infinitive Mood.	Present and Imperfect,	mon-ēri, *to be advised.*
	Perfect and Pluperfect,	monĭtus esse *or* fuisse, *to have been advised.*
	Future,	monĭtum iri, *to be about to be advised.*
Participles.	Present,	(wanting). The meaning '*whilst being advised*' may be rendered by *dum* with Present Indicative, as, dum monetur.
	Perfect,	monĭtus, *advised, being advised*, or *having been advised.*
	Future,	(wanting).
	Gerundive,	mon-endus, *that must be advised.*

§ 54. THIRD CONJUGATION. PASSIVE VOICE.

INDICATIVE MOOD.
Primary Tenses.

PRESENT TENSE.	S. rĕg-or, *I am ruled,* or *am being ruled.* reg-ĕris *or* -ĕre, *Thou art ruled,* etc. reg-ĭtur, *He is ruled.* P. reg-ĭmur, *We are ruled.* reg-ĭmĭni, *Ye are ruled.* reg-untur, *They are ruled.*
FUTURE-SIMPLE TENSE	S. reg-ar, *I shall be ruled.* reg-ēris *or* -ēre, *Thou wilt be ruled.* reg-ētur, *He will be ruled.* P. reg-ēmur, *We shall be ruled.* reg-ēmĭni, *Ye will be ruled.* reg-entur, *They will be ruled.*
PERFECT TENSE.	S. rectus sum [1], *I have been ruled.* rectus es, *Thou hast been ruled.* rectus est, *He has been ruled.* P. recti sŭmus, *We have been ruled.* recti estis, *Ye have been ruled.* recti sunt, *They have been ruled.*
FUTURE-PERFECT TENSE.	S. rectus ĕro [2], *I shall have been ruled.* rectus eris, *Thou wilt have been ruled.* rectus erit, *He will have been ruled.* P. recti erĭmus, *We shall have been ruled.* recti erĭtis, *Ye will have been ruled.* recti erunt, *They will have been ruled.*

[1] *or* fui, etc.   [2] *or* fuero, etc.

INDICATIVE MOOD (continued).
Historic Tenses.

IMPERFECT TENSE.	S. reg-ēbar, *I was being ruled*, or *I was ruled.* reg-ēbāris *or* -ēbāre, *Thou wast being ruled,* reg-ebatur, *He was being ruled.* [etc. P. reg-ebamur, *We were being ruled.* reg-ebamĭni, *Ye were being ruled.* reg-ebantur, *They were being ruled.*
AORIST TENSE.	S. rectus sum [1], *I was ruled.* rectus es, *Thou wast ruled.* rectus est, *He was ruled.* P. recti sŭmus, *We were ruled.* recti estis, *Ye were ruled.* recti sunt, *They were ruled.*
PLUPERFECT TENSE.	S. rectus eram [2], *I had been ruled.* rectus eras, *Thou hadst been ruled.* rectus erat, *He had been ruled.* P. recti erāmus, *We had been ruled.* recti eratis, *Ye had been ruled.* recti erant, *They had been ruled.*

[1] *or* fui, etc.   [2] *or* fuĕram, etc.

SUBJUNCTIVE or CONJUNCTIVE MOOD.
Primary Tenses.

Present Tense.	S. reg-ar, *I may be ruled*, or *may I be ruled*. reg-āris *or* -āre, *Thou mayst be ruled*, etc. reg-atur, *He may be ruled*. P. reg-amur, *We may be ruled*. reg-amĭni, *Ye may be ruled*. reg-antur, *They may be ruled*.
Perfect Tense.	S. rectus sim[1], *I may have been ruled*. rectus sis, *Thou mayst have been ruled*. rectus sit, *He may have been ruled*. P. recti sīmus, *We may have been ruled*. recti sītis, *Ye may have been ruled*. recti sint, *They may have been ruled*.

Historic Tenses.

Imperfect Tense.	S. reg-ĕrer, *I should* or *might be ruled*. reg-ĕrēris *or* -erēre, *Thou wouldst be ruled*, reg-cretur, *He would be ruled*. [etc. P. reg-eremur, *We should be ruled*. reg-eremini, *Ye would be ruled*. reg-erentur, *They would be ruled*.
Pluperfect Tense.	S. rectus essem[2], *I should have been ruled*. rectus esses, *Thou wouldst have been ruled*. rectus esset, *He would have been ruled*. P. recti essēmus, *We should have been ruled*. recti essētis, *Ye would have been ruled*. recti essent, *They would have been ruled*.

Future-Simple Tense. Wanting: see § 296.
Aorist Tense. Rendered variously by *rectus sim*, *regĕrer*, and *rectus essem*. See §§ 205, 206.

[1] or fuĕrim, etc.   [2] or fuissem, etc.

IMPERATIVE MOOD.

PRESENT TENSE.

S. 2 Pers. reg-ĕre, *be thou ruled*, reg-ĭtor, *thou must be ruled.*
3 Pers. reg-ĭtor, *he must be ruled.*
P. 2 Pers. reg-ĭmĭni, *be ye ruled.*
3 Pers. reg-untor, *they must be ruled.*

Note 1. The forms regitor, regitor, reguntor are sometimes reckoned as Future Imperatives.

Note 2. The Present Subjunctive is often used in a Present Imperative sense, as, regar, *let me be ruled*, regaris, *be thou ruled*, regatur, *let him be ruled*, etc.

VERB INFINITE.

Infinitive Mood.
- PRESENT AND IMPERFECT, rĕg-ī, *to be ruled.*
- PERFECT AND PLUPERFECT, rectus esse *or* fuisse, *to have been ruled.*
- FUTURE, rectum iri, *to be about to be ruled.*

Participles.
- PRESENT, (wanting). The meaning '*whilst being ruled*' may be rendered by *dum* with Present Indicative, as, dum regitur.
- PERFECT, rectus, *ruled, being ruled,* or *having been ruled.*
- FUTURE, (wanting).
- GERUNDIVE, regendus, *that must be ruled.*

§ 55. FOURTH CONJUGATION. PASSIVE VOICE.

INDICATIVE MOOD.

Primary Tenses.

PRESENT TENSE.	S. aud-ĭor, *I am heard* or *am being heard.* aud-īris *or* -īre, *Thou art heard*, etc. aud-ītur, *He is heard.* P. aud-īmur, *We are heard.* aud-īmĭni, *Ye are heard.* aud-ĭuntur, *They are heard.*
FUTURE-SIMPLE TENSE.	S. aud-ĭar, *I shall be heard.* aud-ĭēris *or* -ĭēre, *Thou will be heard.* aud-ĭētur, *He will be heard.* P. aud-ĭēmur, *We shall be heard.* aud-ĭēmini, *Ye will be heard.* aud-ĭentur, *They will be heard.*
PERFECT TENSE.	S. audītus sum[1], *I have been heard.* audītus es, *Thou hast been heard.* audītus est, *He has been heard.* P. audīti sŭmus, *We have been heard.* audīti estis, *Ye have been heard.* audīti sunt, *They have been heard.*
FUTURE-PERFECT TENSE.	S. audītus ero[2], *I shall have been heard.* audītus eris, *Thou will have been heard.* audītus erit, *He will have been heard.* P. audīti erĭmus, *We shall have been heard.* audīti erĭtis, *Ye will have been heard.* audīti erunt, *They will have been heard.*

[1] *or* fui, etc.   [2] *or* fuĕro, etc.

INDICATIVE MOOD (*continued*).
Historic Tenses.

Imperfect Tense.	S. aud-iēbar, *I was being heard,* or *I was heard.* aud-iebāris *or* -iebāre, *Thou wast being heard.* aud-iebatur, *He was being heard.* P. aud-iebamur, *We were being heard.* aud-iebamini, *Ye were being heard.* aud-iebantur, *They were being heard.*
Aorist Tense.	S. auditus sum[1], *I was heard.* auditus es, *Thou wast heard.* auditus est, *He was heard.* P. auditi sŭmus, *We were heard.* auditi estis, *Ye were heard.* auditi sunt, *They were heard.*
Pluperfect Tense.	S. auditus eram[2], *I had been heard.* auditus eras, *Thou hadst been heard.* auditus erat, *He had been heard.* P. auditi erāmus, *We had been heard.* auditi erātis, *Ye had been heard.* auditi erant, *They had been heard.*

[1] *or* fui, etc. [2] *or* fuĕram, etc.

SUBJUNCTIVE or CONJUNCTIVE MOOD.
Primary Tenses.

Present Tense.	S. aud-iar, *I may be heard*, or *may I be heard*. aud-iāris *or* -iāre, *Thou mayst be heard*. aud-iatur, *He may be heard*. P. aud-iamur, *We may be heard*. aud-iamini, *Ye may be heard*. aud-iantur, *They may be heard*.
Perfect Tense.	S. auditus sim¹, *I may have been heard*. auditus sis, *Thou mayst have been heard*. auditus sit, *He may have been heard*. P. auditi sīmus, *We may have been heard*. auditi sītis, *Ye may have been heard*. auditi sint, *They may have been heard*.

Historic Tenses.

Imperfect Tense.	S. aud-īrer, *I should* or *might be heard*. aud-irēris *or* -irēre, *Thou wouldst be heard*, aud-iretur, *He would be heard*. [etc. P. aud-iremur, *We should be heard*. aud-iremini, *Ye would be heard*. aud-irentur, *They would be heard*.
Pluperfect Tense.	S. auditus essem², *I should have been heard*. auditus esses, *Thou wouldst have been heard*. auditus esset, *He would have been heard*. P. auditi essēmus, *We should have been heard*. auditi essetis, *Ye would have been heard*. auditi essent, *They would have been heard*.

Future-Simple Tense. Wanting: see § 296.

Aorist Tense. Rendered variously by *auditus sim, audirer,* and *auditus essem.* See §§ 205, 206.

---

¹ or fuĕrim, etc.   ² or fuissem, etc.

IMPERATIVE MOOD.

Present Tense.

S. 2 Pers. aud-īre, *be thou heard,* aud-ītor, *thou must be heard.*
3 Pers.   aud-ītor, *he must be heard.*
P. 2 Pers. aud-īmĭni, *be ye heard.*
3 Pers.   aud-iuntor, *they must be heard.*

Note 1. The forms auditor, auditor, audiuntor, are sometimes reckoned as Future Imperatives.

Note 2. The Present Subjunctive is often used in a Present Imperative sense, as, audiar, *let me be heard,* audiaris, *be thou heard,* audiatur, *let him be heard,* etc.

VERB INFINITE.

Infinitive Mood.

- Present and Imperfect,   aud-īri, *to be heard.*
- Perfect and Pluperfect,   aud-ītus esse *or* fuisse, } *to have been heard.*
- Future,   audītum iri, *to be about to be heard.*

Participles.

- Present, (wanting). The meaning '*whilst being heard*' may be rendered by *dum* with Present Indicative, as, dum auditur.
- Perfect, aud-ītus, *heard, being heard,* or *having been heard.*
- Future, (wanting).
- Gerundive, aud-ĭendus, *that must be heard.*

§ 56. Comparative Table of Endings of the Four Conjugations.

1. INDICATIVE MOOD. Primary Tenses.

Tense.		Active Voice.							Passive Voice.						
PRESENT.	Am- Mon- Reg- Aud-	o, eo, o, io,	as, es, is, is,	at, et, it, it,	āmus, ēmus, ĭmus, īmus,	ātis, ētis, ĭtis, ītis,	ant. ent. unt. iunt.		or, eor, or, ior,	āris(e), ēris(e), ĕris(e), īris(e),	ātur, ētur, ĭtur, ītur,	āmur, ēmur, ĭmur, īmur,	āmĭni, ēmĭni, ĭmĭni, īmĭni,	antur. entur. untur. iuntur.
FUTURE SIMPLE.	Am- Mon- Reg- Aud-	ābo, ēbo, am, iam,	ābis, ēbis, es, ies,	ābit, ēbit, et, iet,	ābĭmus, ēbĭmus, ēmus, iēmus,	ābĭtis, ēbĭtis, ētis, iētis,	ābunt. ēbunt. ent. ient.		ābor, ēbor, ar, iar,	abĕris(e), ebĕris(e), ēris(e), iēris(e),	ābĭtur, ēbĭtur, ētur, iētur,	ābĭmur, ēbĭmur, ēmur, iēmur,	ābĭmĭni, ēbĭmĭni, ēmĭni, iēmĭni,	ābuntur. ēbuntur. entur. ientur.
PERFECT.	Amāv- Monu- Rex- Audiv-	i,	isti,	it,	ĭmus,	istis,	ērunt. or ēre.		Amātus Monĭtus Rectus Audītus	} sum, es, est, -i sŭmus, estis, sunt. } fui, fuisti, fuit, -i fuĭmus, fuistis, fuērunt, or fuēre.				
FUTURE PERFECT.	Amāv- Monu- Rex- Audiv-	ĕro,	eris,	erit,	erĭmus,	erĭtis,	erint.		Amātus Monĭtus Rectus Audītus	} ero, eris, erit, -i erĭmus, erĭtis, erunt. } fuero, fueris, fuerit, -i fuerĭmus, fuerĭtis, fuerint.				

[§ 56.] TABLE OF CONJUGATION ENDINGS.

2. INDICATIVE MOOD (continued). Historic Tenses.

Tense.		Active Voice.		Passive Voice.
IMPERFECT.	Am- Mon- Reg- Aud-	ābam, ābās, ābat, ābāmus, ābātis, ābant. ēbam, ēbās, ēbat, ēbāmus, ēbātis, ēbant. ēbam, ēbās, ēbat, ēbāmus, ēbātis, ēbant. iēbam, iēbas, iēbat, iēbamus, iēbatis, iēbant.		ābar, ābāris(e), ābātur, ābāmur, ābāmĭni, ābantur. ēbar, ēbāris(e), ēbātur, ēbāmur, ēbāmĭni, ēbantur. ēbar, ēbāris(e), ēbātur, ēbāmur, ēbāmĭni, ēbantur. iēbar, iēbāris(e), iēbātur, iēbāmur, iēbāmĭni, iēbantur.
AORIST.	Amāv- Monu- Rex- Audiv-	i, isti, it, īmus, istis, ērunt. or ēre.	Amātus Monĭtus Rectus Audītus	sum, es, est, -i sumus, estis, sunt. Or, fui, fuisti, fuit, -i fuĭmus, fuistis, fuērunt, or fuēre.
PLUPERFECT.	Amāv- Monu- Rex- Audiv-	ĕram, ĕras, ĕrat, ĕrāmus, erātis, ĕrant.	Amātus Monĭtus Rectus Audītus	ĕram, ĕras, ĕrat, -i ĕrāmus, ĕratis, ĕrant. Or, fuĕram, fuĕras, fuĕrat, -i fuĕrāmus, fuerātis, fuĕrant.

TABLE OF ENDINGS OF THE CONJUGATIONS (continued).

3. SUBJUNCTIVE MOOD. Primary Tenses.

Tenses.		Active Voice.	Passive Voice.
PRESENT.	Am- Mon- Reg- Aud-	em, es, et, ēmus, ētis, ent. eam, eas, cat, eāmus, eātis, cant. am, as, at, āmus, ātis, ant. iam, ias, iat, iāmus, iātis, iant.	er, ēris(e), ētur, ēmur, ēmĭni, entur. ear, eāris(e), eātur, eāmur, eāmĭni, eantur. ar, āris(e), ātur, āmur, āmĭni, antur. iar, iāris(e), iātur, iāmur, iāmĭni, iantur.
PERFECT.	Amāv- Monu- Rex- Audīv-	ĕrim, ĕrīs, ĕrit, ĕrĭmus, ĕrītis, ĕrint.	Amātus ⎫ Monĭtus ⎬ sim, sis, sit, -i simus, sītis, sint. Rectus ⎭ Or, Audītus fuĕrim, fuĕris, fuĕrit, fuĕrimus, fuĕrĭtis, fuĕrint.

4. SUBJUNCTIVE MOOD. Historic Tenses.

IMPER- FECT.	Am- Mon- Reg- Aud-	ārem, ārēs, āret, ārēmus, ārētis, ārent. ērem, ēres, ēret, ērēmus, ērētis, ērent. ĕrem, ĕres, ĕret, ĕrēmus, ĕrētis, ĕrent. īrem, īres, īret, īrēmus, īrētis, īrent.	ārer, ārēris(e), ārētur, ārēmur, ārēmĭni, ārentur. ērer, ērēris(e), ērētur, ērēmur, ērēmĭni, ērentur. ĕrer, ĕrēris(e), ĕrētur, ĕrēmur, ĕrēmĭni, ĕrentur. īrer, īrēris(e), īrētur, īrēmur, īrēmĭni, īrentur.
PLUPER- FECT.	Amāv- Monu- Rex- Audīv-	⎫ ⎬ issem, isses, isset, issēmus, issētis, ⎭ issent.	Amātus ⎫ essem, esses, esset, -i essēmus, essētis, essent. Monĭtus ⎬ forem, fores, foret, -i forēmus, forētis, forent. Rectus ⎭ Or, Audītus fuissem, fuisses, fuisset, -i fuissēmus, fuissētis, fuissent.

5. IMPERATIVE MOOD.

Active Voice.

PRESENT.	Am- Mon- Reg- Aud-	ā, ē, ĕ, ī,	āto, ēto, ito, ito,	āte, ēte, ite, ite,	ātōte, anto. ētōte, ento. itōte, unto. itote, iunto.

Passive Voice.

āre, ēre, ĕre, īre,	ātor, ētor, ĭtor, ītor,	ātor, ētor, ĭtor, ītor,	āmĭni, antor. ēmĭni, entor. ĭmĭni, untor. ĭmĭni, iuntor.

6. INFINITIVE MOOD and PARTICIPLES.

Active Voice.

INFINITIVE MOOD.	Pres. and Imperf. {	am-āre. mon-ēre. reg-ĕre. aud-īre.
	Perf. and Pluperf. {	amāv-isse. monu-isse. rex-isse. audīv-isse.
	Future {	amāturus esse. monitūrus esse. rectūrus esse. auditūrus esse.
PARTICIPLES.	Present {	am-ans. mon-ens. reg-ens. aud-iens.
	Future {	amātūrus. monitūrus. rectūrus. auditūrus.
GERUNDS AND SUPINES.	Gerunds {	am-andum, andi, ando. mon-endum, endi, endo. reg-endum, endi, endo. aud-iendum, iendi, iendo.
	Supines {	amāt-um, u. monit-um, u. rect-um, u. aud ītum, u.

Passive Voice.

Pres. and Imperf. {	am-āri. mon-ēri. reg-i. aud-īri.	
Perf. and Pluperf. {	amātus monĭtus rectus audītus	} esse or fuisse.
Future {	amātum monĭtum rectum audītum	} iri.
Perfect {	amātus. monĭtus. rectus. audītus.	
Gerundive {	amandus. monendus. regendus. audiendus.	

§ 57. Conjugation of a Deponent Verb, that is, a Verb which is Passive in Form but Active in Meaning.

INDICATIVE MOOD.
Primary Tenses.

Present Tense.	S. ūt-or, *I use, am using,* or *do use.* ut-ĕris *or* -ĕre, *Thou usest,* etc. ut-ĭtur, *He uses.* P. ut-ĭmur, *We use.* ut-ĭmĭni, *Ye use.* ut-untur, *They use.*
Future-Simple Tense.	S. ut-ar, *I shall use.* ut-ēris *or* -ēre, *Thou will use.* ut-etur, *He will use.* P. ut-emur, *We shall use.* ut-emini, *Ye will use.* ut-entur, *They will use.*
Perfect Tense.	S. ūsus sum[1], *I have used.* usus es, *Thou hast used.* usus est, *He has used.* P. usi sumus, *We have used.* usi estis, *Ye have used.* usi sunt, *They have used.*
Future-Perfect Tense.	S. usus ero[2], *I shall have used.* usus eris, *Thou will have used.* usus erit, *He will have used.* P. usi erimus, *We shall have used.* usi eritis, *Ye will have used.* usi erunt, *They will have used.*

[1] *or* fui, etc.   [2] *or* fuĕro, etc.

INDICATIVE MOOD (*continued*).
Historic Tenses.

Imperfect Tense.	S. ut-ēbar, *I was using*, or *I used*. ut-ēbāris *or* -ēbare, *Thou wast using*, etc. ut-ebatur, *He was using*. P. ut-ebamur, *We were using*. ut-ebamini, *Ye were using*. ut-ebantur, *They were using*.
Aorist Tense.	S. usus sum [1], *I used*. usus es, *Thou usedst*. usus est, *He used*. P. usi sumus, *We used*. usi estis, *Ye used*. usi sunt, *They used*.
Pluperfect Tense.	S. usus eram [2], *I had used*. usus eras, *Thou hadst used*. usus erat, *He had used*. P. usi eramus, *We had used*. usi eratis, *Ye had used*. usi erant, *They had used*.

[1] *or* fui, etc.   [2] *or* fuĕram, etc.

SUBJUNCTIVE or CONJUNCTIVE MOOD.
Primary Tenses.

PRESENT TENSE.	S. ut-ar, *I may use,* or *may I use,* or *let me use.* ut-āris *or* -āre, *Thou mayst use,* etc. ut-atur, *He may use.* P. ut-amur, *We may use.* ut-amini, *Ye may use.* ut-antur, *They may use.*
PERFECT TENSE.	S. usus sim [1], *I may have used.* usus sis, *Thou mayst have used.* usus sit, *He may have used.* P. usi simus, *We may have used.* usi sitis, *Ye may have used.* usi sint, *They may have used.*

Historic Tenses.

IMPERFECT TENSE.	S. ut-ĕrer, *I should* or *might use.* ut-ĕrēris *or* -ĕrēre, *Thou wouldst use,* etc. ut-erētur, *He would use.* P. ut-erēmur, *We should use.* ut-erēmini, *Ye would use.* ut-erentur, *They would use.*
PLUPERFECT TENSE.	S. usus essem [1], *I should* or *might have used.* usus esses, *Thou wouldst have used,* etc. usus esset, *He would have used.* P. usi essemus, *We should have used.* usi essetis, *Ye would have used.* usi essent, *They would have used.*

Future-Simple Tense. Usurus sim *or* essem.
Aorist Tense. Rendered variously by *usus sim, uterer,* and *usus essem.* See §§ 205, 206.

---

[1] or fuĕrim, etc.   [2] or fuissem, etc.

IMPERATIVE MOOD.

PRESENT TENSE.

S. 2 Pers. ut-ĕre, *use thou*, ut-ĭtor, *thou must use.*
   3 Pers.   ut-ĭtor, *he must use.*
P. 2 Pers. ut-ĭmĭni, *use ye.*
   3 Pers.   ut-untor, *they must use.*

Note 1. The forms utitor, utitor, utuntor are sometimes reckoned as Future Imperatives.

Note 2. The Present Subjunctive is often used in a Present Imperative sense.

VERB INFINITE.

Infinitive Mood.
- PRESENT AND IMPERFECT, ūt-i, *to use* (or *using*, in the sense of 'the act of using').
- PERFECT AND PLUPERFECT, ūsus esse, *or* fuisse, *to have used.*
- FUTURE, ūsūrus esse, *to be about to use.*

Gerunds.
- ACCUSATIVE, ut-endum, *using.*
- GENITIVE, ut-endi, *of using.*
- DAT. ABL., ut-endo, *for* or *by using.*

Supines.
- in -um, ūsum, *in order to use.*
- in -u, ūsu, *in using.*

Participles.
- PRESENT, ut-ens, *using* (declined like ingens).
- PERFECT, ūsus, *having used.*
- FUTURE, ūsūrus, *being about to use.*
- GERUNDIVE, ut-endus, *that must be used.*

Note on Deponent Verbs. There are Four Conjugations of Deponent Verbs, as, venor, Inf. venāri, *I hunt*, vereor, Inf. verēri *I fear*, utor, Inf. uti, *I use*, and partior, Inf. partīri, *I divide*, which are conjugated like amor, moneor, regor, and audior respectively.

Deponent Participles used Passively. Many Deponent Perfect Participles are used Passively as well as Actively, as comitatus, *having accompanied* and *accompanied*, from comitor; oblitus, *having forgotten* and *forgotten*, from obliviscor.

Deponents in -ior *of the Third Conjugation.* The Verbs gradior, *I walk*, morior, *I die*, and patior, *I suffer*, belong to the Third Conjugation, and drop the *i* before *i* and short *ĕr*, as

INDIC. PRES.
  { pati-or.
    pat-ĕris *for* pati-ĕris.
    pat-ĭtur *for* pati-ĭtur.
    pat-ĭmur *for* pati-ĭmur.
    pat-ĭmini *for* pati-ĭmini.
    pati-untur.

IMPER. PRES. pat-ĕre *for* pati-ĕre.
SUBJ. IMPERF. pat-ĕrer *for* pati-ĕrer.
INF. PRES.   pat-i *for* pati-i.

Note on the Verbs orior *and* potior. The Verbs orior and potior belong to the Fourth Conjugation of Deponents, but in some tenses they have forms borrowed from the Third, as,

INDIC. PRES.
  { 2 p. S. orĕris.
    3 p. S. orĭtur.
    1 p. Pl. orĭmur.
PART. FUT. orĭturus.

INDIC. PRES.
  { 3 p. S. potĭtur *or* potītur.
    1 p. Pl. potĭmur *or* potīmur.

SUBJ. IMPERF.
  { 1 p. S. potĕrer *or* potīrer.
    2 p. S. potĕrēris *or* potīrēris.
    3 p. S. potĕrētur *or* potīrētur.
    1 p. Pl. potĕrēmur *or* potīrēmur.
    2 p. Pl. potĕrēmini *or* potīrēmini.
    3 p. Pl. potĕrentur *or* potīrentur.

§ 58. Table showing a comparison of the Latin Tenses with the corresponding Tenses in Greek, French, German, and English.

Tenses.		Greek.	Latin.	French.	German.	English.
Present.	Indefinite, or Aorist.	φιλέω	amo	j'aime	Ich liebe	I love.
	Imperfect, or Continuous.					I am loving.
	Perfect, or Completed.	πεφίληκα	amavi	j'ai aimé	Ich habe geliebt	I have loved.
Future.	Indefinite.	φιλήσω	amabo	j'aimerai	Ich werde lieben	I shall love.
	Imperfect.					I shall be loving.
	Perfect.	. . . .	amavero	j'aurai aimé	Ich werde geliebt haben	I shall have loved.
Past.	Indefinite.	ἐφίλησα	amavi	j'aimai	Ich liebte	I loved.
	Imperfect.	ἐφίλεον	amabam	j'aimais		I was loving.
	Perfect.	ἐπεφιλήκειν	amaveram	j'avais aimé	Ich hatte geliebt	I had loved.

§ 59. Conjugation of the Anomalous Verbs.

1. Possum [potis-sum], *to be able.*

Indicative Mood.

PRESENT. possum, pŏt-es, pot-est, pos-sŭmus, pot-estis, pos-sunt.
FUT. SIMP. pot-ĕro, -eris, -erit, -erĭmus, -erĭtis, -erunt.
PERFECT. potu-i, -isti, -it, -ĭmus, -istis, -ērunt *or* -ēre.
FUT. PERF. potu-ĕro, -eris,- erit, -erĭmus, -erĭtis, -erint.
IMPERFECT. pot-ĕram, -eras, -erat, -erāmus, -erātis, -erant.
AORIST. Same in form as Perfect.
PLUPERF. potu-ĕram, -eras, -erat, -erāmus, -erātis, -erant.

Subjunctive Mood.

PRESENT. pos-sim, -sis, -sit, -sīmus, -sitis, -sint.
PERFECT. potu-ĕrim, -eris, -erit, -erĭmus, -erĭtis, -erint.
IMPERFECT. pos-sem, -ses, -set, -sēmus, -setis, -sent.
PLUPERF. potu-issem, -isses, -isset, -issēmus, -issetis, -issent

Infinitive Mood.

PRES. AND IMPERF. posse.
PERF. AND PLUPERF. potu-isse.
PRESENT PARTICIPLE. (wanting [1]).

Note. 'Possum' has no Imperative Mood.

---

2. { Volo, *to wish, be willing.*
     Nolo [non volo], *to be unwilling.*
     Malo [magis volo], *to wish rather, prefer.*

Indicative Mood.

PRESENT. { vŏlo, vis, vult, volŭmus, vultis, volunt.
          nōlo, nonvis, nonvult, nolŭmus, nonvultis, nolunt.
          mālo, mavis, mavult, malŭmus, mavultis, malunt.

FUT. SIMP. { vŏl-
             nōl-   } am, -es, -et, -ēmus, -etis, -ent.
             māl-

---

[1] The form potens is only used as an Adjective, *powerful.*

§ 59.] CONJUGATION OF ANOMALOUS VERBS.

PERFECT. { vŏlŭ- / nōlu- / mālu- } i, -isti, -it, -ĭmus, -istis, -ērunt *or* -ēre.

FUT. PERF. { volu- / nolu- / malu- } ĕro, -cris, -erit, -crĭmus, -erĭtis, -crint.

IMPERFECT. { vol- / nol- / mal- } ēbam, -ebas, -ebat, -ebāmus, -ebatis, -ebant.

AORIST. Same in form as Perfect.

PLUPERF. { volu- / nolu- / malu- } ĕram, -eras, -erat, -erāmus, -eratis, -erant.

Subjunctive Mood.

PRESENT. { vel- / nol- / mal- } im, -is, -it, -īmus, -itis, -int.

PERFECT. { volu- / nolu- / malu- } ĕrim, -eris, -erit, -crĭmus, -crĭtis, -erint.

IMPERFECT. { vell- / noll- / mall- } em, -es, -et, -ēmus, -etis, -ent.

PLUPERF. { volu- / nolu- / malu- } issem, -isses, -isset, -issēmus, -issetis, -issent.

Imperative Mood.

PRESENT. { S. 2 Pers. nolī, nolīto. / 3 Pers. nolīto. / P. 2 Pers. nolīte, nolītōte. / 3 Pers. nolunto.

Note. 'Volo' and 'malo' have no Imperative Mood.

Infinitive Mood.

PRES. AND IMPERF. { velle. / nolle. / malle.

PERF. AND PLUPERF. { voluisse. / noluisse. / maluisse.

Gerunds.	volen-dum, -di, -do. nolen-dum, -di, -do. malen-dum, -di, -do.
Supines.	(wanting).
Pres. Participles.	volens. nolens.

3. Fero, *to bear.*

Indicative Mood.

Present.	fĕro, fers, fert, fĕrĭmus, fĕrtis, ferunt.
Fut. Simp.	fer-am, -es, -et, -ēmus, -etis, -ent.
Perfect.	tŭl-i, -isti, -it, -ĭmus, -istis, -ērunt *or* -ēre.
Fut. Perf.	tul-ĕro, -eris, -erit, -erĭmus, -crĭtis, -erint.
Imperfect.	fĕrē-bam, -bas, -bat, -bāmus, -batis, -bant.
Aorist.	Same in form as Perfect.
Pluperf.	tul-ĕram, -eras, -erat, -erāmus, -eratis, -erant.

Subjunctive Mood.

Present.	fer-am, -as, -at, -āmus, -atis, -ant.
Perfect.	tul-ĕrim, -eris, -erit, -crĭmus, -erĭtis, -crint.
Imperfect.	fer-rem, -res, -ret, -rēmus, -retis, -rent.
Pluperf.	tul-issem, -isses, -isset, -issēmus, -issetis, -issent.

Imperative Mood.

Present.	S. 2 Pers.	fer,	ferto.
	3 Pers.		ferto.
	P. 2 Pers.	ferte,	fertōte.
	3 Pers.		ferunto.

Infinitive Mood.

Pres. and Imperf.	ferre.
Perf. and Pluperf.	tul-isse.
Future.	lāturus esse.
Gerunds.	feren-dum, -di, -do.
Supines.	lātum, latu.
Pres. Participle.	ferens.
Fut. Participle.	laturus.

§ 59.] CONJUGATION OF ANOMALOUS VERBS. 71

4. Feror, *to be borne.*

Indicative Mood.

PRESENT. fĕror, ferris *or* ferre, fertur, ferĭmur, ferimĭni, feruntur.
FUT. SIMP. fer-ar, -ēris *or* -ēre, -etur, -emur, -emini, -entur.
PERFECT. lat-us sum, es, est, -i sŭmus, estis, sunt.
FUT. PERF. lat-us ĕro, eris, erit, -i erĭmus, eritis, erunt.
IMPERFECT. fer-ēbar, -ebāris *or* -ebāre, -ebatur, -ebamur, -ebamini, -ebantur.
AORIST. Same in form as Perfect.
PLUPERF. lat-us ĕram, eras, erat, -i eramus, eratis, erant.

Subjunctive Mood.

PRESENT. fer-ar, -āris *or* -āre, -atur, -amur, -amini, -antur.
PERFECT. lat-us sim, sis, sit, -i sīmus, sitis, sint.
IMPERFECT. fer-rer, -rēris *or* -rēre, -retur, -remur, -remĭni, -rentur.
PLUPERF. lat-us essem, esses, esset, -i essēmus, essetis, essent.

Imperative Mood.

PRESENT.
S. 2 Pers. ferre, fertor.
3 Pers. fertor.
P. 2 Pers. ferimĭni.
3 Pers. feruntor.

Infinitive Mood.

PRES. AND IMPERF. ferri.
PERF. AND PLUPERF. lātus esse.
FUTURE. latum iri.
PERF. PARTICIPLE. latus.
GERUNDIVE. ferendus.

---

5. Eo, *to go.*

Indicative Mood.

PRESENT. eo, is, it, īmus, itis, eunt.
FUT. SIMP. ī-bo, -bis, -bit, -bĭmus, -bitis, -bunt.
PERFECT. īv-i, -isti, -it, -ĭmus, -istis, -ērunt *or* -ēre.
FUT. PERF. iv-ĕro, -eris, -erit, -erĭmus, -crĭtis, -erint.
IMPERFECT. ī-bam, -bas, -bat, -bāmus, -batis, -bant.

AORIST.   Same in form as Perfect.
PLUPERF.   iv-ĕram, -eras, -erat, -erāmus, -eratis, -erant.

Subjunctive Mood.
PRESENT.   e-am, -as, -at, -āmus, -atis, -ant.
PERFECT.   iv-ĕrim, -eris, -erit, -erĭmus, -erĭtis -erint.
IMPERFECT. ī-rem, -res, -ret, -rēmus, -retis, -rent.
PLUPERF.   iv-issem, -isses, -isset, -issēmus, -issetis, -issent.

Imperative Mood.
PRESENT.
- S. 2 Pers. ī,   īto.
-    3 Pers.   īto.
- P. 2 Pers. īte, ītōte.
-    3 Pers.   eunto.

Infinitive Mood.
PRES. AND IMPERF.   īre.
PERF. AND PLUPERF.   ivisse.
FUTURE.   itūrus esse.
GERUNDS.   eun-dum, -di, -do.
SUPINES.   ĭtum, ĭtu.
PRES. PARTICIPLE.   iens. [Gen. eunt-is.]
FUT. PARTICIPLE.   ĭturus.

---

6. **Fĭo**, *to be made, to become.*

Indicative Mood.
PRESENT.   fio, fis, fit, (fimus), (fitis), fiunt.
FUT. SIMP. fi-am, -es, -et, -ēmus, -etis, -ent.
PERFECT.   fact-us sum, es, est, -i sumus, estis, sunt.
FUT. PERF. fact-us ĕro, eris, erit, -i erĭmus, eritis, erunt.
IMPERFECT. fi-ēbam, -ebas, -ebat, -ebāmus, -ebatis, -ebant.
AORIST.   Same in form as Perfect.
PLUPERF.   fact-us ĕram, eras, erat, -i erāmus, eratis, erant.

Subjunctive Mood.
PRESENT.   fi-am, -as, -at, -āmus, -atis, -ant.
PERFECT.   fact-us sim, sis, sit, -i sīmus, sitis, sint.
IMPERFECT. fĭ-erem, -eres, -eret, -erēmus, -eretis, -erent.
PLUPERF.   fact-us essem, esses, esset, -i essēmus, essetis, essent.

Imperative Mood.

PRESENT. { S. 2 Pers. fi.
{ P. 2 Pers. fīte.

Infinitive Mood.

PRES. AND IMPERF.	fĭĕri.
PERF. AND PLUPERF.	factus esse.
FUTURE.	factum iri.
PERF. PARTICIPLE.	factus.
GERUNDIVE.	faciendus.

Note. 'Fio' is the Passive of the Verb facio, *to make*.

---

7. The Verb ĕdo, *I eat*, has irregular forms in certain tenses.

INDIC. PRES.	ĕdo, ĕdis *or* es, ĕdit *or* est, ĕdĭmus, ĕdĭtis *or* estis, ĕdunt.
SUBJ. PRES.	{ edam, edas, edat, etc.; *or* { edim, edis, edit, etc.
IMPERF.	{ edĕrem, edĕres, edĕret, etc.; *or* { essem, esses, esset, etc.
IMPERATIVE.	{ *Sing.* ĕdĕ, ĕdĭto *or* esto. { *Plur.* ĕdĭte *or* este, ĕdĭtote *or* estote, edunto.
INFIN. PRES.	edĕre *or* esse.

In the Passive, estur is found for ĕdĭtur, and essetur for ederetur.

---

8. Queo, *I am able*, and, nequeo, *I am unable*, are conjugated like 'eo,' but have no Imperative or Gerunds.

Table of the chief tenses of the Irregular Verbs.

	Ind. Pres.	*Inf.*	*Perf.*	*Supine.*	
1.	Possum,	posse,	potui,		to be able.
2.	{ Vŏlo,	velle,	volui,		to be willing.
	{ Nōlo,	nolle,	nolui,		to be unwilling.
	{ Mālo,	malle,	malui,		to wish rather.
3.	Fĕro,	ferre,	tŭli,	lātum,	to bear.
4.	Fĕror,	ferri,	latus sum,		to be borne.
5.	Eo,	īre,	īvi *or* ĭi,	ĭtum,	to go. [become.
6.	Fīo,	fĭĕri,	factus sum,		to be made *or*
7.	Ĕdo,	edĕre *or* esse,	ēdi,	ēsum,	to eat.
8.	{ Quĕo,	quīre,	quīvi,	quĭtum,	to be able.
	{ Nequĕo,	nequire,	nequīvi,	nequĭtum,	to be unable.

§ 60. Interrogative Forms of the Verb.

Use of -nĕ. The Indicative and Subjunctive Moods may be made Interrogative (i.e. made to express a question) by adding the Particle -nĕ to the various Numbers and Persons, as,

Indic. Present. amo-nĕ, *do I love?*
amas-nĕ, *dost thou love?* etc.
Future. amabo-nĕ, *shall I love?*
amabis-nĕ, *will thou love?* etc.

and so on throughout the Tenses.

Note. For videsnĕ, audisnĕ, etc., we sometimes find the forms vidĕn, audĭn, etc., in Poetry.

Position of -nĕ. The Particle -ne is not necessarily attached to the *Verb* in an Interrogative sentence. It is usually added to the first word in the sentence, as, puernĕ amat, *does the boy love?*

Use of num. When the answer 'no' is expected num is used in a question instead of -nĕ, as, num amat, *he does not love, does he?*

Use of nonnĕ. When the answer 'yes' is expected nonne is used in a question, as, nonnĕ amo, *do I not love?* or, *I love, do I not?*

Double Questions. If the word *or* occurs in a question to which the answer 'yes' or 'no' is expected, it is translated by an, and one of the Particles utrum, num, -ne must be used for the first part of the question, as,

utrum servus es an liber?
num servus es an liber?   } *Are you a slave or a free man?*[1]
servusnĕ es an liber?

---

[1] Literally '*Whether* are you a slave or a free man?' but the English Interrogative whether is now seldom used in *direct* questions. It appears more frequently in older English, as, Mark ii. 9, '*Whether* is it easier to say to the sick of the palsy, Thy sins be forgiven thee; or to say, Arise, and take up thy bed and walk?'

Interrogative Pronouns, etc. The chief Interrogative Pronouns and Particles in Latin are:—

qualis, *of what sort?*	cur, *why?*
quantus, *how great?*	quoties, *how often?*
uter, *which of two?*	quare, *wherefore?*
quis, *who?*	quam, *how?*
quot, *how many?*	quomodo, *how?*
quŏtus, *which in numerical order?*	num, *whether?*
	-nĕ, *whether?*
unde, *whence?*	ut, *how?*
ubi, *where?*	an, *or whether?*
quando, *when?*	utrum, *whether of the two?*

NOTES ON THE CONJUGATIONS.

§ 61. **Third Person Singular.** The Pronouns *she* and *it* are used, as well as *he*, to translate the 3rd Person Singular of the Verb. Thus amat may mean '*he, she,* or *it* loves.' In Tenses compounded of a Participle and the Verb sum the termination of the Participle will vary according to the Gender of the person or thing spoken of, as,

amatus est, *He has been loved.*
amata est, *She has been loved.*
amatum est, *It has been loved.*

§ 62. **Impersonal Verbs.** Certain Verbs are found only in the 3rd Person Singular, and have the word *it* for their apparent Nominative in English, as, licet, *it is permitted.* These are called Impersonal Verbs[1].

§ 63. **Present Indicative.** A Present Indicative, as **amo**, may be translated *I love, I am loving,* or *I do love.*

---

[1] A list of the chief Impersonals is given in § 78.

The sign *do* is seldom used affirmatively except when emphasis is required, but it constantly occurs in the Negative and Interrogative forms, as, non amo, *I do not love;* amonĕ, *do I love?*

§ 64. **Imperfect Indicative.** An Imperfect Indicative, as **amabam**, may be translated *I was loving, I loved, I used to love*, or *I began to love*. The translation *I loved* can only be used when the meaning is *I was loving at the time*, a sense which is often loosely expressed by the English Past Tense.

§ 65. **Aorist Indicative.** The sign *did* is seldom used affirmatively, except for the sake of emphasis, but it constantly occurs in the Negative and Interrogative forms, as non amavi, *I did not love*, etc.

§ 66. **Present Subjunctive.** This Tense admits of many translations. Thus **amem** means *I may, would*, or *should love, may I love*, and *let me love:* and, further, it has often to be translated as a Present Indicative, *I love, I am loving*, or *I do love*, when it occurs in dependent or subordinate sentences. Thus, quum amem is expressed in English by *since I love*.

§ 67. **Other Subjunctive Tenses.** What has been remarked of the Present holds good with respect to all the other Subjunctive Tenses, viz. that they frequently have to be translated by the corresponding Tense of the Indicative, and not by the signs *would, would have*, etc. Thus, quum audivissem does not mean *when I should have heard*, but *when I had heard*.

§ 68. **Contraction in the Perfect and Pluperfect Tenses.** Perfects ending in -vi, and the Tenses formed from them, may suffer contraction in all Conjugations, the letter **v** being omitted, e. g.—

Conj. 1. Amâsti *for* amavisti; amâssent *for* amavissent.
Conj. 2. Summôsses *for* summovisses.
Conj. 3. Nôrunt *for* novērunt; nôsti *for* novisti.
Conj. 4. Audîsti *for* audivisti. In this Conjugation there is also a form produced by throwing out the v, without any contraction of vowels, as Perf. audii *for* audivi. This form is also found in certain Verbs of the Third Conjugation, as, peto, cupio, etc., which have Perfect in -vi, as, petii *for* petivi.

Note. This contraction is not allowed before -re in the 3rd Person Plural of the Perfect Indicative. We cannot say amâre *for* amavere.

§ 69. **Old Latin Forms sometimes used in Poetry.**

(*a*) In the Pres. Infin. Pass. -ier was used for -i, as, amarier *for* amari.

(*b*) In the Imperf. Indic. of 4th Conjugation e was dropped, as, audibam *for* audiebam.

(*c*) In the Fut. Simp. of 4th Conjugation the regular forms -ibo and -ibor were used, as, audibo, audibor. Afterwards these forms were replaced by forms proper to the 3rd Conjugation, as, audiam, audiar.

(*d*) The Subj. Pres. in the 1st and 3rd Conjugations sometimes ended in -im, as, duim, *let me give*, for dem; edim, *let me eat*, for edam.

§ 70. **Note on certain Imperatives.** Facio, fero, dico, and duco[1], make in the Imperative Present făc, fĕr dīc, dūc. Scio, *I know*, has only scito, never sci, for Imperative.

§ 71. **Note on the termination '-ro' for '-ris.'** The use of -re for -ris as the termination of the 2nd Pers. Sing. in the Passive Voice is common in all the tenses except the Present Indicative, where it might be mistaken for the Infinitive Active or Imperative Passive, as, amare.

[1] *Make, bear, say, lead.*

§ 72. **Gerundive in '-undus.'** The gerundives of the 3rd and 4th Conjugations are sometimes formed in -undus instead of -endus, especially when i precedes, as potiundus, capiundus.

§ 73. **The Periphrastic Conjugation.** The Future Active Participle may be coupled with all the Tenses of the Verb **sum**, and thus a new Active Conjugation, called the Periphrastic, is formed, indicating that a person *has a mind to do a thing* or *is upon the point of doing it*, e.g.

amaturus sum, *I am about to love.*
amaturus eram, *I was about to love.*

And so on throughout all the tenses.

In the same way the Gerundive may be coupled with the Tenses of 'sum' to form a Passive Periphrastic Conjugation, as,

amandus sum, *I ought to be loved* or *I must be loved.*
amandus eram, *I ought to have been loved*, etc.

DEFECTIVE AND OTHER VERBS.

§ 74. Defective Verbs are those of which only certain Moods, Tenses, or Persons are found; e.g.—

(a) **Aio,** *I say* or *affirm.*

Indic. Pres.	Aīo,	aĭs,	aĭt,			aīunt.
,, Imperf.	Ai-ēbam,	-ēbas,	-ēbat,	-ēbāmus,	-ēbātis,	-ēbant.
Subj. Pres.		aīas,	aīat,			aīant.

(b) **Inquam,** *I say.*

Indic. Pres.	Inquam,	inquĭs, inquĭt, inquĭmus, inquĭtis, inquĭunt.	
,, Imperf.	Inquiebat.	Perf. Inquisti, inquit.	
,, Fut.		inquĭes, inquĭet.	
Imperat. Pres.		inquĕ, inquĭto,	inquĭte.

(*c*) **Coepi**, *I have begun*, or *I begin*, **memini**, *I remember*, and **odi**, *I hate*, have, for the most part, only those parts of the Verb which are formed from the Perfect Tense, e. g.

Indic. Perf.	coepi, coepisti, coepit, etc.
„ Pluperf.	coeperam.
„ Fut. Perf.	coepero.
Subj. Perf.	coeperim.
„ Pluperf.	coepissem.
Inf. Perf. and Pluperf.	coepisse.

Note. **Coepi** and **odi** have also a Perf. Part. **coeptus, osus**, and a Fut. Part. **coepturus, ōsūrus**. **Memini**, has an Imperative **memento**, Plur. **mementōte**.

(*d*) **Fari**, *to speak*, has **fātur**, *he speaks*, **fābor**, *I shall speak*, and **fārĕ**, *speak thou*, with Participles **fantem** (no Nominative), **fātus, fandus**, Gerunds **fandi, fando**, and Supine **fatu**.

(*e*) The following Imperatives:

Ăvē (or **hăvē**), **ăvēte**, *hail*. Infin. **ăvēre**.
Salvē, **salvēte**, *hail*. Infin. **salvēre**.
Cĕdŏ, **cĕdĭte** (or **cettĕ**), *give me*.
Apăgĕ, **ăpăgĭte**, *begone*.

§ 75. **Derived Verbs.** Many Verbs are derived either from other Verbs or from Nouns.

Those chiefly derived from Verbs are of four kinds, Inceptive, Desiderative, Frequentative, and Diminutive.

(*a*) **Inceptive** Verbs signify 'to begin to do a thing,' and end in **-sco**, as, **calesco**, *I begin to be warm, grow warm* (from **caleo**), **tenerasco**, *I grow tender* (from **tener**).

(*b*) **Desiderative** Verbs signify 'to desire to do a thing,' and end in **-urio**, as, **ēsŭrio**, *I wish to eat*, or *I am hungry* (from **ĕdo**).

(*c*) **Frequentative** Verbs signify 'to do a thing frequently,' and end in -so, -to, and -ito, as, pulso (from pello, *I drive*), canto (from cano, *I sing*), and clamĭto (from clamo, *I shout*).

(*d*) **Diminutive** Verbs signify 'to do a little thing,' and end in -illo, as, cantillo, *I sing a little song* (from cano).

Verbs derived from Nouns belong usually to the First Conjugation if Transitive, and to the Second if Intransitive, as, fraudāre, *to deceive* [from fraus, *deceit*], albēre, *to be white* [from albus, *white*].

§ 76. **Semi-Deponent** (or **Neuter Passive**) **Verbs.** These are audeo, fido, gaudeo, and soleo¹. They have an Active Present with a Perfect of Passive form, as, audeo, ausus sum; fido, fisus sum; gaudeo, gavīsus sum; soleo, solitus sum.

§ 77. **Quasi-Passive** (or **Neutral Passive**) **Verbs.** These are văpŭlo, vĕnĕo, lĭcĕo, exŭlo, and flo². They are Active in form but Passive in meaning.

§ 78. **Impersonal Verbs.** The chief Impersonal Verbs are the following. They are of the Second Conjugation, and being only found in the 3rd Person Singular of the Finite Verb, and in the Infinitive Mood, may be called Unipersonals.

Pres.	*Perf.*	*Infin.*	
lĭbet, (lubet),	lĭbŭit *or* lĭbĭtum est,	lĭbēre,	*it pleases.*
lĭcet,	lĭcŭit *or* lĭcĭtum est,	lĭcēre,	*it is lawful.*
lĭquet,	lĭcŭit,	lĭquēre,	*it is clear.*
mĭsĕret,	mĭsĕrŭit *or* mĭserĭtum est,	mĭsĕrēre,	*it moves to pity.*
ŏportet,	ŏportuit,	oportēre,	*it behoves or is necessary.*
pĭget,	pĭgŭit *or* pigĭtum est,	pigēre,	*it troubles.*

¹ *Dare, trust, rejoice, am accustomed.*
² *Am beaten, am for sale, am put up to auction, am banished, am made.*

Pres.	*Perf.*	*Infin.*	
paenĭtet,	paenĭtŭit,	paenitēre,	*it repents.*
pŭdet,	pŭdŭit *or* pudĭtum est,	pudēre,	*it shames.*
taedet,	taedŭit *or* pertaesum est,	taedēre,	*it wearies.*

§ 79. The above Verbs are, for the most part, only found in the Impersonal form. But many completely conjugated Verbs are used impersonally, as, juvo, *I assist*, which has juvat, meaning *it delights*, with many others, e. g.

Pres.	*Perf.*	*Infin.*	
accēdit,	accessit,	accedĕre,	*it is added.*
accĭdit,	accĭdit,	accidĕre,	*it happens.*
constat,	constĭtit,	constāre,	*it is well known.*
convĕnit,	convēnit,	convenīre,	*it suits.*
dĕcet,	dĕcŭit,	dĕcēre,	*it becomes* or *beseems.*
dēdĕcet,	dēdĕcŭit,	dēdĕcēre,	*it misbecomes.*
fit,	factum est,	fĭĕri,	*it comes to pass.*

Together with certain Verbs denoting change of weather, as, pluit, *it rains*, fulminat, *it lightens*, tonat, *it thunders*, etc.

§ 80. Intransitive Verbs are used impersonally in the Passive Voice, as, sto, *I stand*, statur, *it is stood* or *a stand is made.* Hence statur a me = *it is stood by me* = *I stand*.

PARTICLES.

§ 81. **Adverbs.** These may express Place, Time, Manner, or Number, as, eo, *thither*, tunc, *then*, sapienter, *wisely*, bis, *twice*.

§ 82. **Derivation of Adverbs.** Most Adverbs are formed from Adjectives. Thus,

From Adjectives in -*us* are formed Adverbs in -*ē*, and (less commonly) -*o*; as digne, *worthily*, from dignus, *worthy*; subito, *suddenly*, from subitus, *sudden*.

From Adjectives of two terminations in -*is*, -*ns*, -*x*, &c.,

are formed Adverbs in *-iter* or *-ter*, as feliciter, *happily*, from felix, *happy;* libenter, *willingly*, from libens, *willing*.

Adjectives in *-us* and *-is* often use their Neuter[1] Adverbially, as horrendum stridens, *sounding horribly;* dulcē ridens, *smiling sweetly*. This is chiefly a Poetic usage.

There is also a termination in *-im*, chiefly from Participles, as separatim, *separately;* and in *-ĭtus*, as divinĭtus, *divinely*.

Adverbs are also formed from Pronouns; thus from hic, *this*, are derived the Adverbs hìc, *here*, huc, *hither*, and hinc, *from hence;* from qui, *who* or *which*, are derived quà, *where*, and quo, *whither*, etc.

For comparison of Adverbs, see §§ 28 and 162 (*d*).

§ 83. **Prepositions.** For a list of the Latin Prepositions see §§ 111 and 122, and for a full account of their usual meanings, with Examples, see §§ 318–363.

§ 84. **Conjunctions.** These are of two kinds, viz.—

- (i.) **Coordinative,** which simply link together words, phrases, or clauses, and do not influence the Mood of the Verb. They are,
    - (*a*) *Copulative*, et, -que, ac, atque, *and;* nec *or* neque, *and not*.
    - (*b*) *Disjunctive*, aut, vel, -ve, *either;* sive, *whether*.
    - (*c*) *Adversative*, sed, autem, verum, vero, ceterum, at, *but*.

Note. Sentences linked together by the above Conjunctions are called Coordinate Sentences.

- (ii.) **Subordinative,** which introduce Subordinate Clauses (§ 94). The chief kinds are as follow. Those marked * are almost always found with a Subjunctive.

---

[1] Masculine and Feminine Adjectives are also used Adverbially, as, invitus (*or* invita) Romam migravit, *he* (or *she*) *has unwillingly removed to Rome*.

Final. Ut*, *in order that*, quo*, *in order that*, nē*, *lest, in order that . . . not*, quominus*, quin*, *in order that . . . not.*

Consecutive. Ut*, *so that*, quin*, *that not.*

Temporal. Quum, ubi, ut, *when;* donec, dum, quoad, *whilst, until;* antequam, priusquam, *before that;* postquam, *after that;* simul, simul ac, *as soon as;* quoties, *as often as.*

Causal. Quum*, quoniam, quandŏquĭdem, *since;* quod, quia, *because.*

Conditional. Si, *if*, nisi, *if not, unless:* dum*, dummŏdo*, *provided that.*

Concessive. Etsi, licet*, quamquam, quamvis*, quum*, ut, *although.*

Comparative. Quasi*, tanquam*, tanquam si*, *as if, as though.*

§ 85. **Interjections.** Interjections express joy, as, io, *hail;* grief, as, heu or eheu, *alas!* astonishment, as, en or ecce, *lo!* and calling or summoning, as heus, *ho!*

A SHORT CATECHISM

OF

LATIN SYNTAX.

Elementary Rules for Construing.

§ 86. *Q.* How do we begin the translation of a Latin sentence?

A. First look for the Finite Verb, and then for its Subject.

§ 87. *Q.* Will *any* Finite Verb do that happens to be in the sentence?

A. No. The Finite Verb of the Sentence is *never* to be looked for in a clause introduced by the Relative qui, quae, quod, or by a Subordinative Conjunction, as, quum, *when*, ut, *that*, ne, *lest*, si, *if*, etsi, *although*, etc.

§ 88. *Q.* What do you mean by 'the Subject'?

A. The Subject is the person or thing *of which something is said.* Thus in the sentence Caesar scribit, *Caesar writes*, it is said of Caesar that he writes; hence Caesar is called the Subject of the sentence.

Note. That which is said of the Subject is called the *Predicate.*

§ 89. *Q.* How do we find the Subject?

A. It is, as a rule, a Noun[1] in the Nominative Case.[2] If

---

[1] Under the head of 'Nouns' are also included words or phrases equivalent to Nouns, e. g. an Infinitive Mood, an Accusative and Infinitive, an Adjective used Substantively, or a whole clause introduced by a Conjunction.

[2] The Subject of an Infinitive Mood is put in the Accusative. See § 112.

there is no Nominative expressed, the Subject is one of the Pronouns *I, thou, he, she, it, we, you,* or *they*, contained in the Verb-ending.

Varieties of the Sentence.

§ 90. *Q.* How many kinds of sentences are there?

A. Three, namely:

    (*a*) The Statement, as, Caesar scribit, *Caesar is writing.*

    (*b*) The Question, as, Scribitnĕ Caesar? *Is Caesar writing?*

    (*c*) The Command or Request, as, Scribe, Caesar, *Write, O Caesar;* Scribat Caesar, *Let Caesar write.*

§ 91. *Q.* What is an Oblique or Indirect Sentence (*Oratio Obliqua*)?

A. A Statement, Question, or Command, which forms the Subject or Object (see § 39) of another Verb,[1] as,

    Ait **Caesarem scribĕre,** *He says that Caesar is writing.* **Scribatnĕ Caesar** nostrā nihil interest, *Whether Caesar is writing is of no importance to us,* or *it is of no importance to us whether Caesar is writing.*

In the first example the words Caesarem scribere are the Object of ait; in the second the words scribatne Caesar are the Subject of interest.

§ 92. *Q.* What is a Complex Sentence?

A. A sentence consisting of a number of clauses joined together in such a manner that one clause is Principal and the others Subordinate.

---

[1] A sentence which does not form the Subject or Object of a verb is said to be in *Oratio Recta* or *Directa.*

§ 93. *Q.* Distinguish between Principal and Subordinate Clauses.

A. The Principal clause contains the main Statement, Question, or Command: Subordinate clauses are added in order to explain some word, usually either a Noun or Verb, in the Principal sentence.

§ 94. *Q.* How are Subordinate clauses introduced?

A. Subordinate clauses are introduced either by the Relative, qui, quae, quod, as, vir **quem video**, bonus est, *The man whom I see is good*, or by a Subordinative Conjunction, as, haec fecit, **ut laudaretur**, *He did this that he might be praised.*

On the Three Concords or Rules of Agreement.

§ 95. *Q.* Name the Three Concords or Rules of Agreement.

A. (*a*) The Finite Verb agrees with its Nominative in Number and Person, as, Rex audit, *The king hears*, or *is hearing;* Reges audiunt, *The kings hear*, or *are hearing*.

Note. We could not in Latin say rex audi*unt* or reges aud*it*, any more than we could say in English, *the king are hearing*, or *the kings is hearing*.

(*b*) The Adjective agrees with its Substantive in Gender, Number, and Case, as,

Bonae matres bonos pueros amant, *Good mothers love good boys.*

Opus perfectum est, *The work is accomplished.*

Illud opus perfectum est, *That work is accomplished.*

Note. Participles and Adjectival Pronouns are here considered as Adjectives.

(c) The Relative **qui, quae, quod,** agrees with its Antecedent in Gender, Number, and Person; but in Case belongs to its own clause, as,

Arbor, **quae** in horto crescit, alta est, *The tree which grows in the garden is high.*

Arbor, **quam** video, alta est, *The tree which I see is high.*

On Copulative Verbs.

§ 96. *Q.* What are Copulative Verbs?

A. The Verb **sum,** and Passive Verbs of *thinking, calling,* or *making,* as, vocor, *I am called,* fio, *I am made,* etc.

§ 97. *Q.* What is the Case-Construction after Copulative Verbs?

A. They take the same Case after them as they have before them, as, dies fit nox, *day becomes night;* sensimus diem fieri noctem, *we perceived that day was becoming night.*

On Apposition.

§ 98. *Q.* What is meant by Apposition?

A. One Substantive added to another to explain some part of its meaning is said to be in Apposition to it, as, Cassandra **vates,** *Cassandra the prophetess.*

§ 99. *Q.* Name the three kinds of Apposition.

A. (*a*) The first kind is where the second Substantive comes close after the first and explains some part of its meaning, as,

Marius **consul** triumphavit, *Marius the consul triumphed;*

(*b*) The second is where the second Substantive is separated from the first by a Copulative Verb, as,

Marius erat **consul,** *Marius was consul.*

Marius **consul** creatus est, *Marius was made consul.*

(c) The third is where both Substantives are in the Accusative after an Active Verb of *thinking, calling,* or *making,* as,

Marium **consulem** creaverunt, *They made Marius consul.*

Note. Apposition of the second and third kind is also explained by Grammarians as forming what is called the *Complement* of the Verb.

§ 100. *Q.* What is the rule for the Case of a Noun in Apposition?

A. It must be in the same Case as the Noun to which it refers.

Rules of Time, Place, and Measure.

§ 101. *Q.* Give the rules for expressing *Duration* of Time [or time *how-long*], and a *Point* of Time [or time *when*].

A. Duration of Time is put in the Accusative, as, multos annos vixit, *he lived many years;* a Point of Time in the Ablative, as, primā luce surgit, *he rises at first dawn.*

§ 102. *Q.* How is *to* a place expressed?

A. By **ad** or **in** with Accusative, unless the place be a town or small island,[1] when the Preposition is omitted, as,

Ad portam eo, *I go to the gate.* But,

Romam eo, *I go to Rome.*

§ 103. *Q.* How is *from* a place expressed?

A. By **ab** or **ex** with Ablative, unless the place be a town or small island,[2] when the Preposition is omitted, as,

---

[1] Except also domum, *home,* rus, *the country,* and foras, *out of doors;* as domum ibo, *I will go home;* rus ibo, *I will go into the country;* foras ibo, *I will go out of doors.*

[2] Or domo, *from home;* rure, *from the country;* humo, *from the ground.*

Ex castris profectus est, *He set out from the camp.* But, Romā profectus est, *He set out from Rome.*

§ 104. *Q.* How is *at* a place expressed?

A. By ad, in, apud, etc., with their cases, unless the place be a town or small island, when the Locative Case must be used, as,

Ad fluvium constitit, *He halted at the river.* But, Cortonae mansit, *He remained at Cortona.*

§ 105. *Q.* What is the Locative Case?

A. An old Case specially used to denote '*at* a place.' It ends like the Ablative, except in the Singular Number of the First and Second Declensions, where it ends like the Genitive, as,

Romae, Sami, Athenis, Carthagine, Gadibus vixit, *He has lived at Rome, Samos, Athens, Carthage, and Cadiz.*

§ 106. *Q.* What Nouns have a Locative Case in use?

A. Names of towns and small islands; the Case also survives in the words domi, *at home,* foris, *out of doors,* humi, *on the ground,* ruri, *in the country,* vesperi, *in the evening,* belli, *at the war,* and militiae, *on military service.*

§ 107. *Q.* How is Measure of Space expressed?

A. Usually by the Accusative, as,

Fossa ducentos pedes longa, *A trench 200 feet long.*

Duo millia passuum progreditur, *He advances two miles.*

But sometimes by the Ablative, as,

Hiberna duobus millibus passuum aberant, *The winter-quarters were two miles distant.*

Note. Measures in the Genitive, as, fossa ducentorum pedum, *a trench 200 feet long,* may be classed as Genitives of Quality. For Ablatives of Measure, as multo major, etc., see § 121 (*g*).

On the Accusative Case.

§ 108. *Q.* Define the Accusative Case.

A. The Accusative is properly the Case of the Direct Object.

§ 109. *Q.* What is the Accusative of the Direct Object?

A. The Accusative which follows Transitive Verbs, as,

Video taurum, *I see a bull.*

§ 110. *Q.* What other uses of the Accusative are there?

A. (*a*) The Cognate Accusative or Accusative of Kindred Meaning, which follows Intransitive Verbs, as,

Duram servit servitutem, *He serves a hard servitude.*

(*b*) The Accusative of Limitation, which is generally an Adjective or Pronoun in the Neuter Gender, and is added chiefly to Intransitive Verbs, as,

Quid refert, *What does it matter?*
Sera comans narcissus, *The late-blooming narcissus.*

(*c*) The Accusative of Respect, which follows certain Verbs, Participles, and Adjectives, and is translated by the sign *with respect to* or *as to*, as,

Latus humeros, *Broad as to his shoulders.*

(*d*) (*e*) (*f*) The Accusatives of Duration of Time, Motion to, and Measure, which have already been noticed (§§ 101, 102, 107).

(*g*) The Accusative of Exclamation, used with or without an Interjection, as,

Me miserum! *Unhappy me!*
Proh deorum atque hominum fidem! *Alas for the faith of Gods and men!*

(*h*) The Accusative after a Preposition.

§ 111. *Q.* What Prepositions govern the Accusative?

A. **Ante, apud, ad, adversus,**
Circum, circa, citra, cis,
Contra, erga, extra, infra,
Inter, intra, juxta, ob,
Penes, pone, post, and praeter,
Prope, propter, per, secundum,
Supra, versus, ultra, trans,
And unto these, if *motion* be intended,
Let **in, sub, super, subter,** be appended.

Note. For the meaning of these Prepositions see §§ 318–347.

§ 112. *Q.* Explain the Accusative and Infinitive construction.

A. The Accusative and Infinitive is used as Subject of Impersonal Verbs, and as Object of Verbs of *declaring, perceiving, knowing, thinking,* or *believing.* The rule for translation is;—begin with the word *that,* and then construe the Accusative as a Nominative, and the Infinitive as a Finite Verb of the same Tense, as,

Caesarem amare constat, *It is well known that Caesar loves.* (Caesarem amare, *Subject;* constat, *Verb.*)

Caesarem amavisse scimus, *We know that Caesar has loved.* (Scimus, *Verb;* Caesarem amavisse, *Object.*)

§ 113. *Q.* Give a rule for translating the Conjunction *that* into Latin.

When *that* means *the fact that* it is usually translated by Accusative and Infinitive, as,

Nuntiat Caesarem rediisse, *He announces (the fact) that Caesar has returned.*

But when *that* means *in order that* or *so that* it is translated by ut with Subjunctive, as,

Hoc fecit ut Caesar redire cogeretur, *He did this that Caesar might be forced to return.*

Tantum bellum exortum est ut Caesar redire cogeretur, *So great a war broke out that Caesar was forced to return.*

§ 114. *Q.* What Verbs take two Accusatives?

A. Verbs of *asking* and *teaching*, and celo, *to conceal*, as,

Me sententiam rogavit, *He asked me my opinion.*

Me hanc rem celavit, *He concealed this matter from me.*

Note. The Accusative of the *thing asked* or *taught* remains even when the Verb is in the Passive Voice, as, Rogatur sententiam, *He is asked his opinion;* Docta est litteras, *She has been taught her letters.*

On the Dative Case.

§ 115. *Q.* Define the Dative Case.

A. The Dative is the Case of the Indirect Object.

Note. The Indirect Object is the person (or thing) *affected* but *not directly acted on* by an action or quality.

§ 116. *Q.* What words can take a Dative of the Indirect Object?

A. (*a*) Transitive Verbs, which already have a Direct Object, as,

Fabio consilium dedi, *I gave counsel to Fabius.*

(*b*) Intransitive Verbs, as,

Plaudunt histrioni, *They applaud the actor.*[1]

(*c*) Adjectives, as,

Mihi amicus est, *He is friendly to me.*

---

[1] Lit. '*clap their hands for* the actor.' Many Verbs which seem from their English translation to be Transitive are really Intransitive in Latin and so require a Dative, e. g. noceo is 'I *am* hurtful' rather than 'I hurt,' &c.

§ 117. *Q.* What other uses of the Dative are there?

A. (*a*) The Dative of Advantage or Disadvantage (Dativus Commodi vel Incommodi), used generally of *persons* after Verbs and Adjectives, as,

Praedia aliis coluit, non sibi, *He cultivated farms for others, not for himself.*

Note. It is very difficult to separate this Dative from the Dative of the Indirect Object. Roughly speaking we may class the Datives that are translated by *to* as Datives of the Indirect Object, and those that are translated by *for*, when referring to a *person*, as Datives of Advantage or Disadvantage.

(*b*) The Ethic Dative; a Dative of the Personal Pronouns, used in order to call particular attention to the person indicated. It admits of many renderings in English according to the sense of the passage, as,

Quid mihi Celsus agit, *Pray tell me, what is Celsus doing?*
Pulset mihi lictorem, *Let me see him strike a lictor.*
Quid tibi vis, *What do* **you** *want?*

(*c*) The Dative after the Verb sum, with the signification of habeo, *I have*, as, est mihi pater, *I have a father;* est tibi frater, *you have a brother.*

(*d*) The Dative of the Agent, which is used with the Gerundive, with Passive Verbs and Participles (in poetry), and with Verbal Adjectives in **-bilis**, as,

Hoc tibi non faciendum est, *This must not be done by you.*
Non intellegor ulli, *I am understood by no one.*
Bella matribus detestata, *Wars abhorred by mothers.*
Nulli flebilior quam tibi, *By none more lamented than by thee.*

(*e*) The Dative of Purpose, as,

Decemviri legibus scribendis creati, *Decemvirs created for the purpose of writing the laws.*

(*f*) The Dative of the Predicate, which in English we express by a Nominative, as,

Ea res impedimento erat, *That matter was a hindrance.*

§ 118. *Q.* What Verbs govern the Dative?

A. (*a*) All the compounds of **sum** except **possum**.

(*b*) Many Verbs compounded with
Bene, male, satis, re,
Ad, ante, con, in, inter, de,
Ob, sub, super, post, and *prae.*

(*c*) 1. A dative put with *shew*, and *give*,
2. *Tell, envy, spare, permit, believe,*
3. *Persuade, command, obey;* to these
4. Add *threaten, pardon, succour, please,*
5. With *vacāre, displicēre,*
6. *Servīre, nubĕre, studēre,*
7. *Heal, favour, hurt, resist,* and *indulgēre*[1].

Note 1. All the above take a Dative of the *person* (also occasionally of the *thing*); some of them, e. g. dico, do, invideo, permitto, persuadeo, ignosco, with some others not mentioned, as, excuso, *I plead in excuse,* defendo, *I ward off,* grātŭlor, *I congratulate,* etc., take a Dative of the *person* and an Accusative of the *thing,* as, do tibi librum, *I give you a book,* minor tibi mortem, *I threaten death to you, threaten you with death.*

Note 2. Jubeo, sino, laedo, delecto, sano[2] take an Accusative: tempĕro and modĕror take an Accusative when they mean *to govern,* but a Dative when they mean *to restrain* or *refrain from.*

§ 119. *Q.* What is the Passive use of Verbs which in the Active Voice govern a Dative only?

A. They are only used *impersonally* in the Passive. Thus, *I persuade* is 'persuadeo,' but *I am persuaded* is not 'persuadeor,' but 'persuadetur mihi'; literally, *it is persuaded to me.*

[1] Line 1. Ostendo, monstro, etc.; do. 2. Dico, etc.; invideo; parco; permitto, concedo, licet, etc.; credo. 3. Persuadeo; impero, mando, etc.; pareo or obedio. 4. Minor; ignosco or condono; succurro, auxilior, subvenio, etc.; placeo or libet. 5. Have leisure for; displease. 6. Be a slave to; be married to; pay attention to. 7. Medeor; faveo; noceo; resisto or repugno; indulge.

[2] Command, permit, hurt, please, heal.

On the Ablative Case.

§ 120. *Q.* Define the Ablative Case.

A. The Ablative is the Case which modifies the meaning of Verbs or Nouns, like an Adverb, especially as regards Place *whence*, Place *where*, and Instrument *with which*. Examples are,

a. **Place whence**, as, Athenis redit, *He returns from Athens* (§ 103).

b. **Place where**, as, terrā marique, *By land and sea*.

Note 1. This Ablative is often hardly distinguishable from the Locative, on account of the similarity of the endings.

Note 2. Here, perhaps, should be noticed the forms magni, *at a great price,* parvi, tanti, quanti, etc., which have lately been classed by etymologists as Locatives, though the old grammarians classed them as Genitives of Value.

c. **Instrument with which**, as, gladio pugnare, *to fight with a sword*.

§ 121. *Q.* What other uses of the Ablative are there?

A. (*a*) Separation, as, oppugnatione desistunt, *They desist from the attack*.

(*b*) Origin, as, clarissimo patre natus, *Born of a most noble father*.

(*c*) Comparison (used after Comparative Adjectives, and translated by *than*), as, Caesar major erat Crasso, *Caesar was greater than Crassus*.

(*d*) Price (or amount *at which*), as, hortum tribus talentis ēmit, *He bought a garden for three talents*.

(*e*) Time *when*, as, tertio anno, *in the third year*. This Ablative has been already noticed in § 101.

(*f*) Respect, as, aetate provectus, *Advanced in age*.

(*g*) Measure, as, tribus millibus passuum abest, *He is three miles distant*. Especially frequent after Comparative Adjectives, as, multo major, *much greater*.

(*h*) Matter *with which*, as, parvo contentus, *contented with a little*.

(*j*) Quality (translated by *of*, and never found except with Adjective in agreement), as, vir summā sapientiā, *a man of the utmost wisdom*.

(*k*) Manner *how* (usually with Adjective in agreement), as, aut vi aut fraude fit injuria, *Injury is caused either by violence or fraud:* suā sponte hoc fecit, *He did this of his own accord*.

(*l*) Cause, as, senectute mortuus est, *He died of old age*.

Note. Of the above uses, *a, b, c* may be referred more or less closely to *Place whence*, *d, e, f, g* to *Place where*, and *h, j, k, l* to *Instrument*.

(*m*) Agent *by whom*, after Passive Verbs, (always used of a *living thing*, and always requiring the Preposition **a** or **ab**,) as, Caesar a Bruto interfectus est, *Caesar was slain by Brutus*.

(*n*) Ablative after a Preposition.

§ 122. *Q.* What Prepositions govern the Ablative?

A. **A (ab), absque, coram, de,**
palam, clam, cum, ex or **e,**
sine, tenus, pro, and **prae.**
And unto these, if *rest at* be intended,
Let **in, sub, super, subter** be appended.

Note. For the meaning of these Prepositions see §§ 348-363.

§ 123. *Q.* What is the Ablative Absolute?

A. A construction formed of a Noun and Participle in agreement in the Ablative Case, as,

Bello orto, Caesar profectus est, *War having arisen, Caesar set out*.

Note. Absolute means independent, and the name is given to the construction because it is independent of the rest of the Sentence, being in fact equivalent to a Subordinate Clause. Thus orto bello is the same as quum bellum ortum esset, and might be rendered '*when* war had arisen,' or '*since* war had arisen,' or '*though* war had arisen,' etc.

§ 124. *Q.* What Verbs govern the Ablative?

A. **Fungor, fruor, utor, vescor, potior, dignor, supersedeo**[1], and Verbs of *wanting, being full, enriching,* or *depriving.*

Note. Impleo, compleo, egeo, indigeo[2] are also found with Genitive

§ 125. *Q.* What Adjectives govern the Ablative?

A. **Dignus, indignus, fretus, extorris, liber**[3], and Adjectives which signify *wanting, being full, enriching,* or *depriving.*

§ 126. *Q.* What Substantives govern the Ablative?

A. **Opus** and **usus**[4].

On the Genitive Case.

§ 127. *Q.* Define the Genitive Case.

A. The Genitive is the Case which qualifies Nouns, like an Adjective. It is also used as the Direct Object of Nouns and Adjectives, and as the Indirect Object of certain Verbs.

§ 128. *Q.* Distinguish between the Subjective and Objective Genitive.

A. The Subjective Genitive is a Genitive dependent on a Substantive, and regarded as the Subject from whence that Substantive proceeds, as, Amor Dei, *the love of God,* i.e. the love which *God* has *for us* (where God is the Subject who loves).

The Objective Genitive is a Genitive dependent on

---

[1] *Perform, enjoy, use, eat, get possession of, deem worthy, desist from.* [Potior also takes a Genitive].

[2] *Fill, fill, be in want, be in want.*

[3] *Worthy, unworthy, relying on, banished, free.* [Dignus and indignus sometimes take a genitive, as, magnorum indignus avorum, *unworthy of my great ancestors*].

[4] *Need, use.*

a Substantive, and regarded as the Object towards which that Substantive, is directed, as, Amor Dei, *love of God*, i.e. the love which *we* have *for God* (where God is the Object of our love).

§ 129. *Q*. Classify the uses of the Genitive.

A. (*a*) Genitive of the Possessor or Author, as, horti Caesaris, *the gardens of Caesar;* pater Bruti, *the father of Brutus*.

(*b*) Partition (when the Genitive of a Noun signifying a *whole* is dependent on a Noun signifying a *part of that whole*), as, magna pars militum, *a great part of the soldiers;* fortissimus Graecorum, *the bravest of the Greeks*.

(*c*) Definition (showing of what a thing consists), as, honos consulatūs, *the honour of the consulship;* cadus vini, *a cask of wine*.

(*d*) Quality (always found with Adjective in agreement), as, vir summae sapientiae, *a man of the utmost wisdom*.

Note 1. Quality is also expressed by the Ablative. See § 121 (*j*).
Note 2. The above are all to be classed as Subjective Genitives.

(*e*) Object of Substantives, as, timor hostium, *fear of the enemy*.

(*f*) Object of Adjectives, as, avidus laudis, *eager for praise*.

(*g*) Indirect Object of Verbs, as, me majestatis accusat, *he accuses me of treason;* datae fidei reminiscitur, *he remembers* [lit. *reminds himself of*] *his promise given*.

(*h*) Respect or Cause (usually in imitation of Greek constructions), as, integer aevi, *unimpaired in age;*

notus in fratres animi paterni, *well known for his paternal affection towards his brothers.*

Note 3. For the Genitive of Value see § 120, *b*, *Note* 2.

§ 130. Sometimes the Substantive on which a Genitive is dependent is omitted; of this there are two cases, (*a*) of place, as, ventum erat ad Vestae, *we had come to Vesta's*, i.e. Vesta's temple; just as we say in English 'to go to St. Paul's,' i.e. St. Paul's Cathedral; (*b*) when the governing Substantive signifies *nature, duty,* or *business,* as, pastoris est tondēre oves, *it is the duty of a shepherd to shear his sheep*. In both these cases the Genitive is known as *Elliptic*.

§ 131. *Q.* What Verbs govern a Genitive?

A. (1) Reminiscor, obliviscor, memini, recordor, misereor, miseresco, potior, interest, and rēfert; together with certain Verbs signifying *want*, as, egeo, indigeo.[1]

Note. Reminiscor, obliviscor, memini, and recordor also take an Accusative; and potior an Ablative.

(2) Verbs of *accusing, convicting, condemning, acquitting, admonishing,* and *reminding*, take an Accusative of the Person and a Genitive of the Thing, as,

Furti me accusat, *He accuses me of theft.*

The Impersonal Verbs.

§ 132. *Q.* What is the construction after the Impersonal Verbs?

A. The Unipersonals take an Accusative of the *Person*, except licet, libet, and liquet, which take a Dative; and they may all take an Infinitive Mood, as,

Abire me oportet, *I ought to go away.*

Abire mihi licet, *I am permitted to go away.*

Note 1. Licet and others sometimes take a Subjunctive with or without ut, as, licet mihi abeam, *or* ut abeam, *I am permitted to go away.*

Note 2. Miseret, piget, paenitet, pudet, and taedet may also take a Genitive of the *thing*, as, taedet me vitae, *I am weary of life*.

[1] *Remember, forget, remember, remember, pity, pity, get possession of, it makes a difference, it concerns, be in want, be in want.*

Other Verbs used Impersonally take a Dative of the Person, often with an Infinitive, or ut Clause, as,

Expědit mihi abire, *or*, ut abeam, *It is expedient for me to go away*.

But decet, dedecet, juvat, delectat, fallit, fugit,[1] take an Accusative, as,

Te pugnare juvat, *You delight in fighting*.

§ 133. *Q*. What is the construction after **interest** and **refert**?[2]

A. They take a Genitive of the Person, often with an Infinitive or ut Clause. But instead of **mei, tui, sui, nostri, vestri,** the forms **meā, tuā, suā, nostrā, vestrā,** are used, as,

Nec Caesaris nec nostrā interest ut venias, *It is neither of importance to Caesar nor to us that you should come*.

On the Infinitive Mood.

§ 134. *Q*. What is the Infinitive Mood?

A. It is, properly speaking, a Verb-Noun, and may be Nominative, as,

Dormire est jucundum, *to sleep is pleasant*, or *sleeping is pleasant*,

or Accusative, as,

Cupio **dormire**, *I wish to sleep*.

§ 135. *Q*. What are the Gerunds?

A. They are Cases of the Infinitive, the Gerund in **-dum** being Accusative (after a Preposition), the Gerund in **-di** Genitive, and the Gerund in **-do** Dative or Ablative.

---

[1] *It becomes* or *beseems, misbecomes, delights, delights, escapes one's notice, escapes one's notice.*

[2] *It is of importance to* or *makes a difference to, it concerns* or *is of importance to.*

§ 136. *Q.* What are the Supines?

A. These are also Cases of the Infinitive, the Supine in -um being Accusative (only used after Verbs of *motion*, as, eo lusum, *I go to play*), and the Supine in -u Ablative (of Respect), after Adjectives, as, horrendum dictu, *horrible to be told*, i. e. horrible in the telling.

§ 137. *Q.* How is the Future Infinitive Passive formed?

A. By the Supine in -um and iri the Present Infinitive Passive of eo, *I go*, used *Impersonally*, as, credo occisum iri Caesarem, *I believe that Caesar will be killed;* literally, credo *I believe*, iri *that there is a going*, occisum *to kill*, Caesarem *Caesar*.

On the Gerund and Gerundive.

§ 138. *Q.* Can the Gerunds take an Object in the Accusative Case?

A. Sometimes[1], as, Efferor studio patres vestros videndi, *I am elated with the desire of seeing your fathers.* But usually the Noun is put into the Case of the Gerund, and instead of the Gerund the Gerundive is used, agreeing in Gender, Number, and Case with the Noun.

§ 139. *Q.* Give an example.

A. Instead of saying, amor exercendi virtutem, *the love of practising virtue*, we usually say, amor exercend*ae* virtut*is*.

---

[1] Especially when a Pronoun or Adjective is the Object, as, studio illud videndi, *with a desire of seeing that thing;* studio multa videndi, *with desire of seeing many things.* This is to prevent ambiguity, because studio illius videndi might mean *with a desire of seeing that man* or *that thing:* studio multorum videndorum, might mean *with a desire of seeing many men,* or *many things.*

§ 140. *Q.* How is the word *must* translated into Latin?

A. In the Passive Voice by the Gerundive; in the Active by the forms **amandum est,** *we must love,* **monendum est,** *we must advise,* etc., which are probably the neuters of the Gerundive.

§ 141. *Q.* Can **amandum est** take an Accusative of the Object after it, as, Amandum est Deum, *We must love God?*

A. No; we must say, Amandus est Deus, *God must be loved.* But after Verbs which only govern the Dative, a Dative of the Object is used, as, Parcendum est hostibus, *We must spare our enemies.*

Note. Fungor, fruor, utor, vescor, and potior, which govern an Ablative, have both Gerund and Gerundive; hence we may say, utendum est aetate, *we must make use of our age,* or, utenda est aetas, (the latter form very rare).

§ 142. *Q.* In what case is the Agent, or *living person* by whom a thing is done, put after the Gerundive?

A. In the Dative, as, Canendum est poetae, *The poet must sing* [literally, 'it is to be sung *by* the poet';] unless the Verb be one of those which only govern a Dative, when a or ab with Ablative must be used, as, Credendum est a poetâ, *The poet must believe.*

Note. This is to prevent ambiguity; nobis credendum est poetae might mean either *the poet must believe us* or *we must believe the poet.*

Rules for Qui, Quum, and Ut.

§ 143. *Q.* What is the rule for the Mood of the Verb after qui?

A. Qui, in its simple sense of *who* or *which,* takes the Indicative, as, qui peccat miser est, *He who sins is miserable.* But if there is implied in it *since, in order that,* or *such that,* it takes the Subjunctive, as,

Stultus es qui huic credas, *You are foolish for believing this man.*

Mittit equites qui agros vastent, *He sends cavalry to lay waste the fields.*

Non est is qui timeat, *He is not the man to be afraid.*

§ 144. *Q.* What is the Rule for **quum**?

A. **Quum**, meaning *since* or *although*, always takes the Subjunctive, as, quae quum ita sint, *Since these things are so;* **quum**, meaning *when*, takes a Subjunctive if the sense requires an Imperfect or Pluperfect Tense; otherwise it takes the Indicative, as,

Quum Athenis essem, *When I was at Athens.*

Quum Athenas pervenisset, *When he had arrived at Athens.*

Vix haec locutus erat quum clamor exortus est, *Scarcely had he said these things when a shout arose.*

§ 145. *Q.* What is the rule for **ut**?

A. **Ut**, meaning *as, when*, or *how*, takes an Indicative, as, ut vales, *How are you?* ut, meaning *in order that*, or *so that*, takes a Subjunctive, as,

Edĭmus ut vivamus, *We eat that we may live.*

Tam potens est Deus ut omnia regat, *God is so powerful that he rules all things.*

Note. The Rules given in the three foregoing sections must be understood to apply only to Oratio Recta, so far as the use of the Indicative is concerned. When the learner has mastered the Note on the Subjunctive given in §§ 197-203, he will understand that wherever a Sentence is Oblique the use of an Indicative is inadmissible.

§ 146. *Q.* How are *in order that . . . not* and *so that . . . not* translated?

A. In order that . . . not by **nē**; *so that . . . not* by **ut non**.

On the Sequence of Tenses.

§ 147. *Q.* What is meant by the Sequence of Tenses?

A. The correspondence regularly observed between the tenses of the Principal Verbs in a sentence and those of the Subordinate or Dependent Verbs.

§ 148. *Q.* What is the rule for the Sequence of Tenses?

A. **Primary Tenses are followed by Primary, Historic by Historic.** Examples are :—

(*a*) *Oblique Statement.*

Affirmat, affirmavit, affirmabit, se scribere, scripsisse, scripturum esse, scripturum fuisse.

He declares or *is declaring, has declared, will declare, that he writes* or *is writing, wrote* or *has written, will write, would have written.*

Affirmabat, affirmavit, affirmaverat, se scribere, scripsisse, scripturam esse, scripturam fuisse.

She was declaring, declared, had declared, that she wrote or *was writing, had written, would write, would have written.*

Note. After Primary Tenses, scribere and esse are Presents, scripsisse and fuisse Aorists or Perfects; after Historic Tenses they are Imperfects or Aorists, and Pluperfects, respectively.

(*b*) *Oblique Question.*

Quaero, quaesivi, quaeram, quid scribat, quid scripserit, quid scripturus sit, quid scripturus fuerit.

I ask or *am asking, I have asked, I shall ask, what he writes* or *is writing, what he wrote* or *has written, what he will write, what he would have written.*

Quaerebam, quaesivi, quaesiveram, quid scriberet, quid scripsisset, quid scriptura esset, quid scriptura fuisset.

I was asking, I asked, I had asked, what she wrote or *was writing, what she had written, what she would write, what she would have written.*

APPENDIX.

A TABLE OF VERBS, SHEWING THE PRESENT, INFINITIVE, PERFECT, AND SUPINE.

Note.—Some Verbs, as lăvo, have forms belonging to more than one Conjugation. These are bracketed and placed in the earliest in order of the Conjugations to which either of the forms can be referred.

*** Forms enclosed in round brackets, as, (jutum) are rarely used.

§ 149. First Conjugation.

	Present.	Infinitive.	Perfect.	Supine.
Regular Form,	-o,	-are,	-avi,	-atum.
as,	amo,	amāre,	amāvi,	amātum.

Exceptions:—

(*a*) Those having -ui in Perfect, -ĭtum or -tum in Supine.

Pres.	Inf.	Perf.	Supine.	Meaning.
1. crĕpo,	crepāre,	crepŭi,	crepĭtum,	*creak.*
2. cŭbo,	cubāre,	cubŭi,	cubĭtum,	*lie down.*
3. dŏmo,	domāre,	domŭi,	domĭtum,	*tame.*
4. ĕnĕco,	enecāre,	enecui,	enectum,	*kill*[1].
5. explĭco,	explicāre,	{ explicŭi, explicāvi,	explicĭtum, explicātum, }	*unfold*[2].
6. frĭco,	fricāre,	fricŭi,	frictum,	*rub.*
7. mĭco,	micāre,	micŭi,	. . .	*glitter*[3]
8. sĕco,	secāre,	secŭi,	sectum,	*cut.*
9. sŏno,	sonāre,	sonŭi,	sonĭtum,	*sound.*
10. tŏno,	tonāre,	tonŭi,	tonĭtum,	*thunder.*
11. vĕto,	vetāre,	vetŭi,	vetĭtum,	*forbid.*

[1] The simple form *neco, to kill,* is regular.
[2] So nearly all compounds of plico, *to fold,* which has no Perfect or Supine. But duplico, *double,* multiplico, *multiply,* supplico, *supplicate,* are regular, not being compounds of plico.
[3] Compounds have -ātum in Supine. Dimico, *contend,* has Perf. -avi or -ui.

(b) Those having -vi in Perfect, -tum in Supine.

Pres.	Inf.	Perf.	Supine.	Meaning.
1. jŭvo,	juvāre,	jūvi,	(jūtum),	help.
2. lăvo,	lavāre, lavĕre,	lāvi, (lavavi),	lautum, lōtum, lavātum,	wash.
3. pōto,	potāre,	potāvi,	potātum, pōtum,	drink.

(c) Those having reduplicated [1] Perfect, -tum in Supine.

1. do,	dăre,	dĕdi,	dătum,	give.
2. sto,	stāre,	stĕti,	stātum,	stand [2].

§ 150. Second Conjugation.

	Pres.	Inf.	Perf.	Supine.
Regular Form,	-ĕo,	-ēre,	-ŭi,	-ĭtum.
as,	monĕo,	monēre,	monŭi,	monĭtum.

Exceptions:—

(a) Those having regular Perf. in -ui, but -tum or -sum in Supine.

Pres.	Inf.	Perf.	Supine.	Meaning.
1. censeo,	censēre,	censŭi,	censum,	reckon, think.
2. dŏceo,	docēre,	docŭi,	doctum,	teach.
3. misceo,	miscēre,	miscŭi,	mixtum, mistum,	mix.
4. rĕtĭnco,	retinēre,	retinŭi,	rĕtentum,	retain [3].
5. torreo,	torrēre,	torrŭi,	tostum,	parch.

(b) Those having -vi (-ui) in Perf., -tum or -itum in Supine.

1. aboleo,	abolēre,	abolevi, abolui,	abolĭtum,	abolish.
2. adoleo, adolesco,	adolēre, adoles- cĕre,	adolevi, adolui,	adultum,	enlarge. grow [4].

---

[1] That is, having the first consonant of the Present, together with a vowel, prefixed to the Perfect Tense, as do, de-di. In the Perfects of compound Verbs the initial consonants of the Verb, not of the Preposition, appear as the reduplication of the Perfect, e.g. consto, con-stĭti.

[2] The compounds make -stĭti in Perf., as, praesto, praestiti, and seldom have a Supine.

[3] So all compounds of 'teneo,' to hold, which has no Supine.

[4] Adoleo (usually in Perf. adolui), to enlarge, hence as sacrificial term (1) to honour by sacrifice, (2) to burn sacrifice. Adolesco (usually in Perf. adolēvi), to grow (intrans.).

APPENDIX. [-150.

Pres.	Inf.	Perf.	Supine.	Meaning.
3. conīveo,	conivēre,	conīvi, conixi,	. . .	*wink.*
4. dēleo,	delēre,	delēvi,	delētum,	*destroy.*
5. ferveo, fervo,	fervēre, fervĕre,	ferbui, fervi,	. . .	*boil.*
6. flĕo,	flēre,	flēvi,	flētum,	*weep.*
7. impleo,	implēre,	implēvi,	implētum,	*fill*[1].
8. neo,	nēre,	nēvi,	nētum,	*spin.*
9. păveo,	pavēre,	pāvi,	. . .	*be afraid.*

(c) Those having -si in Perf., -sum or -tum in Supine.

1. absorbeo,	absorbēre,	absorpsi, absorbui,	(absorptum),	*swallow up*[2].
2. algeo,	algēre,	alsi,	. . .	*be cold.*
3. ardeo,	ardēre,	arsi,	arsum,	*be on fire.*
4. augeo,	augēre,	auxi,	auctum,	*make bigger.*
5. fulgeo, fulgo,	fulgēre, fulgĕre,	fulsi,	. . .	*glitter.*
6. frīgeo,	frigēre,	(frixi),	. . .	*be cold.*
7. haereo,	haerēre,	haesi,	haesum,	*stick.*
8. indulgeo,	indulgēre,	indulsi,	(indultum),	*indulge.*
9. jŭbeo,	jubēre,	jussi,	jussum,	*command.*
10. măneo,	manēre,	mansi,	mansum,	*remain, await.*
11. lugeo,	lugēre,	luxi,	(luctum),	*mourn.*
12. mulceo,	mulcēre,	mulsi,	mulsum,	*soothe.*
13. mulgeo,	mulgēre,	mulsi,	(mulsum), mulctum,	*milk.*
14. rīdeo,	ridēre,	risi,	risum,	*laugh.*
15. suadeo,	suadēre,	suasi,	suasum,	*advise.*
16. torqueo,	torquēre,	torsi,	tortum,	*twist.*
17. tergeo, tergo,	tergēre, tergĕre,	tersi,	tersum,	*wipe.*
18. turgeo,	turgēre,	tursi,	. . .	*swell.*
19. urgeo,	urgēre,	ursi,	. . .	*urge.*

(d) Those having -i in Perf., -tum or -sum in Supine.

1. căveo,	cavēre,	cāvi,	cautum,	*beware.*
2. făveo,	favēre,	fāvi,	fautum,	*favour.*
3. fŏveo,	fovēre,	fōvi,	fōtum,	*cherish.*
4. mŏveo,	movēre,	mōvi,	motum,	*move.*
5. vŏveo,	vovēre,	vōvi,	vōtum,	*vow.*

[1] So all compounds of 'pleo,' *to fill*, which is never found in an uncompounded form.
[2] So all compounds of sorbeo, sorbēre, sorbui, no Sup., *to swallow.*

Pres.	Inf.	Perf.	Supine.	Meaning.
6. prandeo,	prandēre,	prandi,	pransum,	dine.
7. respondeo,	respondēre,	respondi,	responsum,	answer [1].
8. sĕdeo,	sedēre,	sēdi,	sessum,	sit [2].
9. vĭdeo,	vidēre,	vīdi,	visum,	see.

(e) Those having reduplicated Perf., -sum in Supine.

1. mordeo,	mordēre,	mŏmordi,	morsum,	bite.
2. pendeo,	pendēre,	pĕpendi,	pensum,	be suspended.
3. spondeo,	spondēre,	spŏpondi,	sponsum,	promise.
4. tondeo,	tondēre,	tŏtondi,	tonsum,	shear.

(f) Semi-deponent Verbs.

1. audeo,	audēre,	ausus sum,		dare.
2. gaudeo,	gaudēre,	gavīsus sum,		rejoice.
3. sŏleo,	solēre,	solĭtus sum,		be accustomed.

(g) The following have regular Perfect but seldom or never a Supine:—arceo, *ward off*; caleo, *be warm* (calĭtum); egeo, *be in want*; floreo, *flourish*; horreo, *shudder*; lateo, *lie hid*; madeo, *be wet*; niteo, *shine*; oleo, *smell*; pateo, *lie open*; rigeo, *be stiff*; rubeo, *be red*; sileo, *be silent*; studeo, *pay attention to*; stupeo, *be amazed*: tepeo, *be warm*; timeo, *fear*; tumeo, *swell*; vigeo, *flourish*; vireo, *be green*.

§ 151. Third Conjugation.

No regular form. Infinitive ends in -ĕre. The principal varieties of Conjugation are the following:—

(a) Those having -si in Perf., -tum in Supine. [*Note.* Perfects in -xi are considered as ending in -si, since x is only a double letter standing for cs, gs, ks, or qs.]

Pres.	Inf.	Perf.	Supine.	Meaning.
1. allĭcĭo,	allicĕre,	allexi,	allectum,	entice [3].
2. aspĭcĭo,	aspicĕre,	aspexi,	aspectum,	behold [4].
3. carpo,	carpĕre,	carpsi,	carptum,	pluck.
4. cingo,	cingĕre,	cinxi,	cinctum,	surround.
5. cōmo,	comĕre,	compsi,	comptum,	adorn.

[1] So all compounds of spondeo, *to promise*.
[2] The compounds, except circumsedeo and supersedeo, make -sideo, -sēdi, -sessum, as obsideo, *to besiege*.
[3] So all compounds [except 'elicio'] of the unused Verb lacio, *to entice*.
[4] So all compounds of the unused Verb specio, *to see*.

APPENDIX.

	Pres.	Inf.	Perf.	Supine.	Meaning.
6.	contemno,	contemnĕre,	contempsi,	contemptum,	*despise* [1].
7.	cŏquo,	coquĕre,	coxi,	coctum,	*cook.*
8.	dēmo,	demĕre,	dempsi,	demptum,	*take away.*
9.	dīco,	dicĕre,	dixi,	dictum,	*say, tell.*
10.	dūco,	ducĕre,	duxi,	ductum,	*lead.*
11.	emungo,	emungĕre,	emunxi,	emunctum,	*blow the nose.*
12.	extinguo,	extinguĕre,	extinxi,	extinctum,	*extinguish* [2].
13.	fingo,	fingĕre,	finxi,	fictum,	*invent.*
14.	frīgo,	frigĕre,	(frixi),	frictum,	*roast.*
15.	gĕro,	gerĕre,	gessi,	gestum,	*carry on.*
16.	inflīgo,	infligĕre,	inflixi,	inflictum,	*inflict* [3].
17.	jungo,	jungĕre,	junxi,	junctum,	*join.*
18.	(ninguo),	ninguĕre,	(ninxi),	. . .	*snow* [4].
19.	nūbo,	nubĕre,	nupsi,	nuptum,	*be married* [5].
20.	pingo,	pingĕre,	pinxi,	pictum,	*paint.*
21.	plango,	plangĕre,	planxi,	planctum,	*beat the breast.*
22.	prōmo,	promĕre,	prompsi,	promptum,	*draw out.*
23.	rĕgo,	regĕre,	rexi,	rectum,	*rule* [6].
24.	rēpo,	repĕre,	repsi,	(reptum),	*creep.*
25.	{scalpo, sculpo,	scalpĕre, sculpĕre,	scalpsi, sculpsi,	scalptum, sculptum,}	*engrave.*
26.	scrībo,	scribĕre,	scripsi,	scriptum,	*write.*
27.	stringo,	stringĕre,	strinxi,	strictum,	*graze, squeeze.*
28.	strŭo,	struĕre,	struxi,	structum,	*build.*
29.	sūgo,	sugere,	suxi,	suctum,	*suck.*
30.	sūmo,	sumĕre,	sumpsi,	sumptum,	*take.*
31.	tĕgo,	tegĕre,	texi,	tectum,	*cover.*
32.	tinguo,	tinguĕre,	tinxi,	tinctum,	*dye.*
33.	trăho,	trahĕre,	traxi,	tractum,	*draw.*
34.	unguo,	unguĕre,	unxi,	unctum,	*anoint.*
35.	ūro,	urĕre,	ussi,	ustum,	*burn.*
36.	vĕho,	vehĕre,	vexi,	vectum,	*carry.*
37.	vīvo,	vivĕre,	vixi,	victum,	*live.*

[1] The simple form temno, *despise*, is seldom found in Perf. or Supine.

[2] So all compounds of stinguo, *to quench*, which has no Perfect or Supine.

[3] So all compounds of the unused Verb fligo, *to smite*, except profligo, *rout*, which is of the 1st Conjugation.

[4] Not found except as Impersonal ninguit, *it snows*, ninxit, etc.

[5] Lit. *put on a bridal veil*, and always, therefore, used of a *woman*.

[6] The compounds make -rigo, -rexi, -rectum, as dirigo, *direct*. Pergo, *proceed*, and surgo, *rise*, are for perrigo, surrigo (per-rego, sub-rego), and make pergĕre, perrexi, perrectum, surgĕre, surrexi, surrectum.

(b) Those having -si in Perf., -sum in Supine.

Pres.	Inf.	Perf.	Supine.	Meaning.
1. cēdo,	cedĕre,	cessi,	cessum,	*go, yield.*
2. claudo,	claudĕre,	clausi,	clausum,	*shut* [1].
3. concŭtĭo,	concutĕre,	concussi,	concussum,	*shake* [2].
4. dīvĭdo,	divĭdĕre,	divīsi,	divīsum,	*divide.*
5. ēvādo,	evādĕre,	evāsi,	evāsum,	*go out* [3].
6. fīgo,	figĕre,	fixi,	fixum,	*fix.*
7. flecto,	flectĕre,	flexi,	flexum,	*bend.*
8. flŭo,	fluĕre,	fluxi,	fluxum,	*flow.*
9. laedo,	laedĕre,	laesi,	laesum,	*hurt.*
10. lūdo,	ludĕre,	lūsi,	lūsum,	*play.*
11. mergo,	mergĕre,	mersi,	mersum,	*plunge.*
12. mitto,	mittĕre,	misi,	missum,	*send.*
13. necto,	nectĕre,	{ nexi, nexui, }	nexum,	*bind.*
14. pecto,	pectĕre,	pexi,	pexum,	*comb.*
15. plaudo,	plaudĕre,	plausi,	plausum,	*clap the hands* [4].
16. plecto,	plectĕre,	. . .	plexum,	*plait.*
17. plecto,	plectĕre,	. . .	. . .	*punish.*
18. prĕmo,	premĕre,	pressi,	pressum,	*press* [5].
19. rādo,	radĕre,	rāsi,	rāsum,	*scrape.*
20. rōdo,	rodĕre,	rōsi,	rōsum,	*gnaw.*
21. spargo,	spargĕre,	sparsi,	sparsum,	*sprinkle* [6].
22. trūdo,	trudĕre,	trūsi,	trūsum,	*thrust.*

(c) Those having a reduplicated Perf., -tum or -sum in Supine.

1. cădo,	cădĕre,	cĕcĭdi,	cāsum,	*fall.*
2. caedo,	caedĕre,	cĕcīdi,	caesum,	*cut, kill.*
3. căno,	cănĕre,	cĕcĭni,	cantum,	*sing.*
4. curro,	currĕre,	cŭcurri,	cursum,	*run.*
5. disco,	discĕre,	dĭdĭci,	. . .	*learn.*
6. fallo,	fallĕre,	fĕfelli,	falsum,	*deceive.*
7. pango,	pangĕre,	{ pēgi, pĕpĭgi, }	pactum,	{ *fasten, bargain.* }

[1] The compounds make -cludo, as, reclūdo, -ĕre, -si, -sum, *open.*
[2] So all compounds of quatio. *to shake*, which has no Perfect.
[3] So all compounds of vado, *to go*, which has no Perf. or Sup. in use.
[4] The compounds, except applaudo, make -plodo, -plodĕre, -plōsi, -plōsum, as explōdo, *hiss off the stage.*
[5] The compounds make -primo, -primĕre, -pressi, -pressum, as exprimo, *express.*
[6] The compounds make -spergo, -spersi, -spersum, as aspergo, *besprinkle.*

APPENDIX.

Pres.	Inf.	Perf.	Supine.	Meaning.
8. parco,	parcĕre,	pĕperci,	parsum,	*spare.*
9. părĭo,	părĕre,	pĕpĕri,	{ parĭtum, partum, }	*bring forth.*
10. pello,	pellĕre,	pĕpŭli,	pulsum,	*drive.*
11. pendo,	pendĕre,	pĕpendi,	pensum,	*weigh.*
12. perdo,	perdĕre,	perdĭdi,	perdĭtum,	*lose, destroy* [1].
13. posco,	poscĕre,	pŏposci,	. . .	*demand.*
14. pungo,	pungĕre,	pŭpŭgi,	punctum,	*prick* [2].
15. rĕsisto,	resistĕre,	restĭti,	restĭtum,	*resist* [3].
16. sisto,	sistĕre,	(stĕti),	(stătum),	*place, stop.*
17. tango,	tangĕre,	tĕtĭgi,	tactum,	*touch.*
18. tendo,	tendĕre,	tĕtendi,	{ tensum, tentum, }	*stretch.*
19. tollo,	tollĕre,	. . .	. . .	*lift, take away* [4].
20. tundo,	tundĕre,	(tŭtŭdi),	{ tunsum, tūsum, }	*beat, pound.*

(*d*) Those having -i in Perf., -tum in Supine.

1. attingo,	attingĕre,	attĭgi,	attactum,	*touch* [5].
2. ăgo [6],	agĕre,	ēgi,	actum,	*act, drive.*
3. bĭbo,	bĭbĕre,	bĭbi,	bĭbĭtum,	*drink.*
4. căpĭo [7],	căpĕre,	cēpi,	captum,	*take.*
5. contendo,	contendĕre,	contendi,	contentum,	*strive* [8].
6. ĕmo [9],	ĕmĕre,	ēmi,	emptum,	*buy.*

[1] So most compounds of the unused Verb do, dĕre, *to place* [probably a form of do, dāre]; as, addo, *add;* abdo, *hide;* condo, *found;* crēdo, *believe;* dēdo, *give up;* ēdo, *give forth;* prōdo, *betray;* reddo, *restore;* trādo, *deliver up;* vendo, *sell.* But circumdo, *surround;* pessumdo, *ruin;* satisdo, *give security;* and venumdo, *offer for sale,* are compounds of do, dăre, *to give,* and belong to the 1st Conjugation.

[2] The compounds, as expungo, *to expunge,* make -punxi in the Perfect.

[3] So all compounds of sisto, *to stop* [itself a reduplicated form of 'sto'].

[4] Sustuli, sublatum, from suffĕro [sub-fero], are used for the Perfect and Supine cf this Verb. The compounds, as attollo, extollo, have no Perfect or Supine.

[5] So all compounds of tango, *to touch.*

[6] The compounds, except circumago, perago, satago, make -ĭgo, -ĭgĕre, -ēgi, -actum, as exigo, *exact.* Cogo, coēgi, coactum, *collect* or *compel,* is for co-ago Dēgo (de-igo), dēgi, *to spend time,* has no Supine.

[7] The compounds, except antecapio, make -cipio, -cipĕre, -cēpi, -ceptum, as accipio, *receive.*

[8] So all compounds of tendo, *to stretch.* Extendo, *extend,* ostendo, *shew,* and some others, have -sum as well as -tum in the Supine.

[9] Most compounds (except como, demo, promo, sumo, § 151, *a*) make -ĭmo, -imĕre, -ēmi, -emptum, as adĭmo, *take away.*

Pres.	Inf.	Perf.	Supine.	Meaning.
7. făcio[1],	facĕre,	fēci,	factum,	*make, do.*
8. frango[2],	frangĕre,	frēgi,	fractum,	*break.*
9. fŭgio,	fugĕre,	fūgi,	fugĭtum,	*fly.*
10. impingo,	impingĕre,	impēgi,	impactum,	*strike upon*[3].
11. jăcĭo[4],	jăcĕre,	jēci,	jactum,	*throw.*
12. lambo,	lambĕre,	lambi,	. . .	*lick.*
13. lĕgo[5],	lĕgĕre,	lēgi,	lectum,	*choose, read.*
14. refello,	refellĕre,	refelli,	. . .	*refute.*
15. rĕlinquo,	relinquĕre,	relīqui,	relictum,	*leave*[6].
16. rumpo,	rumpĕre,	rūpi,	ruptum,	*burst through.*
17. vinco,	vincĕre,	vīci.	victum,	*conquer.*

(*e*) Those having -i in Perf., -sum in Supine.

1. accendo,	accendĕre,	accendi,	accensum,	*set on fire*[7].
2. contundo,	contundĕre, contŭdi,		contunsum, contūsum,	*bruise*[8].
3. defendo,	defendĕre,	defendi,	defensum,	*defend*[9].
4. ĕdo,	ĕdĕre,	ēdi,	ēsum,	*eat.*
5. excūdo,	excudĕre,	excūdi,	excūsum,	*hammer out*[10].
6. făcesso,	facessĕre,	făcessi,	facessītum,	*execute.*
7. findo,	findĕre,	fĭdi,	fissum,	*cleave.*
8. fŏdĭo,	fŏdĕre,	fŏdi,	fossum,	*dig.*
9. fundo,	fundĕre,	fūdi,	fūsum,	*pour.*
10. mando,	mandĕre,	mandi,	mansum,	*chew.*
11. occĭdo,	occĭdĕre,	occĭdi,	occāsum,	*fall*[11].
12. occīdo,	occīdĕre,	occīdi,	occīsum,	*kill*[12].

[1] Facio, when compounded with a Preposition, makes -ficio, -ficĕre, -fēci, -fectum, and the Passive is formed regularly in -or, as afficio, *affect*, Pass. afficior. But when compounded with bene, satis, male, or a Verb, the form -facio is retained, and the Passive is -fio, as benefacio, *benefit*, patefacio, *lay open*, Pass. benefio, patefio.

[2] The compounds make -fringo, -fringere, -frēgi, -fractum, as effringo.

[3] From pango, *to fasten*. Some compounds retain the *a*, as depango.

[4] The compounds make -jicio, -jicĕre, -jeci, -jectum, as conjicio.

[5] The compounds are sometimes written -lego, as perlĕgo, *read through*, sometimes -lĭgo, as deligo, *choose*. Most make -lēgi, -lectum in Perfect and Supine; but diligo, *love*, intellego, *understand*, and neglego, *neglect*, make -lexi, -lectum.

[6] So all compounds of linquo, Perf. liqui, *to leave*, which has no Supine.

[7] So all compounds of the unused Verb cando, *to set on fire*.

[8] So most compounds of tundo, *to beat* or *pound*.

[9] So all compounds of the unused Verb fendo, *to strike*.

[10] So all compounds of cūdo, cūdi, cūsum, *to hammer* (rarely used).

[11] So all compounds of cado, *to fall*; but the Supine is rarely found.

[12] So all compounds of caedo, *to cut* or *kill*.

APPENDIX.

	Pres.	Inf.	Perf.	Supine.	Meaning.
13.	pando,	pandĕre,	pandi,	pansum, passum,	unfold.
14.	percello,	percellĕre,	percŭli,	perculsum,	strike down.
15.	prehendo,	prehendĕre,	prehendi,	prehensum,	seize.
16.	rĕpello,	rĕpellĕre,	rēpŭli,	rĕpulsum,	repel [1].
17.	scando [2],	scandĕre,	scandi,	scansum,	climb.
18.	scindo,	scindĕre,	scĭdi,	scissum,	cut.
19.	sīdo,	sīdĕre,	sīdi.	. . .	settle.
20.	succurro,	succurrĕre,	succurri,	succursum,	succour [3].
21.	suspendo,	suspendĕre,	suspendi,	suspensum,	suspend [4].
22.	vello,	vellĕre,	velli, vulsi,	vulsum,	pluck.
23.	verro,	verrĕre,	verri,	versum,	sweep.
24.	verto,	vertĕre,	verti,	versum,	turn.
25.	vīso,	vīsĕre,	vīsi,	vīsum,	visit.

(*f*) Those having -ui in Perf., -tum or -sum in Supine.

	Pres.	Inf.	Perf.	Supine.	Meaning.
1.	accumbo,	accumbĕre,	accŭbui,	accubĭtum,	sit at meat [5].
2.	ălo,	alĕre,	alŭi,	alĭtum, altum,	nourish.
3.	cŏlo,	cŏlĕre,	cŏlŭi,	cultum,	cultivate.
4.	compesco,	compescĕre,	compescui,	. . .	restrain.
5.	concĭno,	concinĕre,	concinui,	(concentum),	sing in harmony [6].
6.	consŭlo,	consŭlĕre,	consŭlŭi,	consultum,	consult.
7.	ēlĭcĭo,	ēlĭcĕre,	ēlĭcŭi,	ēlĭcĭtum,	elicit.
8.	excello,	excellĕre,	excellui,	excelsum,	excel [7].
9.	frĕmo,	frĕmĕre,	frĕmŭi,	frĕmĭtum,	roar.
10.	frendo,	frendĕre,	(frendui),	frēsum, fressum,	gnash the teeth.
11.	fŭro,	furĕre,	(furui),	. . .	rage.
12.	gĕmo,	gĕmĕre,	gĕmŭi,	gĕmĭtum,	groan.
13.	gigno,	gignĕre,	gĕnŭi,	gĕnĭtum,	beget.

[1] So all compounds of pello. Rĕpuli is also spelt reppuli.
[2] Scando becomes scendo in compounds, as, descendo, descendi, descensum, *to descend*.
[3] So all compounds of curro, *to run*. But some have the reduplicated form also, as, decurro, *to run down*, which has Perf. decurri *and* decucurri.
[4] So all compounds of pendo, *to weigh*.
[5] So all compounds of the unused Verb cumbo, *to lie* (a form of cŭbo, cubāre).
[6] So most compounds of cano, *to sing*.
[7] So all compounds, except percello, § 151 *e*, of the unused Verb cello, *to impel*.

114   *LATIN GRAMMAR.*   [§§ 151–

Pres.	Inf.	Perf.	Supine.	Meaning.
14. mĕto,	mĕtĕre,	messŭi,	messum,	*reap.*
15. mŏlo,	mŏlĕre,	molŭi,	molĭtum,	*grind.*
16. occŭlo,	occŭlĕre,	occŭlŭi,	occultum,	*hide.*
17. pōno,	pōnĕre,	pŏsŭi,	pŏsĭtum,	*put, place.*
18. răpĭo[1],	răpĕre,	răpŭi,	raptum,	*seize.*
19. sĕro,	sĕrĕre,	sĕrŭi,	sertum,	*sew.*
20. sterto,	stertĕre,	(stertui)	. . .	*snore.*
21. strĕpo,	strĕpĕre,	strĕpŭi,	strĕpĭtum,	*make a noise.*
22. texo,	texĕre,	texŭi,	textum,	*weave.*
23. trĕmo,	trĕmĕre,	trĕmŭi,	. . .	*tremble.*
24. vŏmo,	vŏmĕre,	vŏmŭi,	vŏmĭtum,	*vomit.*

(*g*) Those having -vi in Perf., -tum in Supine.

1. abolesco,	abolescĕre,	abolēvi,	(abolĭtum),	*decay.*
2. adscisco,	adsciscĕre,	adscivi,	adscītum,	*take.*
3. arcesso,	arcessĕre,	arcessivi,	arcessītum,	*summon*[2].
4. cerno,	cernĕre,	crēvi,	crētum,	*discern.*
5. cognosco,	cognoscĕre,	cognōvi,	cognĭtum,	*know*[3].
6. cresco,	crescĕre,	crēvi,	crētum,	*grow.*
7. cŭpĭo,	cŭpĕre,	cŭpīvi,	cŭpītum,	*desire.*
8. incesso,	incessĕre,	incessīvi,	. . .	*attack.*
9. lĭno,	lĭnĕre,	{ lēvi, līvi, }	lĭtum,	*smear.*
10. nosco,	noscĕre,	nōvi,	nōtum,	{ *become acquainted with.*
11. pasco,	pascĕre,	pāvi,	pastum,	*feed.*
12. pĕto,	pĕtĕre,	pĕtīvi,	pĕtītum,	*seek.*
13. quaero[4],	quaerĕre,	quaesīvi,	quaesītum,	*ask.*
14. quĭesco,	quĭescĕre,	quĭēvi,	quĭētum,	*rest.*
15. rŭdo,	rudĕre,	rudīvi,	(rudītum),	*bray.*
16. scisco,	sciscĕre,	scīvi,	scītum,	*ratify.*
17. sĕro,	sĕrĕre,	sēvi,	sătum,	*sow.*
18. sĭno,	sĭnĕre,	sīvi,	(sĭtum),	*allow.*
19. sperno,	spernĕre,	sprēvi,	sprētum,	*despise.*
20. sterno,	sternĕre,	strāvi,	strātum,	*throw down.*

[1] The compounds make -rĭpio, -rĭpere, -ripui, -reptum, as, dirĭpio, *to tear in pieces.*
[2] So capesso, *take in hand,* and lacesso, *provoke.* Arcesso and lacesso sometimes have -īri for -i in Present Infinitive Passive. Arcesso is sometimes written accerso.
[3] So agnosco, *to recognise.* Other compounds of nosco, *to become acquainted with,* have no Supine, except ignosco, *pardon,* which has ignotum.
[4] The compounds make -quiro, -quirĕre, -quisīvi, -quisītum, as exquiro.

Pres.	Inf.	Perf.	Supine.	Meaning.
21. suēsco,	suēscĕre,	suēvi,	suētum,	*be accustomed.*
22. tĕro,	tĕrĕre,	trīvi,	trītum,	*rub.*

(*b*) Those ending in **-uo** in Present Indicative First Person Singular, which [with the exception of some already mentioned, as, struo, struxi, etc.] make **-ŭi** in Perf. and **-ūtum** in Supine, as, trĭbŭo, trĭbŭĕre, trĭbŭi, trĭbūtum, *assign.* Pluo, *to rain*, has Perf. plui *or* pluvi. In this class must be included

1. solvo,	solvĕre,	solvi,	solūtum,	*loose, pay.*
2. volvo,	volvĕre,	volvi,	volūtum,	*roll.*

Ruo, *rush down*, makes Supine rŭtum. The following have no Supine: annuo, *assent;* congruo, *agree;* metuo, *fear;* pluo, *rain.*

(*j*) Inceptives in **-sco.** These Verbs are formed (*a*) from Verbs chiefly of the Second Conjugation, (*b*) from Nouns. The former have no Perfects, except those of the Verbs from which they are derived, as, pallesco [*from* palleo], *I grow pale*, Perf. pallŭi; the latter either have no Perfects or form them in the same way in **-ui**, as, dūresco [*from* durus], *I grow hard*, Perf. durŭi. Few Inceptives have any Supine.

Of the exceptions to the above rule some, as abolesco, adolesco, scisco, suesco, have already been given. Notice the following:—

1. concupisco, concupiscĕre, concupīvi, concupītum, *desire.*
2. exardesco, exardescĕre, exarsi, exarsum, *blaze forth.*
3. expavesco, expavescĕre, expāvi, . . . *grow alarmed.*
4. illucesco, illucescĕre, illuxi, . . . *grow light.*
5. inveterasco, inveterascĕre, inveteravi, . . . *grow old.*

(*k*) The Semi-Deponent, fido, *trust*, has Perfect fisus sum. The compounds confīdo, *trust confidently*, and diffīdo, *mistrust*, have Perfects confīdi *and* confisus sum, diffīdi *and* diffisus sum.

§ 152. The Fourth Conjugation.

	Pres.	Inf.	Perf.	Supine.
Regular Form,	**-ĭo,**	**-īre,**	**-īvi,**	**-ītum.**
as,	audĭo,	audīre,	audīvi,	audītum.

Exceptions:—

(*a*) Those having regular Perf., but **-tum** in Supine.

Pres.	Inf.	Perf.	Supine.	Meaning.
1. ĕo,	īre,	īvi (ii),	ĭtum,	*go* [1].
2. sĕpĕlĭo,	sepelīre,	sĕpĕlīvi,	sĕpultum,	*bury.*

[1] The compounds usually make ii in Perf. Vēneo, *am for sale*, has no Supine.

(b) Those having -i in Perf., -tum in Supine.

Pres.	Inf.	Perf.	Supine.	Meaning.
1. compĕrĭo,	compĕrīre,	compĕri,	compertum,	*ascertain.*
2. rĕpĕrĭo,	rĕpĕrīre,	rĕpĕri,	rĕpertum,	*find.*
3. vĕnĭo,	vĕnīre,	vēni,	ventum,	*come.*

(c) Those having -si in Perf., -tum or -sum in Supine.

1. confercĭo,	confercīre,	confersi,	confertum,	*press together*[1].
2. ferĭo,	ferīre,	...	...	*strike*[2].
3. fulcĭo,	fulcīre,	fulsi,	fultum,	*prop.*
4. haurĭo,	haurīre,	hausi,	haustum,	*draw up.*
5. sancĭo,	sancīre,	sanxi,	sanctum,	*decree.*
6. sarcio,	sarcīre,	sarsi,	sartum,	*mend.*
7. sentĭo,	sentīre,	sensi,	sensum,	*feel.*
8. saepĭo,	saepire,	saepsi,	saeptum,	*fence round.*
9. vincĭo,	vincīre,	vinxi,	vinctum,	*bind.*

(d) Those having -ui in Perf., -tum in Supine.

1. amicio,	amicīre,	{ amicui, amixi, }	amictum,	*clothe.*
2. ăpĕrĭo,	ăpĕrīre,	ăpĕrŭi,	ăpertum,	*uncover, open.*
3. ŏpĕrĭo,	ŏpĕrīre,	ŏpĕrŭi,	ŏpertum,	*cover.*
4. sălĭo[3],	sălīre,	salŭi,	(saltum),	*leap.*

(e) Desideratives (§ 75) have no Supine, and with the exception of esurio, nupturio, parturio, no Perfect.

§ 153. Deponent Verbs.

(a) Deponents of the First Conjugation are all regular, making Infin. in -āri and Perfect Participle in -ātus.

(b) Deponents of the Second Conjugation make Inf. in -ēri and Perf. Part. in -ĭtus, except

Pres.	Inf.	Perf. Part.	Meaning.
1. fătĕor[4],	fatēri,	fassus,	*acknowledge.*
2. mĭsĕrĕor,	mĭsĕrēri,	mĭsĕrĭtus *or* mĭsertus,	*pity.*
3. rĕor,	rēri,	rătus,	*think.*

---

[1] So all compounds of farcio, farcire, farsi, fartum, *to stuff.*

[2] Percussi, percussum, from percutio, are used for the Perfect and Supine of this Verb.

[3] The compounds make -silio, -silire, -silui *or* -silii, -sultum, as, rĕsĭlĭo, *to leap back.*

[4] The compounds make -fĭtĕor, -fĭtēri, -fessus, as confĭtĕor, *to confess.*

(c) Deponents of the Third Conjugation have no regular form. A great number end in -scor in Pres. Indic., e. g. :—

Pres.	Inf.	Perf. Part.	Meaning.
1. ădĭpiscor,	ădĭpisci,	ădeptus,	*obtain* [1].
2. commĭniscor,	commĭnisci,	commentus,	*devise.*
3. expergiscor,	expergisci,	experrectus,	*awake.*
4. īrascor,	īrasci,	īrātus,	*become angry.*
5. nanciscor,	nancisci,	nactus *or* nanctus,	*obtain.*
6. nascor,	nasci,	nātus,	*be born.*
7. oblīviscor,	oblīvisci,	oblītus,	*forget.*
8. păciscor,	pacisci,	pactus,	*bargain.*
9. pascor,	pasci,	pastus,	*feed.*
10. prŏfĭciscor,	prŏfĭcisci,	prŏfectus,	*set out, march.*
11. reminiscor,	reminisci,	. . .	*remember.*
12. vescor,	vesci,	. . .	*eat.*
13. ulciscor,	ulcisci,	ultus,	*avenge.*

The others are :—

14. amplector,	amplecti,	amplexus,	*embrace.*
15. frŭor,	frŭi,	fructus *and* frŭĭtus,	*enjoy.*
16. fungor,	fungi,	functus,	*perform.*
17. grădĭor [2],	grădi,	gressus,	*march.*
18. lābor,	lābi,	lapsus,	*glide.*
19. lŏquor,	lŏqui,	locūtus,	*speak.*
20. mŏrĭor,	mŏri,	mortŭus,	*die.*
21. nītor,	nīti,	nīsus *or* nixus,	*strive.*
22. pătĭor [3],	păti,	passus,	*suffer, allow.*
23. quĕror,	quĕri,	questus,	*complain.*
24. sĕquor,	sĕqui,	secūtus,	*follow.*
25. ūtor,	ūti,	usus,	*use.*

(d) Deponents of the Fourth Conjugation make Inf. in -īri, and Perf. Part. in -ītus, except

1. assentĭor,	assentīri,	assensus,	*assent.*
2. expĕrĭor,	expĕrīri,	expertus,	*make trial of.*
3. mētĭor,	mētīri,	mensus,	*measure.*
4. oppĕrĭor,	oppĕrīri,	oppertus,	*wait for.*
5. ordĭor,	ordīri,	orsus,	*begin.*
6. ŏrĭor,	ŏrīri,	ortus,	*rise.*

---

[1] So all compounds of apiscor, apisci, aptus, *to obtain.*
[2] The compounds make -grĕdĭor, -grĕdi, -gressus, as aggrĕdior, *to attack*
[3] The compounds make -petior, -peti, -pessus, as perpetior.

A TABLE OF RULES FOR THE GENDERS OF LATIN NOUNS.

§ 154. **General Rules.**

(*a*) **Males, Mountains, Months**, the **Winds**, the **Stream**,
And **People** Masculine we deem:
Isles are Feminine; to these
Add **Females, Cities, Countries, Trees**:
Indeclinables we call
Neuter Gender, one and all.

Note. For exceptions see Madvig §§ 28-31.

(*b*)   1. Common are to either sex
    2. Artĭfex, and opĭfex,
    3. Convīva, vates, advĕna,
    4. Testis, civis, incŏla,
    5. Parens, sacerdos, custos, vindex,
    6. Adolescens, infans, index,
    7. Judex, heres, comes, dux,
    8. Princeps, municeps, conjux,
    9. Obses, ales, interpres,
   10. Auctor, exul; and with these
   11. Bos, dama, talpa, tigris, grus,
   12. Canis and anguis, serpens, sus [1].

§ 155. **Genders of the Five Declensions.**

(*a*) *First Declension.* Feminine, except names of men, as Publicola, *Publicola*, and designations of men, as poëta, *a poet*, nauta, *a sailor*, together with Hadria, or Adria, *the Adriatic Sea*, and Greek Nouns in -as and -es, as Aeneas, Atrides, which are Masculine.

(*b*) *Second Declension.* -us and -er, Masculine; -um, Neuter.
Exceptions:—
-us.]   1. Alvus, colus, carbăsus,
    2. hŭmus, vannus, pampĭnus,

---

[1] Line 2. *artificer, workman;* 3. *guest, prophet, new-comer;* 4. *witness, citizen, inhabitant;* 5. *parent, priest* or *priestess, guardian, avenger;* 6. *young man* or *woman, infant, informer;* 7. *judge, heir, companion, guide;* 8. *chief, burgess, husband* or *wife;* 9. *hostage, bird, interpreter;* 10. *author, exile;* 11. *ox* or *cow, deer, mole, tiger, crane;* 12. *dog, snake, serpent, swine.* Some other words, as hospes, *guest* or *host,* miles, *soldier,* hostis, *enemy,* etc., which from their *meaning* may be of either sex, are sometimes, but rarely, Feminine. (Copied by permission from the Public Schools Latin Primer.)

3. domus [Fourth as well as Second[1]],
4. and jewels, Feminine are reckoned.
5. Then come pelăgus [*the sea*],
6. Vulgus[2], virus, Neuters three[3].

(c) *Third Declension.* Gender various, according to termination of Nom. Case.

(1) Masculine terminations:—

{ Masculines -er, -or, and -o,
  -os, and -es *increasing*, shew.

Exceptions:—

-er.] 1. Cadāver, and all *plants* in -er,
       2. With iter, uber, verber, ver,
       3. To the Neuters we refer;
       4. One is Feminine, linter[4].

-or.] 1. Four in -or, are Neuter, cor,
       2. Marmor, aequor, and ador;
       3. One is Feminine, arbor[5].

-o.]   1. Caro, *flesh*, and endings three,
       2. -do, -io, -go, must reckoned be
       3. In Feminino Genere.

-os.] 1. Feminine are cos and dos,
       2. With the Neuters reckon os[6].

-es, increasing.] 1. Feminine are compes, teges,
                   2. Merces, merges, quies, seges.
                   3.   Aes [aeris], is Neuter[7].

(2) Feminine terminations:—

{ Feminines -do, -io, -go,
  -is, -as, -aus, and -x, will shew,
  -es, if no *increase* is needed,
  -s by Consonant preceded.

---

[1] 'Domus' is declined like both the Second and Fourth Declensions, except that it avoids the endings, -*me*, -*mu*, -*mi* [in Plural], and -*mis*. Hence the memorial line,
    Sperne *me, mu, mi, mis,* si declinare *domus* vis.
[2] 'Vulgus' is once or twice found masculine also.
[3] Line 1. *belly, distaff, canvas;* 2. *ground, winnowing-fan, vine-leaf;* 3. *house;* 6. *common people, poison.*
[4] Line 1. *corpse;* 2. *journey, udder, whip, spring;* 4. *boat.*
[5] Line 1. *heart;* 2. *marble, sea, spelt;* 3. *tree.*
[6] Line 1. *whetstone, dowry;* 2. *bone* [ŏs, G. ossis] or *mouth* [ōs, G. ōris].
[7] Line 1. *fetter, mat;* 2. *reward, corn-sheaf, rest, crop;* 3. *brass.*

Exceptions:—

-do, -go, -io.]
1. Males are ligo, vespertilio,
2. Cardo, ordo, and papilio,
3. Pugio, scipio, and quaternio,
4. Curculio, harpăgo, and ternio[1].

Note. Besides ternio and quaternio, all names of numbers, as unio, binio, quinio, senio, etc., are Masculine. Optio, *an adjutant*, is, by meaning, Masculine. Margo, *edge*, is common.

-is.]
1. Many Latin Nouns in -is
2. Are Masculini Generis.
3. Amnis, axis, fascis, follis,
4. Callis[2], caulis, crinis, collis,
5. Fustis, ignis, orbis, ensis,
6. Panis, piscis, postis, mensis,
7. Torris, unguis, and annālis,
8. Glis, natālis, and canālis,
9. Vectis, vermis, cucŭmis,
10. Lapis, pulvis, and cinis[2],
11. Sanguis, sentis[2], and vomis.
12. *Chiefly* Masculine are clunis,
13. Corbis, torquis, finis, funis[3].

-as.]
1. As, adamas, and elephas,
2. Are Masculina; Neuter vas[4].

x.]
1. Most are Male in e *plus* x,
2. Save nex, supellex, forfex, lex.
3. Common imbrex, and obex,
4. Pumex, cortex, and silex.
5. Three are Masculine in -ix,
6. Fornix, phoenix, and călix[5].

-es not increasing.]
1. Two are Masculine in -es,
2. Verres and acīnaces[6].

---

[1] Line 1. *spade, bat;* 2. *hinge, order, butterfly;* 3. *dagger, staff, the number four;* 4. *weevil, grappling-hook, the number three.*

[2] Callis, cinis, and sentis are sometimes Feminine, but *very* rarely.

[3] Line 3. *river, axle, bundle, pair of bellows;* 4. *path, cabbage, hair, hill;* 5. *club, fire, circle, sword;* 6. *bread, fish, doorpost, month;* 7. *torch, nail, chronicle;* 8. *dormouse, birthday, canal;* 9. *lever, worm, cucumber;* 10. *stone, dust, cinder;* 11. *blood, thorn, ploughshare;* 12. *haunch;* 13. *basket, necklace, end, rope.*

[4] Line 1. *as* [a Roman coin], *adamant, elephant;* 2. *vase.* [But vas, vădis, *bail, surety,* is Masc.]

[5] Line 2. *murder, furniture, shears, law;* 3. *tile, bolt;* 4. *pumice-stone, bark, flint-stone;* 6. *arch, phoenix, cup.*

[6] Line 2. *boar, scimitar.*

-s preceded by a Consonant.]	1. Masculine are fons and mons,
	2. Rudens, torrens, dens, and pons,
	3. Chalybs, hydrops, tridens, cliens,
	4. Fractions of the as, as triens,
	5. Bidens [*hoc*] and confluens,
	6. Oriens and occidens.
	7. Common Gender is forceps,
	8. Common also stirps, adeps[1].

(3) Neuter terminations:—

{ Neuters end in -a, -c, -e, -ar, -ur, -us, -l, -n, and -t.

Exceptions:—

-ur.]	1. Four are Masculine in -ur,
	2. Furfur, turtur, vultur, fur[2].
-us.]	1. Feminine are some in -us
	2. Increasing long, as servitus,
	3. Tellus, juventus, incus, palus,
	4. Virtus, senectus, *atque* salus;
	5. And [Genitive, pecudis] pecus.
	6. Masculine are lepus, mus[3].
-l.]	1. Masculines in -l are mugil.
	2. Sal and consul, sol and pugil[4].
-n.]	1. Males in -n are delphin, splen,
	2. Lien, pecten, attagen[5].

(*d*) *Fourth Declension.* -us, Masculine; -u, Neuter.

Exceptions:—

-us.]	1. Feminine are *trees* in -us,
	2. With tribus, acus, porticus,
	3. Domus, Idus and manus[6].

(*e*) *Fifth Declension.* Feminine, except dies, *a day*, which is Common in the Singular, Masculine in the Plural.

---

[1] Line 1. *fountain, mountain;* 2. *rope, torrent, tooth, bridge;* 3. *steel, dropsy, trident, client;* 4. *third part;* 5. *confluence;* 6. *east, west;* 7. *pincers;* 8. *stock, fat.*

[2] Line 2. *bran, turtle-dove, vulture, thief.*

[3] Line 2. *slavery;* 3. *earth, youth, anvil, marsh;* 4. *virtue* or *valour, old age, safety;* 5. *beast;* 6. *hare, mouse.*

[4] Line 1. *mullet;* 2. *salt, consul, sun, boxer.*

[5] Line 1. *dolphin, spleen;* 2. *spleen, comb, woodcock.*

[6] Line 2. *tribe, needle, portico;* 3. *house, Ides, hand.*

NOTES ON THE DECLENSIONS.

§ 156. First Declension.

(*a*) Several Greek Proper Names in -as and -es, all Masculine, as, Aeneas, *Aeneas*, Atrides, *son of Atreus*, and some Feminine Nouns in -e, as, Circe, *Circe*, crambe, *cabbage*, belong to this Declension.

N.	Aenēas,	Atrīdes,	Circē,
V.	Aeneā,	Atridē [ă *or* ā, *rare*],	Circē,
Acc.	Aeneān [*or* -am],	Atridēn [*or* -am],	Circēn,
G.	Aeneae,	Atridae,	Circes [*or* -ae],
D.	Aeneae,	Atridae,	Circae,
Ab.	Aeneā.	Atridē [*or* -ā].	Circē.

Notes. The termination -ides or -ades means 'son of.' Nouns ending thus, as Atrides, are called *Patronymics*[1] (i.e. *father-named*).

The above Greek Nouns are declined in the Plural like 'mensa,' but, with the exception of the Patronymics [which have -um in Gen. Pl.], are rarely found in this Number.

(*b*) The old Latin Genitive Singular of this Declension ended in -as. Hence paterfamilias, *father of a family*. Another ending, used chiefly by poets, is -āi, as, aulāi for aulae.

(*c*) -um for -arum appears as Genitive Plural (1) of Patronymics, (2) of drachma and amphora, (3) in poetry of certain peoples, as, Lapithûm, Teleboûm, (4) of compounds of colo and gigno, as, coelicolûm, terrigenûm. Duum for duarum is frequent.

(*d*) Dea, filia, liberta[2], make -abus for -is in Dative and Ablative Plural, to distinguish them from the Datives and Ablatives of deus, filius, libertus.

§ 157. Second Declension.

(*a*) Several Greek Nouns in -os and -on belong to this Declension.

N. V.	Dēlŏs,	Androgeōs,	Pelion,
Acc.	Delŏn [*or* -um],	Androgeōn [ō *or* ōna],	Pelion,
Gen.	Deli,	Androgei [*or* -ō],	Pelii,
D. Ab.	Delo.	Androgeo.	Pelio.

---

[1] Feminine Patronymics end in -is or -ias, as Thesēis, *daughter of Theseus*, Pleias, *daughter of Pleione*.

[2] *Goddess, daughter, freedwoman.*

(*b*) Vir, *a man*, makes Acc. vir-um, Gen. vir-i, and so throughout. Deus, *God*, is thus declined:—

	N. V.	Acc.	Gen.	D. Abl.
Sing.	Deus,	Deum,	Dei,	Deo,
Plur.	Di [*or* dii],	Deos,	Deûm [*or* deorum],	Dis [*or* diis].

(*c*) -um for -orum appears as Genitive Plural (1) of trades, coins, weights, measures, and distributive numerals, as fabrûm, talentûm, denûm[1]; (2) in poetry, of names of people, as Rutulûm; (3) of deus, vir, and liberi[2], as deûm, virûm, liberûm, and some others, chiefly in poetry. Duum for duorum is frequent.

§ 158. Third Declension.

(*a*) The stems of the Nouns of this Declension are very various, and can only be completely learnt by practice. The following are examples of the principal varieties:—

-A.	pŏēma,	*poem*	Gen.	poemăt-is.
-C.	lac,	*milk,*	„	lact-is.
-E.	rētĕ,	*net,*	„	rĕt-is.
-L.	ănĭmal,	*animal,*	„	animāl-is.
	sal,	*salt,*	„	săl-is.
	mel,	*honey,*	„	mell-is.
	exul,	*exile,*	„	exŭl-is.
-N.	carmen,	*song,*	„	carmĭn-is.
-O.	latro,	*robber,*	„	latrōn-is.
	orātio,	*speech,*	„	oratiōn-is.
	Măcĕdo,	*Macedonian,*	„	Macedŏn-is.
	hŏmo,	*man,*	„	homĭn-is.
	hĭrundo,	*swallow,*	„	hirundĭn-is.
	Carthāgo,	*Carthage,*	„	Carthagĭn-is.
	căro,	*flesh,*	„	carn-is.
-AR.	calcar,	*spur,*	„	calcār-is.
	Caesar,	*Caesar,*	„	Caesăr-is.
	far,	*corn,*	„	farr-is.
-ER.	carcer,	*prison,*	„	carcĕr-is.
	păter,	*father,*	„	patr-is.
	ĭter,	*journey,*	„	ĭtĭnĕr-is.
	ver,	*spring,*	„	vēr-is.

[1] From faber, *smith*, talentum, *talent*, deni, *ten apiece*.
[2] *God, man, children.*

			Gen.	
-OR.	lăbor,	*labour,*		labōr-is.
	arbor,	*tree,*	,,	arbŏr-is.
	cor,	*heart,*	,,	cord-is.
-UR.	fulgur,	*lightning,*	,,	fulgŭr-is.
	rōbur,	*strength,*	,,	robŏr-is.
	fur,	*thief,*	,,	fūr-is.
-AS.	cīvĭtas,	*state,*	,,	civĭtāt-is.
	ănas,	*duck,*	,,	anăt-is.
	as,	*as* (a coin),	,,	ass-is.
	mas,	*male,*	,,	măr-is.
	vas,	*surety,*	,,	văd-is.
	vas,	*vase,*	,,	vās-is.
-ES.	nubes,	*cloud,*	,,	nūb-is.
	merces,	*pay,*	,,	mercēd-is.
	pes,	*foot,*	,,	pĕd-is.
	obses,	*hostage,*	,,	obsĭd-is.
	Cĕres,	*Ceres,*	,,	Cerĕr-is.
	aes,	*copper,*	,,	aer-is.
	sĕges,	*cornfield,*	,,	segĕt-is.
	quies,	*rest,*	,,	quiēt-is.
	mīles,	*soldier,*	,,	milĭt-is.
-IS.	ăvis,	*bird,*	,,	av-is.
	tigris,	*tiger,*	,,	tigr-is, tigrĭd-is.
	lăpis,	*stone,*	,,	lapĭd-is.
	sanguis,	*blood,*	,,	sanguĭn-is.
	cĭnis,	*ash,*	,,	cinĕr-is.
	glis,	*dormouse,*	,,	glīr-is.
	sēmis,	*half-an-as,*	,,	semiss-is.
	lis,	*lawsuit,*	,,	līt-is.
-OS.	custos,	*guardian,*	,,	custōd-is.
	săcerdos,	*priest,*	,,	sacerdōt-is.
	os,	*mouth,*	,,	ōr-is.
	os,	*bone,*	,,	oss-is.
-US.	ŏpus,	*work,*	,,	opĕr-is.
	corpus,	*body,*	,,	corpŏr-is.
	pălus,	*marsh,*	,,	palūd-is.
	pĕcus,	*beast,*	,,	pecŭd-is, pecŏr-is.
	tellus,	*earth,*	,,	tellūr-is.
	virtus,	*virtue,*	,,	virtūt-is.
	sus,	*sow,*	,,	su-is.
-BS.	urbs,	*city,*	,,	urb-is.
-MS.	hiems,	*winter,*	,,	hiĕm-is.
-NS.	frons,	*leaf,*	,,	frond-is.
	frons,	*forehead,*	,,	front-is.

-PS.	stirps,	*stem,*	Gen.	stirp-is.
	princeps,	*chief,*	„	princĭp-is.
	auceps,	*birdcatcher,*	„	aucŭp-is.
-RS.	pars,	*part,*	„	part-is.
-T.	caput,	*head,*	„	capĭt-is.
-AX.	pax,	*peace,*	„	pāc-is.
	fax,	*torch,*	„	făc-is.
-EX.	pollex,	*thumb,*	„	pollĭc-is.
	nex,	*death,*	„	nĕc-is.
	lex,	*law,*	„	lēg-is.
	grex,	*herd,*	„	grĕg-is.
	senex,	*old man,*	„	sĕn-is.
-IX.	sălix,	*willow,*	„	salĭc-is.
	rādix,	*root,*	„	radīc-is.
	strix,	*screech-owl,*	„	strĭg-is.
	nix,	*snow,*	„	nĭv-is.
-OX.	vox,	*voice,*	„	vōc-is.
	nox,	*night,*	„	noct-is.
-UX.	nux,	*nut,*	„	nŭc-is.
	lux,	*light,*	„	lūc-is.
	conjux,	*wife,*	„	conjŭg-is.
-RX.	arx,	*citadel*	„	arc-is.

(*b*) List of Nouns having -im in Accusative, and -i in Ablative.

1. Vis, ravis, pelvis, sitis, tussis,
2. Sināpis, cŭcŭmis, ămussis,
3. Praesēpis, cannăbis, secūris,
4. Charybdis, tigris, *atque* būris,
5. *Et Propria Nomina in* -IS,
6. *Ut* Syrtis, Tibris, Tamĕsis[1].

(*c*) List of Nouns having -em or -im in Accusative, and -e or -i in Ablative.

1. Restis, puppis, turris, navis,
2. Sementis, strigilis, *et* clavis,
3. Messis, febris, *et* aqualis,
4. -em *vel* -im *dant, utrum malis*[2].

---

[1] Line 1. *force, hoarseness, basin, thirst, cough;* 2. *mustard, cucumber, carpenter's rule;* 3. *enclosure, hemp, axe;* 4. *charybdis, tiger, plough-tail;* 5. and Proper Names in -is, 6. as Syrtis, Tiber, Thames.

[2] Line 1. *rope, stern, tower, ship;* 2. *seed-sowing, flesh-scraper,* and *key;* 3. *harvest, fever, washing-basin,* 4. give -em or -im, whichever you prefer.

(d) List of Nouns having regular Accusative in -em but Ablative in -e or -i.
1. Amnis, anguis, avis, bilis,
2. Civis, ignis, imber, finis,
3. Neptis, orbis, patruelis,
4. Postis, unguis, -i *si velis* [1].

(e) All Nouns which were originally Adjectives in -is follow tristis, and make Acc. -em, Abl. -i, as, Atheniensis [sc. 'homo'], *an Athenian;* Aprīlis [sc. mensis], *April;* annālis [sc. liber], *chronicle.* September, October, November, December [sc. mensis], follow 'acer.' Nouns of this class when they become Proper Names, as Juvenalis, Martialis, have only -e in Abl.

(f) Neuters in -e, -al, -ar, as, cubīle, *bed,* animal, *animal,* calcar, *spur,* make -i in Abl. Sing., -ia in N. V. Acc. Pl. Rēte, *net,* makes Abl. rete, *rarely* reti: mare, *sea,* makes Abl. marĕ in Poetry only. Note also the following exceptions,
1. *Ablatives in* -e *are* far,
2. Baccar, nectar, *and* jubar [2].

(g) **Rules for the Genitive Plural.**
(A) Nouns *not increasing* make -ium, *except* apis, *a bee,* and
1. Vates, *and* proles, juvenis, senex, canis,
2. Accĭpĭter, pater, mater, frater, panis [3].

(B) Nouns *increasing* make -um, *except,*
1. Monosyllabic Nouns of which the stem ends in two Consonants, as, dens, *tooth,* dent-, Gen. Pl. dent-ium.
2. 1. Glis, mas, mus, lis,
2. Compes, palus * *and* penātes,
3. Nix, strix, faux, vis,
4. Servitus *, *and* optimates [4].
3. Neuters in -al and -ar, as, animal, *animal,* calcar, *spur.*
4. Nouns in -as, Gen. atis, as civitas, *state,* and many Nouns and Participles in -ns, as sapiens, *wise,* have both -ium and -um in Gen. Pl.
5. 1. *Sans* Plural Genitives we class
2. Cor, cos, *and* rus, sal, sol, *and* vas [5].

---

[1] Line 1. *river, snake, bird, bile;* 2. *citizen, fire, shower, end;* 3. *granddaughter, circle, cousin;* 4. *door-post, nail,* -i if you like.

[2] Line 1. *Spelt* (a kind of grain); 2. *baccar* (a plant), *nectar, sun-beam.*

[3] Line 1. *Prophet, offspring, young man, old man, dog;* 2. *hawk, father, mother, brother, bread.* [Mensis, *a month,* makes mensum, rarely -ium.]

[4] Line 1. *dormouse, male, mouse, lawsuit;* 2. *fetter, marsh, household gods;* 3. *snow, screech-owl, throat, force;* 4. *slavery, aristocrats.* Those marked * have both -ium and -um.

[5] Line 2. *Heart, whetstone, country, salt, sun, surety.* Sans means *without.*

(*b*) Greek Nouns of this Declension in -as, -er, -is, and -os, make Acc. -em *or* -a, as, hēros, *hero*, Acc. hērōem *or* hērōa; aër, *air*, Acc. aërem *or* aërä. The Acc. Pl. usually ends in -ăs.

Greek Nouns in -is and -ys make -i and -y in Voc. Poēsis, *poesy*, has Acc. poēsim *or* -in, Voc. poēsi.

Greek Nouns in -es have the regular Latin form, and also, in certain cases, duplicate forms derived from the Greek, e. g. Acc. -ēn, -ĕă, or -ētă, Gen. -i, -ei, or -ētis.

Orpheus is thus declined :—

Nom. Orpheus,   Acc. Orpheum *or* -ea,   D. Orpheo, -ëi, -ei,
Voc. Orpheu,   Gen. Orphei *or* -eos,   Ab. Orpheo.

(*j*) The Acc. Pl. of Nouns *not increasing* is often spelt -is instead of -es, as, nubis for nubes.

§ 159. Fourth Declension.

Nouns which take -ŭbus in Dat. Abl. Pl. are dissyllables in -cus, as, arcus, *bow;* also, tribus, *tribe;* partus, *birth;* portus, *harbour;* veru, *spit;* artus, Pl. *limbs.* Several have both forms.

§ 160. Fifth Declension.

(*a*) The -e of the Genitive -ei is said to be long when preceded by a vowel, as facieï; reï and fideï are perhaps doubtful, but the form is altogether rare.

(*b*) Only 'dies' and 'res' in this Declension have the Plural complete : the others either have N. V. Acc. Cases only, or no Plural at all.

§ 161. Adjectives.

(*a*) Present Participles are declined like 'ingens.' In the Ablative Absolute construction they make -e in Abl. Sing.; when used as epithets, -i. But in Poetry this distinction hardly exists.

(*b*) Many Adjectives belonging to the same class as 'ingens' and 'felix' have no Nom. Voc. Acc. Neuters Plural, and are scarcely ever used in the Nom. Voc. Acc. Neuter Singular. They make -e, not -i, in Abl. Sing., and -um instead of -ium in Gen. Plural. Such are dives, *rich*, and the following :—

1. Pauper, puber, hospes, compos,
2. Superstes, senex, sospes, impos,
3. Ales, deses, and reses,
4. *Compounds add of* corpus, pes,
5. *As* bicorpor, quadrupes [1].

---

[1] Line 1. *poor, grown up, friendly, master of;* 2. *surviving, old, safe, not master of;* 3. *winged, inactive, inactive;* 5. *double-bodied, four-footed.*

The following are like the above, but have -i in Ablative Sing.
1. Degener, inops, memor,
2. Vigil, uber, immemor[1].

Note. Celer, *swift*, hebes, *blunt*, and teres, *smoothly-rounded*, are not found in the Gen. Plural. Celeres, *the body-guard* of the Roman kings, has Gen. Plural Celerum. Vetus, *old*, has Neut. Plural vetera.

(*c*) Plus, *more*, is defective in the Singular.

	SINGULAR.		PLURAL.	
	M. F.	N.	M. F.	N.
N. V. A.	...	plus.	plures.	plura.
Gen.	pluris.		plurium.	
Dat.	...		pluribus.	
Ab.	(plure).		pluribus.	

Pluris is only found as an expression of value: pluris hoc, inquam, mihi eris, *you will be the more valued by me, I replied*. Complures, *several*, has Neut. complura, *rarely* compluria.

(*d*) Satur, *full* (of food), makes satur, satŭra, satŭrum, etc., the endings throughout being like those of tener.

(*e*) The Adjectives (cētĕrus), cetera, ceterum, *the rest*, and (ludĭcer *or* ludĭcrus), ludĭcra, ludĭcrum, *sportive*, have their Declension complete, with the exception of the Singular Nominative Masculine, which is not found in any writer.

§ 162. Comparison of Adjectives.

(*a*) The following instances of irregular Comparison, in addition to those given in § 27, are to be noticed. N.B. Square brackets, as [egentior], denote that the degree of Comparison is borrowed from some word of equivalent meaning; round brackets, as (piissimus), denote that the word is rare in Classical Latin.

mātūrus, *ripe*,	maturior,	maturissimus. ⎱ maturrimus. ⎰
ĕgĕnus, *needy*,	[egentior],	[egentissimus].
prōvĭdus, *provident*,	[providentior],	[providentissimus].
⎰ dīves, *rich*, ⎱ (dis), *rich*,	divitior, ditior,	divitissimus. ditissimus.
vetus, *old*,	⎰ [vetustior] ⎱ ⎱ (veterior) ⎰,	veterrimus.
(potis, *able*),	potior, *preferable*,	potissimus.
[ὠκύς, *swift*],	ocior,	ocissimus.
frugi, *virtuous*,	frugalior,	frugalissimus.

---

[1] Line 1. *Degenerate, needy, mindful*; 2. *wakeful, fruitful, unmindful.*

rusticus, *rustic*,	rusticior,	...
falsus, *false*,	...	falsissimus.
novus, *new*,	...	novissimus.
inclĭtus, *famous*,	...	inclitissimus.

(*b*) There are several exceptions to the rule given in § 26 (*c*) respecting Adjectives in -us preceded by a vowel. The chief are—

assiduus, *constant*,	assiduior,	assiduissimus.
egregius, *eminent*,	egregior,	...
pius, *dutiful*,	magis pius,	⎧ maxime pius. ⎨ (piissimus). ⎩ (pientissimus).
strenuus, *active*,	strenuior,	strenuissimus.

(*c*) Many Adjectives have no Comparative or Superlative. It is impossible to give comprehensive rules for these, but the following classification will assist the learner.

(1) Adjectives derived from Substantives, and signifying *made of*, *endowed with*, and *of* or *belonging to*, as, ligneus, *wooden*, aurītus, *long-eared*, Gallicus, *Gallic*. See § 169, *b*.

(2) Most Adjectives compounded of Verbs or Substantives, as, armiger, *armour-bearing*, degener, *degenerate*, inops, *poor*.

Note. The exceptions are Adjectives ending in -dicus, -ficus, -volus, § 26, (4), and compounds of ars, mens, and cor, as iners, *inactive*, demens, *mad*, vecors, *foolish*, which are compared regularly, as, inertior, dementior, etc.

(3)   1. Ferus, mirus, gnarus, gnavus,
         2. Rudis, trux, *non habent gradus* [1].

(*d*) Comparison of Adverbs.

bene, *well*,	melius,	optĭmē.
male, *badly*,	pejus,	pessime.
magnopere, *greatly*,	magis,	maxime.
parum, *too little*,	minus, *less*,	minime.
multum, *much*,	plus,	plurimum.
diu, *for a long time*,	diūtius,	diutissime.
intus, *within*,	interius,	intime.
nuper, *lately*,	...	nuperrime.
[prae, *before*],	prius,	primum.
prope, *near*,	propius,	proxime.
saepe, *often*,	saepius,	saepissime.
satis, *enough*,	satius,	...
secus, *otherwise*,	setius,	...

[1] Line 1. *Fierce, wonderful, knowing, active;* 2. *unpolished, savage*, have no degrees (of comparison).

§ 163. Anomalous and other Substantives.

(a) The following are a few Declensions to be noticed:—

N. V. Jūpĭter, *Jupiter*, has Acc. Jŏvem, Gen. Jŏvis, etc.
N. V. Bos, *ox*, Acc. bŏvem, has Gen. Pl. bŏum, Dat. Abl. bōbus or būbus.
N. V. Paterfamilias, *father of a family*, Acc. patremfamilias, Gen. patrisfamilias, etc. Here familias is an old form of the Gen., but there is also a form paterfamiliae, Acc. patrem familiae, etc. In the Pl. we find patres familias, patres familiae, and patres familiarum. So mater familias, filius familias, etc.
N. V. Acc. Jusjurandum, *oath*, Gen. jurisjurandi, Dat. jurijurando, etc. No Plural.
N. V. Respublica, *state*, Acc. rempublicam, Gen. reipublicae.
N. V. Supellex, *furniture*, Acc. supellectĭlem, Gen. supellectĭlis, Abl. supellectili *or* -e.

(b) Heteroclite Nouns are Nouns of varied declension. They are of two kinds:—

(1) Those having one form of the Nom. but more than one of the Oblique Cases. Thus, many names of trees in -us, as, cupressus, *cypress*, ficus, *fig-tree*, laurus, *bay*, pinus, *pine*, are declined like both 2nd and 4th Declensions. (*Note.* Quercus, *oak*, is 4th Declension only, except Gen. Pl. quercorum.) Notice also,

fĕmur,	*thigh*,	Gen.	femŏris and femĭnis.
jĕcur,	*liver*,	„	jecŏris, and jecĭnŏris.
jūgĕrum,	*acre*,	„	jugĕri, but Pl. Gen. jugerum (3rd Decl.), D. Abl. jugeribus (*rarely* jugeris).
rĕquies,	*rest*,	„	requiētis, but Acc. requiētem *and* requiem, Abl. requiete *and* requie (3rd and 5th Declensions).
vas,	*vessel*	„	vasis, but Pl. vasa, vasorum, vasis (2nd Decl.).

Note. Many other instances will be found under the head of Heterogeneous Nouns, § 163, *c*.

(2) Those having two or more forms of Declension, as, ĕlĕphantus, G. -i, 2, and ĕlĕphas, G. -antis, 3, *an elephant*. Many Nouns of the 2nd Declension have forms in -us, and -um, as, jūgŭlus *and* jugulum, *throat*. Many names of qualities follow both the 1st and 5th Declensions, as, luxuria *and* luxuries, *luxury*. Notice also,

pĕnus,   Gen. penŏris, 3, ⎫
pĕnus,   „ penūs, 4,   ⎬ *provisions.*
pĕnum,   „ peni, 2,   ⎭

§ 163.]   APPENDIX.   131

plebs,	Gen. plēbis, 3,	⎫
plēbes,	„ plebis, 3,	⎬ *the common people.*
plūbes,	„ plebei, 5,	⎭
praesēpe,	„ praesepis, 3,	⎫
praesēpes,	„ praesepis, 3,	⎬ *manger.*
praesēpium,	„ praesepii, 2,	⎭
tăpes,	„ tapētis, 3,	⎫
tapēte,	„ tapētis, 3,	⎬ *carpet.*
tapētum,	„ tapeti, 2,	⎭
vespĕra,	Gen. vesperae, 1,	⎫
vesper,	Acc. vesperum, 2,	⎬ *evening.*
vesper,	Abl. vespere, *or* -i, 3,	⎭

(*c*) Heterogeneous Nouns are such as have different Gender (accompanied almost always by different form also) in Pl. from Sing., as,

carbăsus, f.,	*canvas,*	Pl. carbăsă, n., *sails.*
caelum, n.,	*heaven,*	„ caeli, m.
frenum, n.,	*bit,*	„ freni, m., *and* frena, n.
jŏcus, m.,	*a jest,*	„ joci, m., *and* joca, n.
lŏcus, m.,	*place,*	„ loci, m., *and* loca, n.
ostrea, f.,	*oyster,*	„ ostreae, f., *and* ostrea, n.
Pergămus, m.,	*Pergamus,*	„ Pergama, n.
rastrum, n.,	*harrow,*	„ rastri, m., *and* rastra, n.
sībĭlus, m.,	*hissing,*	„ sibili, m., *and* sibila, n.
Tartărus, m.,	*Tartarus,*	„ Tartara, n.

Note. The Pl. balneae, *a public bath,* has no Sing. except balneum, *a private bath,* pl. balnea; and, on the other hand, epŭlae, *a private banquet,* has no Sing. except epŭlum, *a public entertainment.*

(*d*) The following Nouns (commonly called Indeclinable Nouns), have no flexions (§ 12); fas, *right,* nĕfas, *wrong;* names of letters of the alphabet, as, alpha, beta; together with the Adjectives frugi, *virtuous,* and nequam, *worthless,* and the Numerals from quattuor, *four,* to centum, *a hundred.*

(*e*) Some Nouns are found only in one Oblique Case in the Singular, as,
  verbĕre, Abl., full pl., from (verber), *whip.*
So ambāge, from (ambages), *roundabout way,* compĕde, from (compes), *fetter,* fauce, from (faux), *throat,* obĭce, from (obex), *bolt,* have full plural but are only found in Ablative in the Singular.

Note. Round brackets, as (verber), denote that the word is not found in classical Latin.

Sponte, *by impulse,* noctu, *by night,* jussu, *by order,* injussu, *without orders,* natu, *by birth,* are only found in Abl. Sing., and have no plural.

(*f*) Some Nouns have only two cases in the Singular, as—
fors, *chance,* Abl. forte, no plural.
impĕtis, impete, no pl., from (impes), *violence.*
sordem, sorde, full pl., from (sordes), *filth.*
veprem, vepre, full pl., from (vepres), *bramble.*

(*g*) Some have only three cases in the Singular, as—
fĭdem, fidis, fide, full pl., from (fides), *lyre.*
lues (*Nom.*), luem, lue, no pl., *a pestilence.*
ŏpem, opis, ope, full pl., in the sense of *riches, power,* from (ops), *help.*
precem, preci, prece, full pl., from (prex), *a prayer.*
vĭcem, vicis, vice, pl. vices, vicibus, no Gen., from (vicis), *change.*
vis (*Nom.*), vim, vi, *violence.* Pl. vīres, virium, viribus, *strength.*

(*h*) Some have only four cases in the Singular, as—
dăpem, dapis, dapi, dape, full pl., from (daps), *a feast.*
dicion-em, -is, -i, -e, full pl., from (dicio), *dominion.*
frug-em, -is, -i, -e, full pl., from (frux), *fruit.*
internecion-em, -is, -i, -e, full pl., from (internecio), *destruction.*

(*j*) Nouns used only in the Singular.

Names of Qualities, as sapientia, *wisdom,* senectus, *old age,* and of Materials, as ferrum, *iron,* aes, *bronze,* lignum, *wood,* are, from their meaning, only used in the Singular. Names of materials are, however, sometimes found in the Plural signifying objects made of the material, as aera, *works in bronze,* ligna, *logs;* and names of qualities are sometimes used in the Plural to denote instances of the quality, as omnes avaritiae, *all forms of avarice.* Proper Names are, of course, Singular, but may be used in the Plural to denote a class of names, just as in English.

Pelagus, *the sea,* vulgus, *the common people,* virus, *poison,* supellex, *furniture,* have no Plural. Many other Nouns have been already noticed as occurring only in the Singular.

(*k*) Nouns used only in the Plural.

There are very many nouns of this class in Latin. See Madvig, Lat. Gr. § 51. The following are a few:—

1. Artus, īlia, majōres,   3. *Towns, as* Veii; *inter alia*
2. Casses, mānes, *and* primōres,   4. *Festivals, as* Saturnalia[1].

[1] Line 1. *Limbs, flanks, ancestors;* 2. *net, ghost, chief men;* 3. *Veii;* 4. *Saturnalia.*

(*l*) List of Nouns which vary their meaning in the Plural:—

S.	Aedes, *a temple.*	Impedīmentum, *hindrance.*	
P.	Aedes, *a house.*	Impedimenta, *baggage.*	
S.	Auxilium, *help.*	Littĕra, *letter of the alphabet.*	
P.	Auxilia, *auxiliary forces.*	Litterae, *epistle, literature.*	
S.	Carcer, *prison.*	Ludus, *play.*	
P.	Carcĕres, *starting place.*	Ludi, *public games.*	
S.	Castrum, *fort.*	Lustrum, *space of five years.*	
P.	Castra, *camp.*	Lustra, *dens, lairs.*	
S.	Copia, *plenty.*	Opĕra, *labour.*	
P.	Copiae, *forces.*	Operae, *work-people.*	
S.	Finis, *end.*	Opem [Acc.], *help.*	
P.	Fines, *boundaries.*	Opes, *power, wealth.*	
S.	Gratia, *favour, popularity.*	Sal, *salt.*	
P.	Gratiae, *thanks* or *the Graces.*	Sales, *wit.*	

NUMERAL ADJECTIVES AND ADVERBS.

§164. Numerals are of various kinds.

(*a*) *Cardinal*, as, unus, *one*, duo, *two*, etc. The first three Cardinals have been already declined (see § 23). From quattuor, *four*, to centum, *a hundred*, they are indeclinable.

(*b*) *Ordinal*, as, primus, *first*, sĕcundus, *second.*

(*c*) *Distributive*, as, singŭli, *one apiece*, bini, *two apiece.*

(*d*) *Multiplicative*, as, simplex, *simple*, duplex, *twofold*, triplex, *threefold.*

(*e*) *Adverbial Numerals*, as, sĕmel, *once*, bis, *twice.*

(*f*) There are also *Proportional Numerals*, ending in -plus, and meaning 'how many times as great,' as, duplus, *twice as great*, triplus, *three times as great*; and a class of Adverbs formed from the Ordinals and ending in -o or -um, as, primo or primum, *for the first time.*

(*g*) The principal Numerals are given in the following Table:—

Arabic Numbers.	Roman Symbols.	Cardinals.	Ordinals.	Distributives.	Multiplicatives.	Adverbs.
1	I	ūnus	prīmus, -a, -um	singŭli, -ae, -a	simplex	sĕmĕl
2	II	dŭŏ	sĕcundus *or* alter	bīni	dŭplex	bĭs
3	III	trēs	tertius	terni *or* trīni	trĭplex	tĕr
4	IV	quāttŭor	quartus	quăterni	quadrŭplex	quătĕr
5	V	quinque	quintus	quīni	quincŭplex	quinquĭes
6	VI	sex	sextus	sēni	. . .	sexĭes
7	VII	septem	septĭmus	septēni	septemplex	septĭes
8	VIII	octo	octāvus	octōni	. . .	octĭes
9	IX	nŏvem	nōnus	nŏvēni	. . .	nŏvĭes
10	X	dĕcem	dĕcĭmus	dēni	dĕcemplex	dĕcĭes
11	XI	undĕcim	undĕcĭmus	undēni	. . .	undĕcĭes
12	XII	dŭŏdĕcim	dŭŏdĕcĭmus	dŭŏdēni	. . .	dŭŏdĕcĭes
13	XIII	trĕdĕcim	tertius dĕcĭmus	terni deni	. . .	trĕdĕcĭes
14	XIV	quāttŭordĕcim	quartus decimus	quăterni deni	. . .	quatŭordĕcĭes
15	XV	quindĕcim	quintus decimus	quini deni	. . .	quindĕcĭes
16	XVI	sēdĕcim	sextus decimus	seni deni	. . .	sēdĕcĭes
17	XVII	septemdĕcim	septĭmus decimus	septeni deni	. . .	septĭes decies
18	XVIII	dŭŏdēvīginti	dŭŏdēvīcēsĭmus	dŭŏdēvīcēni	. . .	dŭŏdēvīcĭes
19	XIX	undēvīginti	undēvīcēsĭmus	undēvīcēni	Few Multi-	undēvīcĭes
20	XX	vīginti	vīcēsĭmus	vīceni	plicatives of	vīcĭes
21	XXI	vīginti ūnus *or* unus et viginti	vīcēsĭmus prīmus *or* unus et vīcesimus	vīceni singuli	high numbers are found in Latin, except	sĕmĕl et vicies
22	XXII	vīginti dŭŏ *or* duo et viginti	vīcesimus sĕcundus *or* alter et vīcesimus	viceni bini	centŭplex, *a*	bĭs et vicies

[§ 164.] APPENDIX. 135

					hundred-fold,
30	XXX	trīgintā	trīgēsimus	trīcēni	tricīes
40	XL	quādrāgintā	quadrāgēsimus	quadrāgēni	quadrāgies *and one or*
50	L	quinquāgintā	quinquāgēsimus	quinquāgēni	quinquāgies *two more.*
60	LX	sexāgintā	sexāgēsimus	sexāgēni	sexāgies
70	LXX	septūāgintā	septūāgēsimus	septūāgēni	septūāgies
80	LXXX	octōgintā	octōgēsimus	octōgēni	octōgies
90	XC	nōnāgintā	nōnāgēsimus	nōnāgēni	nōnāgies
100	C	centum	centēsimus	centēni	centies
101	CI	centum et ūnus	centēsimus primus	centēni singuli	centies sĕmĕl
200	CC	dūcenti, -ae, -a	dūcentēsimus	dūcēni	dūcenties
300	CCC	trĕcenti, -ae, -a	trĕcentēsimus	trĕcēni	trĕcenties
400	CCCC or CD	quadringenti, -ae, -a	quadringentēsimus	quadringēni	quadringenties
500	D or IƆ	quingenti, -ae, -a	quingentēsimus	quingēni	quingenties
600	DC	sexcenti, -ae, -a	sexcentēsimus	sexcēni	sexcenties
700	DCC	septingenti, -ae, -a	septingentēsimus	septingēni	septingenties
800	DCCC	octingenti, -ae, -a	octingentēsimus	octingēni	octingenties
900	DCCCC	nongenti, -ae, -a	nongentēsimus	nongēni	nongenties
1,000	M or CIƆ	mille *or* milliă	millēsimus	singŭlā millia	milliēs
2,000	MM or IIM	bis mille *or* duo millia	bis millēsimus	bīna millia	bis milliēs
5,000	VM or CCIƆ	quinquies mille *or* quinque millia	quinquies millesimus	quina millia	quinquies millies
10,000	XM or CCIƆƆ	dĕciēs mille *or* decem millia	decies millesimus	dena millia	decies millies
1,000,000	CCCIƆƆƆ	dĕciēs centum millia	decies centies millesimus	decies centēnā millia	decies centies millies.

§ 165. Notes on the Numerals.

(a) Cardinal Numerals.

(1) Mille is an indeclinable Adjective meaning *one thousand*, as, mille equites, 1000 *horsemen*: millia is a Neuter Plural Substantive of the Third Declension, meaning *thousands*, and takes a dependent Genitive, as, tria millia equitum, 3000 *horsemen*. Such phrases as tria millia quadringenti quadraginta sex milites interfecti sunt, 3446 *soldiers were killed*, are for tria millia militum et quadringenti quadraginta sex milites.

(2) bis mille, ter mille, etc., are found instead of duo, tria, etc., millia, chiefly in poetry; also with anni, as, bis mille anni, 2000 *years*, rather than duo millia annorum.

(3) When the smaller number is put first et is generally used, as, quattuor et viginti, like our 'four *and* twenty;' when the greater is put first et is omitted, as, viginti quattuor.

(4) Cardinals used *partitively* take a Genitive, '300 of the ships were lost,' trecentae navium amissae sunt.

(5) In translating twenty-one, thirty-one, etc., unus must be kept in the Singular. 'We sent twenty-one soldiers,' milites viginti unum, *or*, unum et viginti milites, misimus [i.e. unum milit*em* et viginti milit*es*].

(b) Ordinal Numerals.

(1) For 'the first and second legions,' say, prim*a* et secund*a* [*not* prim*ae* et secund*ae*] legiones.

(2) For 'thirteenth,' 'fourteenth,' etc., say, tertius decimus, quartus decimus, not decimus tertius, etc., except when following higher numbers, as, ducentesimus decimus tertius, *the* 213*th*.

(3) For 'forty-fifth,' 'seventy-eighth,' etc., say, fortieth fifth, seventieth eighth, quadragesimus quintus, etc., not quadraginta quintus. The Cardinals are not joined with Ordinals in Latin, as they are in English, except that unus is sometimes used for primus, as, unus et vicesimus, *the* 21*st*.

(4) The date of a year is expressed in Ordinals: For 'in the year 2875 B.C.,' say, 'in the year before Christ born twice-thousandth, eight-hundredth, seventieth, fifth,' anno ante Christum natum bis millesimo octingentesimo septuagesimo quinto.

(5) Fractions are expressed by 'pars' with Ordinals, as, septima pars, *one-seventh*, duae septimae partes, *two-sevenths*, etc. Pars is often omitted, only tertia, quarta, etc., being used. One-half is pars dimidia. When the denominator exceeds the numerator by 1 only, it is often omitted, as, duae partes, *two-thirds*, quattuor partes, *four-fifths*, etc. For fractions of the *as* see § 173.

(*c*) **Distributive Numerals.**

(1) Distributives shew that the number spoken of applies to each individual of a class. They are often indicated in English by the words *each, every*, or *apiece*. 'He gave each [*or*, every one] of them five books,' or, 'he gave them five books *apiece*,' quinos libros iis dedit. Quinque libros iis dedit would mean 'he gave them five books *in all*,' i.e. five books among the whole number.

(2) Use Distributives for Cardinals (1) with Substantives that have no Singular, (2) with Substantives that have a different meaning in the Plural from the Singular, as una littera, *one letter* (of the alphabet), but binae litterae, *two epistles*. Unus, however, is an exception: 'one camp,' una castra, not singula castra.

TABLE OF RELATIVE, INTERROGATIVE, AND INDEFINITE PRONOUNS.

§ 166. The Simple Forms.

The Relative Pronoun,   Qui, quae, quod, *who* or *which*.

The Interrogative Pronoun, { Quis, (quis), quid, } *who?* or *what?*
                            { Qui, quae, quod, }

The Indefinite Pronoun, { Quis, quă, quid, } *any*.
                         { Qui, quae, quod, }

Note. These duplicate forms of the Interrogative and Indefinite should be carefully remembered. The first is the *Substantival* Form, as, Quis hoc fecit? *Who did this?* Si quis hoc faciat, *If any one should do this*; the second is the *Adjectival*, used when some Substantive is introduced agreeing with the Pronoun, as, Qui puer hoc fecit? *What boy did this?* Si qui puer hoc faciat, *If any boy should do this* [1]. The same distinction is preserved in many of the following Compounds.

§ 167. The Compounds.

Quidam, *a certain per-*   Quidam, quaedam, quiddam, Subst. }
       son.   quoddam, Adj. }
Quivis, }   Quivis, quaevis, quidvis, Subst. }
        } *any you*   quodvis, Adj. }
Quilibet, } *please.*   Quilibet, quaelibet, quidlibet, Subst. }
                                            quodlibet, Adj. }

---

[1] These distinctions are by no means rigidly observed among Latin writers, e.g. 'si *quis* Deus, en! ego, dicat,' Hor., but they should be noticed by beginners.

Quicunque, } *whoso-* Quicunque, quaecunque, quodcunque.
Quisquis, } *ever.*   The forms in use of quisquis are—
   Sing. N. Quisquis, *neut.* quidquid *or* quicquid.
         Acc.   *neut.* quidquid *or* quicquid.
         Abl. Quoquo, quâquâ, quoquo.
Note. Quisquis is generally used as a Substantive, quicunque as an Adjective.

Quisque, *each.*   Quisque, quaeque, quicque *or* quidque, Subst. }
                                                   quodque, Adj.   }
Unusquisque, *each one.* Unusquisque, unaquaeque, unumquicque *or* -dque, Subst. }
                                                   unumquodque, Adj.   }
Aliquis, *some.*   Aliquis, aliquâ, aliquid, Subst. }
                          Aliqui, aliquae, aliquod, Adj.   }
Quispiam, *any one.*   Quispiam, quaepiam, quidpiam *or* quippiam, Subst. }
                                                   quodpiam, Adj.   }
Quisquam, *any one at* } Quisquam, quidquam *or* quicquam.
         all.   }
Note. Quisquam is generally a Substantive; the Adjective is ullus, -a, -um, *any at all.*

Ecquis, ecqua,   ecquid, }
Ecqui, ecquae *or* -ă, ecquod, } *any?* is an Interrogative-Indefinite Pronoun.

The Interrogative part is translated by throwing the sentence in which the Pronoun occurs into the form of a question, and the Indefinite part by supplying the word *any*, as Ecqua puero cura est? *Has the* boy *any* care?

TERMINATIONS OF DERIVED NOUNS.

§ 168. Derived Substantives are formed, (*a*) from Verbs, (*b*) from other Substantives, (*c*) from Adjectives.

(*a*) Substantives derived from Verbs.

(1) **-tor** and **-sor** express the *person who does* the action denoted by the Verb, as, amator, *a lover,* from amo; suasor, *an adviser,* from suadeo. A feminine form in **-trix** is sometimes found, as, victrix.

Note. Some Substantives in **-tor** are derived immediately from other Substantives, as viator, *a traveller,* from via.

(2) **-tio, -tus, -sio,** and **-sus,** express *the action of the Verb,* as, motio *and* motus, *a moving,* from moveo; visus *and* visio, *a seeing,* from video.

(3) **-ium, -or,** and **-us** express the *effect* of the action denoted by the Verb as, gaudium, *joy,* from gaudeo; amor, *love,* from amo; usus, *use,* from utor.

(4) **-mentum** and **-men** express *means of attaining* that which the Verb denotes, as, documentum, *means of teaching*, from doceo; tutamen, *means of defence*, from tutor.

(5) **-ulum, -bulum, -culum,** denote *instrument*, as, jac-ulum, *instrument for throwing*, from jacio.

(b) Substantives derived from other Substantives.

(1) **-lus, -la, -lum** [the termination varies according to the gender of the Primitive Substantive], express *diminutives*. These terminations assume various forms, e.g. **-ŭlus, -cŭlus, -ellus, -illus**; as, cornic-ŭla, *a little crow*, from cornix; corni-cŭlum, *a little horn*, from cornu; libellus, *a little book*, from liber; lapillus, *a little stone*, from lapis.

Note. **-leus** is sometimes a diminutive ending, as, equuleus, *a colt*, from equus.

(2) **-ium** denotes either *an office*, as, sacerdotium, *priesthood*, the office of the sacerdos; or an *assemblage of individuals*, as, collegium, *a college*, or assembly of collēgae.

(3) **-ētum** denotes a *place where plants grow*, as quercētum, *a grove of oaks*, from quercus; salictum (*for* salicētum), *a willow-bed*, from salix.

(4) **-arium** denotes a *receptacle*, as, armarium, *a cupboard*, from arma.

(5) **-ile** denotes a *place where animals are kept*, as, ovīle, *a sheepfold*, from ovis.

(6) **-ia** denotes a country, and is usually derived from the name of its people, as, Italia, *the country of the Itali*.

(7) **Patronymics** end in **-ădes**, if derived from Nouns of 1st Decl., or of 2nd Decl. in *-ius*, as Aeneades, *son of Aeneas*; Thestiades, *son of Thestius*; in **-ides** if from Nouns of 2nd Decl. in *-us*, as Priamīdes, *son of Priam*; in **-īdes**, if from Nouns in *-eus*, as Atrīdes, *son of Atreus*. The feminines end in **-is**, as, Nereis, *daughter of Nereus*; or **-as**, as, Thestias, *daughter of Thestius*.

(c) Substantives derived from Adjectives.

These all denote the *quality* which the Adjective expresses attributively. The chief terminations are:

(1) **-ĭtas** or **-tas**, as, bonitas, *goodness*, the quality of the bonus.

(2) **-ia**, as, audacia, *boldness*, the quality of the audax.

(3) **-itia**, as, justitia, *justice*, the quality of the justus.

(4) **-tudo**, as, fortitudo, *bravery*, the quality of the fortis.

§ 169. Derived Adjectives are formed, (a) from Verbs, (b) from Substantives, (c) from Adverbs and Prepositions.

(a) Adjectives formed from Verbs.
These usually have the force of Participles. The following are the principal terminations:
(1) -bundus and -cundus. These = Present Active Participles, with intensive meaning, as, lacrymabundus, *weeping profusely*, from lacrymor; iracundus, *full of wrath*, from irascor.
(2) -ax denotes *active inclination*, as, pugnax, *fond of fighting*, from pugno.
(3) -idus, chiefly from Intransitive Verbs, denotes *activity*, as, fervidus, *glowing*, from ferveo.
(4) -ilis and -bilis denote *capacity*, and are generally used Passively, as, docilis, *teachable*, from doceo; mobilis (*for* movibilis), *movable*, from moveo. But some are used Actively, as, terribilis, *terrible* (i. e. *capable of terrifying*), from terreo.
(5) -tivus denotes a *state resulting from* verbal action, as, captīvus, *captive* (i.e. in a state of having been taken), from capio.
(6) -tilis and -silis have the force of Perfect Passive Participles, as, sectilis, *cut*, from seco; pensilis, *hung up*, from pendo.

(b) Adjectives formed from Substantives.
These express, (a) *made of*, (b) *full of*, (c) *endowed with*, (d) *of* or *belonging to*. The last class is by far the most numerous.
(1) The chief terminations expressing *made of* are:
    1. -eus, as, ligneus, *wooden*, from lignum.
    2. -nus, as, quernus, *oaken*, from quercus.
Note. These terminations may, however, express *of* or *belonging to*, when the Noun from which they are derived is not a Noun of Matter, as, virgineus, maternus.
(2) The chief terminations expressing *full of* are:
    1. -osus, as, nivōsus, *full of snow*, from nix, nivis.
    2. -lentus, as, vinŏlentus, *full of wine*, from vinum.
(3) Adjectives signifying *endowed with* end in -tus, and have the nature of Perfect Passive Participles, as, aurātus, *gilded*, from aurum; aurītus, *long-eared*, from auris; nasūtus, *long-nosed*, from nasus.
(4) The terminations expressing *of* or *belonging to* are very numerous. The following are the most common:
    1. -ius, as, regius, *royal*, from rex.
    2. -icus, as, Gallicus, *Gallic*, from Gallus.
    3. -lis (or -ris), preceded by a vowel, as, mortalis, *mortal*, from mors; popularis, *popular*, from populus;

fidelis, *faithful*, from fides; hostilis, *hostile*, from hostis.

Note. The termination -ris is the same as -lis in meaning, and seems to be used in order to avoid a repetition of the letter l, as, solaris *for* solalis.

4. **-nus** preceded by a vowel, as, montānus, *mountainous*, from mons; terrēnus, *of earth*, from terra; canīnus, *canine*, from canis.

5. **-ter** or **-tis**, as, pedester, *pedestrian*, from pes; caelestis, *heavenly*, from caelum.

6. **-as** and **-ensis** are usually confined to Adjectives derived from names of Places, as Aquinas, *of Aquinum*; Atheniensis, *Athenian*.

(*c*) A few Adjectives are derived from Adverbs and Prepositions, as, diuturnus, *lasting*, from diu; postěrus, *next*, from post.

The terminations of derived Verbs are given above, § 75.

THE ROMAN CALENDAR.

§ 170. The Roman Calendar agreed with our own in the number of months, and of the days in each; but their manner of dating was very different.

Each month had three distinctive days, namely:—

The Kalends [Kalendae, Gen. -arum], which fell on the 1st.
The Nones [Nonae, Gen. -arum], which fell on the 5th, *usually*.
The Ides [Idūs, Gen. -uum], which fell on the 13th, *usually*.
But in March, May, July, and October, the Nones fell on the 7th and the Ides on the 15th.

§ 171. In dating:—

(*a*) The 1st, 5th, and 13th were denoted by the Ablatives, Kalendis, Nonis, Idibus, with the name of the month added in agreement, as Kalendis Ianuariis, *the 1st of January*. But in March, May, July, and October, Nonis and Idibus stood for 7th and 15th respectively.

(*b*) The day before the Kalends, Nones, or Ides, was denoted by the Adverb pridie, *the day before*, used like a Preposition governing an Accusative Case, as, pridie Kalendas Ianuarias, *the 31st of December*, pridie Idus Ianuarias, *the 12th of January*, pridie Idus Martias, *the 14th of March*.

(*c*) All other days were denoted by reckoning *back* from the next ensuing Kalends, Nones, or Ides. The reckoning included not only the day reckoned *from* but the day reckoned *to;* thus the 30th of December was called the *third* not the *second* day before the Kalends of January. The form for expressing the date thus found is as follows:—

Ante diem tertium Kalendas Januarias, *the 30th of December.*
Ante diem octavum Idus Januarias, *the 6th of January.*
Ante diem quartum Nonas Martias, *the 4th of March.*
Ante diem duodevicesimum Kalendas Maias, *the 14th of April.*

§ 172. A short form for expressing the above dates is as follows:—

a. d. III. Kal. Jan., *the 30th of December.*
a. d. VIII. Id. Jan., *the 6th of January.*
a. d. IV. Non. Mart., *the 4th of March.*
a. d. XVIII. Kal. Mai., *the 14th of April.*

Note 1. An easy method of finding the Roman date corresponding to an English is by adding 1 to the Nones or Ides, or 2 to the days of the month, and then subtracting the English date from the result. Thus, to find the Roman date for the 6th of January:—13 + 1 = 14, and 14 − 6 = 8. Hence our 6th of January is the Roman 8th day before the Ides. So, the 4th of March is 7 + 1 − 4 = 4; the 14th of April is 30 + 2 − 14 = 18, etc.

Note 2. In leap-year the 24th of February [ante diem sextum Kalendas Martias, *or* a. d. VI. Kal. Mart.] was reckoned for two consecutive days. Hence this day was called dies bissextus, and leap-year itself annus bissextus. In such years the additional day was not reckoned in calculating the date from the 14th to the 24th of February. Thus a.d. X. Kal. Mart. stood for the 20th of February, whether the year was leap year or not.

Note 3. The phrase for expressing a date was considered as a single word admitting of government by the Prepositions in and ex, as, Supplicationes edictae sunt in antediem quartum et tertium et pridie Kalendas Novembres, *Public thanksgivings were decreed for the 29th, 30th, and 31st of October;* Supplicatio indicta est ex antediem quintum Idus Octobres, *A public thanksgiving was decreed, beginning from the 11th of October.*

Note 4. The names of the months were Januarius, Februarius, Martius, Aprilis, Maius, Junius, Julius, Augustus, September, October, November, December. These are Adjectives, but may be used as Substantives, mensis being understood. See § 158, *e.*

Note 5. The months of July and August were called Quintilis and Sextilis before the time of the Emperor Augustus.

ROMAN WEIGHTS AND MONEY.

§ 173. **The as,** or *pound,* also called **libra,** which served as the standard unit both for weights and coins, was divided into twelve parts.

Assis Romani partes sunt **uncia, sextans, Quadrans, atque triens, quincunx, et semis, et inde Septunx, bes, dodrans; dextanti junge deuncem.**

Uncia	= $\frac{1}{12}$		of an as	= 1 ounce.	
Sextans	= $\frac{2}{12}$	= $\frac{1}{6}$	of an as	= 2 ounces.	
Quadrans	= $\frac{3}{12}$	= $\frac{1}{4}$	,,	= 3	,,
Triens	= $\frac{4}{12}$	= $\frac{1}{3}$	,,	= 4	,,
Quincunx	= $\frac{5}{12}$		,,	= 5	,,
Semis	= $\frac{6}{12}$	= $\frac{1}{2}$	,,	= 6	,,
Septunx	= $\frac{7}{12}$		,,	= 7	,,
Bes	= $\frac{8}{12}$	= $\frac{2}{3}$	,,	= 8	,,
Dodrans	= $\frac{9}{12}$	= $\frac{3}{4}$	,,	= 9	,,
Dextans	= $\frac{10}{12}$	= $\frac{5}{6}$	,,	= 10	,,
Deunx	= $\frac{11}{12}$		,,	= 11	,,

Terms used in bequeathing property. **Heres ex asse,** *heir to the whole estate;* **heres ex deunce, dextante,** etc., heir to eleven twelfths, five sixths, etc.

§ 174. **Interest.** In the later times of the republic the Romans reckoned interest by the month, not by the year. Hence, asses usurae = 1 *as* per cent. per mensem = 12 per cent. per annum; deunces usurae = $\frac{11}{12}$ of an *as* per cent. per mensem = 11 per cent. per annum, and so on. Instead of asses usurae we sometimes find the phrase centesimae usurae, or simply centesimae, i. e. hundredth parts of the principal paid monthly, or 12 per cent. per annum. Binae centesimae = 24 per cent.

Note. For the phrase fenus unciarium see Smith's Dictionary of Antiquities.

§ 175. The Sestertius, or nummus sestertius, was a coin of the value of $2\frac{1}{2}$ asses, being rather more than twopence of our money before the reign of Augustus, and rather less than that sum afterwards. It is denoted by the symbol HS. (i.e. L(ibra) L(ibra) S(emis), or perhaps IIS(emis), $2\frac{1}{2}$ *pounds).*

The sum of 1000 Sestertii was called Sestertium, roughly equivalent to about £8 English money. This also was denoted by the symbol HS.

The expression for a million sestertii was decies centena millia sestertiûm (for -orum); for 1,100,000 sestertii, undecies centena millia sestertiûm, etc. The words centena millia are often understood; hence, decies sestertium, *a million;* millies HS., *a hundred millions,* etc.

In order to distinguish HS. meaning sestertia from HS. meaning sestertii, a line is sometimes written over the subjoined numeral. Thus, HS.MD.= 1500 sestertii, but HS.M̄D.= 1500 sestertia, i. e. 1,500,000 sestertii. To indicate centena millia sestertiûm a line is sometimes placed over the whole expression, as H̄S̄.M̄D̄.= millies et quingenties centena millia sestertiûm = 150,000,000 sestertii or 150,000 sestertia.

ABBREVIATIONS.

§ 176. Proper Names.

A.	Aulus.	N.	Nŭmĕrius.
C., G.	Caius, Gaius.	P.	Publius.
Cn., Gn.	Cnaeus, Gnaeus.	Q.	Quintus.
D.	Decimus.	S., or Sex.	Sextus.
K.	Kaeso.	Ser.	Servius.
L.	Lūcius.	Sp.	Spŭrius.
M.	Marcus.	T.	Titus.
M'.	Mānius.	Ti.	Tĭbĕrius

For women's names these letters are inverted, as Ↄ. Gaia.

Note. All the above are **praenomina** or individual names. Besides his praenomen, a Roman had a **nomen** which showed his **gens**, and a **cognomen** showing to what branch or family of the gens he belonged. Thus, Marcus Tullius Cicero denotes 'Marcus of the Cicero branch of the Tullia gens.' An **agnomen** was usually a title of honour, e. g. Africanus, Magnus, etc., or a title denoting adoption, as Octavianus (being the name of his *former* gens with the termination -*anus*), assumed by C. Octavius after being adopted by C. Julius Caesar, whose praenomen, nomen and cognomen he also assumed, and became known as Caius Julius Caesar Octavianus.

§ 177. Miscellaneous.

A. U. C.	Anno urbis conditae.		P. C.	Patres conscripti.
Cos.	Consul, -e.		P. R.	Populus Romanus.
Coss.	Consul-es, -ibus.		S. C.	Senatūs consultum.
D.O.M.	Deo Optimo Maximo.		S.	Salutem.
D. D.	Dono dedit.		S. P. D.	Salutem plurimam dicit (*or* dat).
F.	Filius.			
HS.	Sesterti-us, -um.		S.P.Q.R.	Senatus Populusque Romanus.
Imp.	Imperator.			
Id.	Idus.		S.V.B.E.E.V.	Si vales bene est, Ego valeo.
Kal.	Kalendae.			
Non.	Nonae.			

Note. For a more complete list of Abbreviations see Roby's Latin Grammar, vol. i. Appendix G, or Public Schools Lat. Gr., Appendix K.

EXPLANATION OF CERTAIN TERMS USED BY GRAMMARIANS.

§ 178. Letters.

Uncial letters. Capitals.
Cursive letters. Small letters.
Mutes. The letters *c* (*k, q*), *g, h; t, d; p, b, f* (*v*).
Nasals. The letters *m, n.*
Liquids. The letters *l, r.*
Spirants. The letters *f, h, j, s, v.*
Double Letters. The letters *x, z.*
Gutturals. The throat sounds, viz. *c, g, h, n, q, x.*
Dentals. The teeth sounds, viz. *d, j, l, n, r, s, t, z.*
Labials. The lip sounds, viz. *p, b, m, f, v.*

§ 179. Syllables, etc.

Ultima. The last syllable of a word.
Penultima. The last syllable but one.
Antepenultima. The last syllable but two.
Enclitic. A name given to words which are attached to the end of some other word in the sentence, as -que, *and.*

§ 180. Nouns.

Parisyllabic. Having the same number of syllables in the Oblique Cases as in the Nominative, i. e. not increasing.
Imparisyllabic. Increasing in the Oblique Cases.
Root. The Root of a word is that part which it has in common with other kindred words. Thus the root of bellator, *a warrior,* is *bell,* which it has in common with bellum and bellare.
Nouns of Common Gender. Nouns which can be used either as Masculine or Feminine, to suit the sex referred to, as, parens, *a parent;* see § 154 *b.*
Nouns of Epicene Gender. Certain names of animals having only one Gender, whichever be the sex referred to, as, passer, Masc. *a sparrow;* vulpes, Fem. *a fox,* aquila, Fem. *an eagle.* To indicate sex, when necessary, the words mas or femina are used, as mas passer, *cock-sparrow.*
Nouns of Doubtful Gender. Nouns which are used either Masculine or Feminine, without regard to the sex signified, as, talpa, Masc. or Fem., *a mole.*

§ 181. Verbs.

Aorist (= Indefinite). Properly the Tense denoting Indefinite Time, whether Past, Present, or Future (see p. 67), but in Latin restricted to Past Time.

Protăsis and Apodŏsis. In a Conditional Sentence, as, Si voluisset, fecisset, the si clause is called the Protasis, the other the Apodosis.

§ 182. Etymological Figures.

Assimilation. When a consonant changes itself to one which follows it, or to one like that which follows; thus, sub-pono becomes suppono; in-berbis becomes imberbis.

Aphaerĕsis. Cutting off letters from beginning, as, nosco *for* gnosco.

Syncŏpè. Taking away from middle, as, periclum *for* pericŭlum.

Apocŏpè. Cutting off from end, as, dic *for* dice.

Antithesis. Changing one letter for another, as, būbus *for* bōbus.

Metathĕsis. Transposition of a letter or syllable, as, colurnus *for* corulnus, accerso *for* arcesso.

Tmesis. Separation of parts of a compound word by the insertion of one or more words between the parts, as, septem subjecta trioni *for* subjecta septemtrioni.

§ 183. Syntactical Figures.

Ellipse. Omission of something, e.g. of a Substantive, as, ferina, *venison* [supply caro]; of a Verb, as, Nam Polydorus ego, *For I am Polydorus* [supply sum].

Pleonasm. Using more words than are necessary to express the meaning, as, sic *ore* locutus est, where 'ore' is redundant.

Zeugma. When two words or two clauses have the same Verb, which does not apply equally to both; so that for one of them another Verb (to be gathered from the sense of the passage) must be mentally supplied, as, Inceptoque et sedibus haeret in isdem, *He abides by his resolve, and remains seated in the same place.*

Asyndĕton. Omission of Conjunctions, as, veni, vidi, vici.

Hendiădys. Use of two Substantives instead of Substantive and Adjective to express one object, as, pateris libamus et auro *for* libamus aureis pateris.

Enallăgè. Use of one word for another, e.g. one Part of Speech for another, one Case for another, use of Singular for Plural, etc.

Hypallăgè. Interchange of Cases, as, dare classibus Austros *for* dare classes Austris, or using an Adjective in agreement with a Noun other than that to which it belongs in sense, as, sagitta *celeres* transilit umbras.

Prolepsis. The poets sometimes put an Adjective or Participle in agreement with a Substantive, though the quality implied cannot belong to it until the action of the Verb to which the Substantive belongs is completed; as, Scuta *latentia* condunt, which means, *They stow away the shields so that they become hidden,* i. e. *hide the shields out of sight;* where latentia is said to belong to scuta *proleptically,* that is, by anticipation. Compare the English phrases 'to strike a man *dead,*' 'to beat him *black* and *blue,*' etc., and Macbeth, Act iii. Sc. 4, 'Ere humane statute purged the *gentle* weal.'

Synĕsis or *Constructio ad Sensum.* When the Verb agrees not in grammar but in sense with its Subject, the Adjective with its Substantive, or the Relative with its Antecedent, as, fatale monstrum, *quae,* etc., Hor. Od. I, xxxvii. 21. See also §§ 216, 220.

Anacolŭthon. When the latter part of a sentence does not agree in syntax with the former; which sometimes happens when a parenthetical clause has intervened, so that the author has lost sight of the construction with which he set out.

§ 184. Prosody.

Foot. A name given to a set of two or more syllables by which lines of Latin poetry are divided.

Scansion. ⎱ The distribution of a verse of poetry into its proper
Scanning. ⎰ feet.

Dactyl. A foot consisting of one long and two short syllables, as, cārmĭnă.

Spondee. A foot consisting of two long syllables, as, mēnsās.

Other kinds of feet. Pyrrhic, ⏑ ⏑; Iambus, ⏑ –; Trochee, – ⏑; Anapaest, ⏑ ⏑ –; Tribrach, ⏑ ⏑ ⏑.

Hexameter (ἕξ, *six;* μέτρον, *measure*). A verse of six feet, of which the first four may be either Dactyls or Spondees, the fifth must be a Dactyl, and the sixth a Spondee, as,

Tītўrĕ | tū pătŭ lae rēcŭ bāns sūb | tēgmĭnĕ | fāgī‖.

Pentameter (πέντε, *five*). A verse of five feet. It has two divisions, each consisting of two feet and a long syllable, the two long syllables virtually constituting the fifth foot. The first half may have either Dactyls or Spondees, the second half Dactyls only, as,

Rēs ēst | sōllĭcĭ | tī ‖ plēnă tĭ | mōrĭs ă | mŏr ‖.

Note 1. The last syllable of a verse may be either long or short, but a short *vowel*-ending should be avoided, especially in the Pentameter.

Note 2. A Hexameter should end with a trisyllable or dissyllable word. A Pentameter should end with a dissyllable, which should be either a Substantive, Verb, or Personal or Possessive Pronoun.

Caesura. The point in a verse where a word ends, so as to cut [caedo] the foot in two, and the voice pauses a little. In a Hexameter line a Caesura should usually occur in the third foot, as,

Tītўrĕ | tū pătŭ | *lāé* rĕcŭ | bans, etc.

Penthemimeral Caesura (πέντε, *five*, ἡμί, *half*, μέρος, *a part*). A Caesura after the fifth half-foot, as in the line just given.

Hepthemimeral Caesura (ἑπτά, *seven*). A Caesura occurring after the seventh half-foot, as,

Fōrmō | sām rĕsŏ | nārĕ dŏ | *cēs* Āmă | rȳllĭdă | sīlvās‖.

Strong and Weak Caesura. In the Hexameter last given the 3rd foot contains what is called a *weak*, the 4th a *strong* Caesura.

Catalectic. A name given to a verse which is incomplete by one syllable. Thus, each of the two divisions of the Pentameter is said to be Catalectic.

Metre or *Measure* (μέτρον) is used in two senses;—(*a*) A definite system or combination of particular *Verses*; e. g. the Elegiac Metre, the *Iambic* Metre, etc. (*b*) A definite portion of a particular Verse. In Verses made up of Dactyls and Spondees, like the Hexameter and Pentameter, *one* Foot makes a Metre, (hence the name *Hexameter*, *the six-measure verse*, and *Penta*meter, *the five-measure verse*). But in Verses made up of Anapaests, Tribrachs, Iambics, or Trochees, a Metre consists of *two* feet. Hence the Iambic *senarius*, or Verse of six Feet, is called an Iambic *Trimeter.*

Arsis and Thesis (ἄρσις, θέσις). The syllable on which the Ictus or *stress* of the voice falls is said to be in Arsis. In Dactylic Verses the first syllable of each foot is in Arsis, the other syllable or syllables being in Thesis. A short syllable in Arsis is sometimes lengthened by the force of the Ictus, as,

Līmĭnă | *que* laūr | ūsquĕ dĕ | i, etc.

Synaloepha. Elision (or cutting off) of a final vowel before another vowel or *h* at the beginning of the following word, as, sūrg' ăg' ĕt, *for* sūrgĕ ăgĕ ĕt, and pōllŭĕr' hŏspĭtĭŭm *for* pōllŭĕrĕ hŏspĭtĭŭm. Heu and O are never elided.

Ecthlipsis. Elision of *m* and its vowel in the same way, as, mōnstr' hŏrrēnd' īnfōrme, etc., *for* mōnstrŭm, hŏrrēndŭm īnfōrme.

Synaeresis. Contraction of two vowels into one, as, deĭndĕ *for* deïndĕ.

Diaerĕsis. Resolution of one vowel into two, or of a diphthong into two vowels, as, ēvŏlüĭssĕ *for* ēvolvīssĕ, aquāï *for* aquae.

LAWS OF QUANTITY.

§ 185. General Rules.

(*a*) Most monosyllables are long, as, mē, pār, hīc (the Adverb).

Exceptions. Words in b, d, l, and t,
Words enclitic, -quĕ, -nĕ, -vĕ,
Ĕs (from sum), the Pronoun ĭs,
Nominatives hĭc and quĭs,
Ăn and cŏr, nĕc, făc, and fĕr,
Ĭn, vĭr, cĭs, pĕr, bĭs, and tĕr.

(*b*) A vowel before another vowel, or before h, in the same word, is short, as mĕus, prŏhibĕo.

Exceptions. (*a*) Many Greek words, as Aenēas; (*b*) dīci, aulāi, and the like; dīus, ēheu, ōhe, Dīana; (*c*) the i in fīo, except before ĕr, as, omnia jam fīunt, fīeri quae posse negabam; (*d*) the i of Genitives in -ius, which is sometimes doubtful, as unīus, illīus, but short in alterius, utrius, long in alīus, solīus, totīus.

(*c*) All diphthongs and contracted syllables are long, as aut, praeter, nīl (for nihil).

Exception. Prae is shortened before a vowel, as prăeustus.

(*d*) A vowel before two consonants, or before j, x, z, in the same word, is long *by position*, as vēntus, Ājax, rēxi, Amāzon.

Exceptions. Bĭjugus, quadrĭjugus.

Note 1. This rule applies also to final syllables ending in a Consonant, when the next word in the verse begins with a Consonant. Thus the syllables -*or*, -*at*, *nec*, *sit* in the following line are long *by position*:—

Tālis ăm | ōr tĕnĕ | āt nĕc | sĭt mihi | cūrā mĕd | ĕrī ‖.

Note 2. A short final vowel cannot remain short before any word beginning with sc, sm, sp, sq, st, x, or z, except smaragdus, Scamander, Xanthus, Zacynthus. Virgil has *lengthened* such a vowel once, perhaps, in the doubtful reading dătĕ | tĕlā | scăndĭtĕ | mūrōs‖. Æn. ix. 37, but this is a licence which must never be imitated. Avoid the position altogether.

(*e*) A vowel *short by nature* becomes doubtful before a *mute* (§ 178) when followed by *l* or *r*, rarely when followed by *m* or *n*. Thus păter has Gen. pătris. (But a long vowel always remains long: thus, the Gen. of māter is always mātris, never mătris.)

Exceptions. In compound words this rule is not often observed: thus, *ab* and *ob* in āb-luo ōb-ruo, are never shortened; the *re* in rĕ-pleo, rĕ-primo, etc., is never lengthened.

(*f*) Derived words usually follow the quantity of their primitives, as perlĕgo from lĕgo, legĕre, but ablēgo from lēgo, legāre. There are however many exceptions to this rule.

(*g*) Dissyllabic Perfects are long, as vīdi.

Exceptions. Bĭbi, dĕdi, fĭdi,
Stĕti, tŭli, scĭdi.

(*b*) Dissyllabic Supines are long, as vīsum.

Exceptions. Dătum, ĭtum, lĭtum, quĭtum,
Rătum, rŭtum, sătum, sĭtum.
Also cĭtum from cieo, cītum from cio; stătum from sisto, stātum from sto.

(*j*) Pro in composition is generally long, as prōcedo.

Exceptions. Prŏcella, prŏnepos, prŏpero, prŏtervus; and generally where *f* follows, as prŏficiscor, prŏfundus. But prōfero, prōficio, prōfui.

(*k*) Re in composition is short, as rĕfert (from refero).

Exceptions, Rēfert (the Impersonal), rēligio, rēliquiae, rēperit, rēpulit, rētulit. (The last three are often written repperit, reppulit, rettulit.)

§ 186. Final Syllables.

(*a*) Rule for long final syllables;—

Final A, I, O, U, C,
AS, ES, OS, must lengthened be.

(1) Exceptions to *a* long are ită, quiă, ejă, and Nominative, Vocative, and Accusative Cases (except Vocatives of Greek Nouns in -as).

(2) Exceptions to *i* long are nisi, quasi; Greek Vocatives and Datives, as Alexĭ. Palladĭ; and the doubtful vowels mihĭ, tibĭ, sibĭ, ubĭ, ibĭ. Compounds of ubi, except ubīque, are short, as ubivis.

(3) Exceptions to *o* long are citŏ, egŏ, modŏ, quomodŏ, duŏ, homŏ. The o of the First Person Singular of Verbs is said to be common, but except in sciō, nesciō, volŏ, putŏ, it is almost always found long.

(4) Exceptions to *c* long are făc, nĕc, donĕc, hĭc.

(5) Exceptions to *as* long are anăs, văs (vădis), and most Greek Cases of the 3rd Declension in -as.

(6) Exceptions to *es* long are penĕs, ĕs (from sum) and its compounds, and -es of the 3rd Declension *increasing short* as segĕs. But ariēs, abiēs, pariēs, Cerēs, pēs.

(7) Exceptions to *os* long are compŏs, impŏs, ŏs (ossis), and Greek words in -*os*, as epŏs.

(*b*) Rule for short final syllables:—

Finals reckoned short are E,
B, D, L, R, N, and T,
IS and US; nor place deny
To words from Greek in YS and Y.

(1) Exceptions to *e* short are the final *e* of 5th Decl., as diē, and Adverbs derived therefrom, as hodiē, quarē; 2nd Sing. Imperative of 2nd Conj., as monē; Adverbs (except benĕ, malĕ) derived from Adjectives in -us and -er; Greek Nouns in -η.

(2) Exceptions to *l* short are sāl and sōl.

(3) Exceptions to *r* short are făr, fūr, vēr, cūr, pār. with its compounds; Greek nouns in -ηρ.

(4) Exceptions to *n* short are ēn, nōn, quin, and Greek words in -ην or -ων.
(5) Exceptions to *is* short are Dat. and Abl. Plural; Nouns of 3rd Decl. in -is *increasing long*, as Samnīs (itis); 2nd Pers. Sing. of Tenses which have 2nd Pers. Pl. in -ītis, as audīs. The 2nd Sing. Fut. Perf. and Perf. Subj. is doubtful, as amavěrĭs.
(6) Exceptions to *us* short are all the cases of 4th Decl. except Nom. and Voc. Sing.; Nouns of 3rd Decl. in -us *increasing long*, as servitūs; Greek Nouns in -ους, Lat. -us, as Panthūs.

PARSING FORMS.

§ 187. Substantive.

—— is a Substantive, from —— (*state here what it makes in the Genitive*), —— Gender, —— Number, —— Case. Account for the Case, by reference to the explanations given in the Syntax; for example, if the word be in the Genitive Case, state what kind of Genitive it is, and on what word it is dependent.

§ 188. Adjective.

—— is an Adjective of —— Terminations, from ——, —— Gender, —— Number, —— Case, agreeing with ——.
Note. If it be a Comparative or Superlative Adjective, state the fact, and give the Positive; thus, 'digniori is an Adjective of two Terminations, from dignior, the Comparative of dignus, etc.' If it be a Numeral or Quasi-numeral, state the fact.

§ 189. Personal or Reflexive Pronoun.

—— is a —— Pronoun, from ——, —— Gender, —— Number, —— Case. Account for the Case, as with Substantives.

§ 190. Adjectival Pronoun.

—— is a —— Pronoun, from ——, —— Gender, —— Number, —— Case, agreeing with ——. If it be a Relative Pronoun, or a Demonstrative used as a Personal Pronoun, account for the Case, as with Substantives.

§ 191. Verb.

—— is a —— Verb, from —— (*here give the chief parts of the Verb*), —— Voice, —— Mood,[1] —— Tense, —— Number, —— Person,[2] agreeing with its Nominative ——.
If an Infinitive, omit Number, Person, and Agreement.
For an Impersonal Verb, omit Person and Agreement, and after the word 'Number' add the words 'used Impersonally.'

---

[1] Account for the Mood, if a Subjunctive.
[2] Or —— Person, —— Number, —— Tense, —— Mood, —— Voice.

§ 192. Participle.

—— is from ——, the (*here state the Tense and Voice*) Participle of the Verb —— (*here give the chief parts of the Verb*), —— Gender, —— Number, —— Case, agreeing with ——.

Note. If a Gerundive, omit Tense and Voice. In parsing the forms amandum est, monendum est, etc., there is no agreement with any Substantive; therefore, after the word 'Case' add the words 'Neuter Gerundive Construction, implying necessity.'

§ 193. Gerund or Supine.

—— is a Gerund (*or* Supine) in ——, from the Verb —— (*give chief parts of the Verb*), —— Case. Account for the Case.

§ 194. Particles.

(*a*) —— is an Adverb. (If Comparative or Superlative Degree, name the Positive). State what word it modifies.
(*b*) —— is a Preposition governing the —— Case.
(*c*) —— is a —— Conjunction, connecting —— and ——.
(*d*) —— is an Interjection.

§ 195. Example.
Tum senex recitavit judicibus eam fabulam quam proximè scripserat, *then the old man read out to the judges the play which he had last written.*

Note. This example is parsed in a shortened form to show the abbreviations which may be used.

Tum, Adv. of Time, modifying recitavit.
senex, Subst. f. senex, senis, Masc. Sing. Nom. being Subj. to recitavit.
recitavit, Trans. Vb. f. recit-o, -are, -avi, -atum, Act. Ind. Aor. 3rd Sing., agreeing with Nom. senex.
judicibus, Subst. f. judex, judicis, Masc. Pl. Dat. being Ind. Obj. of recitavit.
eam, Demonst. Pron. f. is, ea, id, Fem. Sing. Acc. agr. w. fabulam.
fabulam, Subst. f. fabula, -ae, Fem. Sing. Act. being Direct Object of recitavit.
quam, Rel. Pron. f. qui, quae, quod, Fem. Sing. 3rd Pers. agr. w. antecedent fabulam; Acc. Case, being Direct Object of scripserat.
proxime, Adv. modifying scripserat, Superl. degree from prope, Comp. propius.
scripserat, Trans. Vb. f. scribo, scribĕre, scripsi, scriptum, Act. Ind. Plpf. 3rd Sing., agreeing with Pronoun of 3rd Pers. implied in its ending.

SUPPLEMENTARY RULES

AND

EXAMPLES.

§ 196. **Note on the Subjunctive.** The Subjunctive denotes actions which are *thought of as happening*, whereas the Indicative denotes those which *actually do happen*. Hence,

Rule. The Indicative expresses a *fact*, the Subjunctive a *conception*.

§ 197. The uses of the Subjunctive may conveniently be classified according as they occur in Principal Clauses of Oratio Recta, in Subordinate Clauses of Oratio Recta, in Principal Clauses of Oratio Obliqua, and in Subordinate Clauses of Oratio Obliqua. The use of the Mood in continuous Speeches reported in Oratio Obliqua will also have to be noticed.

§ 198. IN PRINCIPAL CLAUSES OF ORATIO RECTA.

(*a*) **Potential Use**, as, dicat aliquis, *Some one may say*.
Note. Nearly all the instances where the Subjunctive in Principal Clauses is translated by the signs, *may, might, can, could, would, should*, are to be explained as Potential. The Hypothetical and Dubitative uses, to be noticed below in (*b*) and (*c*) are mere varieties of the Potential.

(*b*) **Hypothetical Use**, where a Subjunctive forms the apodosis (§ 181) of a Conditional Sentence, as, fecissem si jussisses, *I should have done it, if you had ordered me.*

(*c*) **Dubitative Use**, found chiefly in questions, as, quid faciam, *what am I to do?*

(*d*) **Optative Use** (often introduced by utinam), as, moriar, *may I die!* utinam mortuus essem, *would that I had died!*

(*e*) **Jussive, Hortative**, or **Imperative Use**, as, abeat, *let him begone;* ne dixeris, *don't say so*.

§ 199. IN SUBORDINATE CLAUSES OF ORATIO RECTA.

Subordinate Clauses are introduced either by the Relative, qui, quae, quod, or by Conjunctions. The Mood in such Clauses *is not always Subjunctive*, but when it is, it is usually explained grammatically as being *governed* by the Relative or Conjunction, though the expression is not strictly correct, the real reason for the Mood being that it refers to a *supposed case* rather than an *actual fact*, e.g. Paetus omnes libros, quos frater suus reliquisset, mihi donavit, *Paetus has given me all the books which his brother left him*, i.e. which his brother, *as he believed*, had left. (For a more complete account of the Relative in its simple sense of *who* or *which* followed by a Subjunctive see Madvig §§ 368, 369.) Of Subordinate Clauses introduced by Conjunctions, the chief kinds are,

(*a*) **Final** (indicating a *purpose*), expressed in English by *that* or *in order that*, *lest*, and in Latin by ut, *that*, nē, *lest*, quo (before Comparatives), *that*, qui = ut, and quominus, quin, *in order that . . . not*.

(*b*) **Consecutive** (indicating a *result*), expressed in English by *that*, after a preceding so or *such*, and in Latin by ut after talis, tam, etc.; also by quin, *so that . . . not*, and qui = talis ut.

(*c*) **Temporal** (indicating *time*), expressed in English by *when*, etc., and in Latin by quum, ut, ubi, and other Temporal Conjunctions already mentioned in § 84.

(*d*) **Causal**, expressed in English by *since*, *as*, or *because*, and in Latin by quum, quia, quod, and other Causal Conjunctions mentioned in § 84.

(*e*) **Conditional**, expressed in English by *if* or *unless*, and in Latin by si, nisi, and other Conditional Conjunctions mentioned in § 84.

(*f*) **Concessive**, expressed in English by *although*, and in Latin by etsi, quanquam, etc. See § 84.

(*g*) **Comparative**, expressed in English by *as if* or *as though*, and in Latin by tanquam, quasi, etc. See § 84.

§ 200. IN PRINCIPAL CLAUSES OF ORATIO OBLIQUA.

(*a*) **Oblique Statement**. A simple Statement, as voluit, *he wished*, becomes Oblique when it forms the Object of a Verb, as dicit se voluisse, *he says that he wished*, or the Subject of a Verb, as constat eum voluisse, *it is well known that he wished*, i.e. that he wished (Subject) is well known (Verb). Here the Infinitive is used. But sometimes we find ut with Subjunctive, as accidit ut vellet, *it happened that he wished*. Hence

Rule. *The Principal Clauses in Oblique Statement are the Subjects of Impersonal Verbs or the Objects of Verbs of declaring, knowing, perceiving, thinking, or believing, and are usually expressed by the Infinitive, but occasionally by* **ut** *with Subjunctive after certain Impersonals*, e.g.

Restat, abest, accidit,
Evēnit, contingit, fit,
Licet, sequitur, *and* est,
Placet, refert, interest.

(*b*) **Oblique Question.** Questions, as, ridesne *are you laughing?* quid rides, *what are you laughing at?* become Oblique when they form the Object of a Verb, as, rideasne scire volumus, *we want to know whether you are laughing*, or the Subject of a Verb, as, quid rideas dictu difficile est, *it is difficult to say what you are laughing at*.

Rule. *All Clauses introduced by an Interrogative Pronoun or Particle* (§ 60, p. 75) *must have their Verb in the Subjunctive if they form the Subject or Object of a Verb.*

Note. This Rule will require some modification when we come to the rule respecting whole Speeches reported in Oratio Obliqua (see § 203).

(c) **Oblique Command.** Properly speaking the only instances of Oblique Command are those which occur in a whole Speech reported in Oratio Obliqua, *where they are always put in the Subjunctive*, as will be seen below, § 202. It is convenient however to include under this head Clauses introduced by ut or ne which follow Verbs expressing such ideas as
To ask or wish, command, contrive,
Allow, forbid, advise, and strive;
as, imperavi tibi ut hoc faceres, *I commanded you to do this;* suasi tibi ne hoc faceres, *I advised you not to do this.* [See § 301.]

§ 201. IN SUBORDINATE CLAUSES OF ORATIO OBLIQUA.

Rule. *A Subordinate Clause in Oratio Obliqua, whether belonging to an Oblique Statement, Question, or Command, must under all circumstances be put in the Subjunctive.*

Note. Such sentences as, nuntiant Belgas, qui cis Rhenum incolunt, in armis esse, are no exception to this rule. The clause 'qui cis Rhenum incolunt' formed no part of the speaker's original words, and does not therefore belong to the Oblique Sentence, but is added by the author for the information of his readers.

§ 202. SPEECHES REPORTED IN ORATIO OBLIQUA.

A whole Speech containing Statements, Questions, and Commands intermingled is sometimes reported Obliquely, being dependent on the words dixit, dicit, or their equivalents expressed or understood.

Rule for Speeches in Oratio Obliqua. *The Statements are put in the Infinitive; the Questions, if of the First or Third Person, are also in the Infinitive, but if of the Second Person they are usually in the Subjunctive; the Commands are put in the Subjunctive; and, lastly, all Subordinate Clauses must be Subjunctive.*

Example:—

Direct. Deinde dux, 'Arcem hostium,' exclamavit, 'statim expugnare mihi in animo est. Quis mecum erit, comites? Expectatisne donec hostes ultro arma tradant? Utrum dux an servus vester sum? Expergiscimini, festinate, arma parate, ne occasionem, quam nunc fors obtulit, belli conficiendi amittamus!'

Oblique. Deinde dux exclamavit, Sibi esse in animo arcem hostium statim expugnare. Quem comitum secum fore? Expectarentne donec hostes ultro arma traderent? Utrum ducem eorum an servum sese esse?

Thereupon the general exclaimed, 'I purpose storming the enemy's citadel immediately. Who will go with me, comrades? Are you waiting until the enemy voluntarily give up their arms? Am I your general or your slave? Wake up! Make haste! Get ready your arms, lest we lose the opportunity which chance has now presented of finishing the war!'

Thereupon the general exclaimed that he purposed storming the enemy's citadel immediately. Which of his comrades would go with him? Were they waiting until the enemy voluntarily gave up their arms? Was he their general or their slave?

Expergiscerentur, festinarent, arma pararent, ne occasionem quam nunc fors obtulisset, belli conficiendi amitterent. *They must wake up, make haste, and get ready their arms, lest they should lose the opportunity which chance had now presented of finishing the war.*

Note. The Subjunctive Mood is sometimes distinguished as *Con*junctive when it occurs in Principal Clauses of Oratio Recta, *Sub*junctive when it occurs in Subordinate or Oblique Sentences.

§ 203. The Subjunctive is also used in Causal and Relative Sentences to denote an *alleged* reason or act, as, Laudat Panaetius Africanum, quod fuerit abstinens, 'Panaetius praises Africanus because *he says that* he was self-restraining.' Fuit for fuerit would mean 'because he *actually was* self-restraining,' without implying that Panaetius said so. So, injuria quae tibi facta *est*, 'the injury which *has* been done you,' but injuria quae tibi facta *sit*, 'the injury which *you say has* been done you,' Cic. in Caecil. 58.

§ 204. **Additional Notes on the Sequence of Tenses.** The general rule for Sequence of Tenses, as stated in § 148, is that Primary Tenses are followed by Primary, and Historic by Historic.

Note. The Rule here given applies equally to both Subjunctive and Infinitive Moods. Remember that what is called the Present Infinitive, as amare, is both Present *and Imperfect*, and that what is called the Perfect Infinitive, as amavisse, is both Perfect *and Pluperfect*. Note the following examples of Infinitive :—

ait se verum dicere, *He says that he is speaking the truth.*
ait se verum dixisse, *He says that he spoke, or has spoken, the truth.*
aiebat se verum dicere, *He said that he spoke, or was speaking, the truth.*
aiebat se verum dixisse, *He said that he had spoken the truth.*

§ 205. The difficulty which most troubles beginners in the rule for Sequence of Tenses is the translation of an English Aorist when requiring to be put into the Subjunctive or Infinitive Mood in Latin. The following rule may be followed in most cases :

After a Primary Tense the Aorist is translated by a Perfect Subjunctive or Infinitive, as,
nescio an verum dixerit, *I know not whether he spoke the truth.*
ait se verum dixisse, *He says that he spoke the truth.*
After a Historic Tense the Aorist is translated by an Imperfect Subjunctive or Infinitive, as,
nesciebam an verum diceret, *I knew not whether he spoke the truth.*
aiebat se verum dicere, *He said that he spoke the truth.*

§ 206. Often however the rule given in § 205 will not apply ; e. g.

(*a*) By a laxity in English usage the Aorist is often used where a Pluperfect ought to stand. Thus, we find such sentences as 'A said that B *told* him so and so,' where *told* of course means *had told*. In all such cases, where the action takes place *before* that of the governing verb, a Pluperfect must be used after a Historic Tense.

(*b*) The Latins often preferred to represent Aorist Time by a Perfect Subjunctive rather than an Imperfect after Historic Tenses : this usage, where it occurs, is intended perhaps to mark the occurrence of an *actual fact* rather than a supposed case. It is especially frequent after ut Consecutive; thus, '*he was so prudent that he avoided these things*' might be translated tam prudens erat ut haec vitaret, or tam prudens erat ut haec vitaverit; the former would mean 'he was so prudent *as to* avoid,' &c., the latter 'he was so prudent that he *did actually* avoid.'

(c) A Pluperfect is often used in Subordinate Clauses of Oratio Obliqua, where an Imperfect would stand if it were Oratio Recta; thus, si flumen *transiret*, hostem vinceret, *if he crossed the river he would conquer the enemy*, becomes, in the Oblique form, putavit se, si flumen *transiisset*, hostem esse victurum.

§ 207. Cicero constantly uses an Imperfect Subjunctive after a Perfect Indicative. Thus in 1 Verr. i. 3 he says, huic ego causae actor *accessi* non ut *augerem* invidiam ordinis, sed ut infamiae communi *succurrĕrem*, *I have come forward as prosecutor in this case, not to increase the unpopularity of your order but to retrieve the ill-repute we suffer from in common.*

§ 208. After a Historic Present, i.e. a Present used for an Aorist, like our 'says he' for 'said he,' the Tenses in Subordinate or Dependent Sentences sometimes follow the *rule*, sometimes the *sense*, as, 'though so great a defeat had been sustained, the general nevertheless exhorts the soldiers not to lose heart,' quum tanta clades esset accepta, dux tamen milites hortatur ne animo deficiant *or* deficerent.

*** The following Examples, as far as § 290, follow the order of the Rules of Syntax, pp. 84-104, which they are intended both to illustrate and supplement. The numbering of the paragraphs is made with a view to facilitating reference, and has nothing to do with the Syntax Rules.

Phrases and words requiring special notice in the Examples are printed in italics without any reference being necessarily intended to the particular rule of Syntax which the example illustrates.

The Three Concords.

(See § 95, a and b.)

§ 209. The Gauls are attacking the city.	Galli urbem oppugnant.
They announce that the Gauls are attacking the city.	Gallos urbem oppugnare nuntiant.
I know not why the Gauls are attacking the city.	Cur Galli urbem oppugnent nescio.
§ 210. What sort of man is Milo?	Qualis est Milo?
I *know not* what sort of man Milo *is*.	Nescio qualis sit Milo.

158   LATIN GRAMMAR.   [§§ 210–

I *know not* what sort of man Milo *was*.   Nescio qualis *fuerit* Milo. (See § 205.)
I *knew not* what sort of man Milo *was*.   Nescivi qualis *esset* Milo. (See § 205.)

§ 211. He is happy.   Beatus est.
He says that he is happy.   Ait se beatum esse.
She says that she is happy.   Ait se beatam esse.
He *says that he is not* happy.   Negat se beatum esse.
They say that he *was* happy.   Aiunt eum beatum *fuisse*.
They *said that he was not* happy.   Negârunt eum beatum *esse* (or *fuisse* by § 206 a).

§ 212. Caesar will come.   Caesar veniet.
I *almost think* [or *perhaps*] Caesar will come.   Haud scio an Caesar venturus sit.
It is well known that Caesar will come.   Caesărem venturum esse constat.
They said that Caesar would come.   Caesarem venturum esse dicebant.
Caesar hopes to come.   Caesar se venturum esse sperat.
Caesar promised to come.   Caesar se venturum esse pollicĭtus est.

§ 213. Is he wise or foolish?   Utrum sapiens an stultus est?
We wish to know whether he is wise or foolish.   Scire volŭmus utrum sapiens an stultus sit.
We *wish* to know whether he *was* wise or foolish.   Scire volumus utrum sapiens an stultus *fuerit* (§ 205).
We *wished* to know whether he *was* wise or foolish.   Scire voluimus utrum sapiens an stultus *esset* (§ 205).

§ 214. Marcus has returned.   Marcus rediit.
Marcus *has been* persuaded [or, *is* persuaded, § 376] to return.   Marco persuasum est ut *redeat* (§§ 200, c, and 205).
Marcus *was* persuaded to return.   Marco persuasum est ut *rediret* (§§ 200, c, and 205).
Marcus was persuaded *not* to return.   Marco persuasum est *ne* rediret.

§ 215. The soldiers had taken the town.   Milites oppĭdum ceperant.
We asked whether the soldiers had taken the town.   Militesnĕ oppidum cepissent quaesivimus.

§ 216. Part load the tables with food.   Pars epulis onĕrant mensas.
Part seek the seeds of flame.   Quaerit pars semĭna flammae.

    Rule. A Noun of Multitude in the Singular Number may have either a Singular or (by *constructio ad sensum*, § 183) a Plural Verb.

§ 217. Caesar and Crassus will soon be at the gates.

Caesar et Crassus mox ad portas erunt.

They *informed me* that Caesar and Crassus would soon be at the gates.

Me certiorem fecerunt Caesarem et Crassum mox ad portas futuros esse.

Rule. When the Subject is Composite, that is, formed of two or more Nouns united by Conjunctions, the Verb is usually Plural, as above. But,

Note 1. If the Composite Subject denote a *Singular idea*, it takes a Singular Verb, as, senatus populusque Romanus hoc decrevit.

Note 2. If the Conjunctions be Disjunctive, as, *nec—nec, utrum—an, sive—sive, vel—vel, aut—aut*, etc., the Verb usually follows the Number and Person of the *nearest* Noun, as, nec Caesar nec legati hoc *fecerunt;* nec legati nec vos hoc *fecistis*.

§ 218. Both *you and I* were happy.

Et *ego et tu* beati fuimus.

They say that both you and I were happy.

Et me et te beatos fuisse ferunt.

You and Marcus will be accused.

Tu et Marcus accusabimini.

We believe that you and Marcus will be accused.

Te et Marcum accusatum iri credimus.

Rule. If the *Persons* in a Composite Subject are different, the Verb *follows the prior Person;* the First Person being considered prior to the Second, and the Second to the Third.

Note. There is often a tendency, however, to make the Verb agree with the Noun *nearest* to it, as, ego et Cicero meus flagitabit. In such cases the Verb is said to be *attracted* to the Person of the nearest Noun.

§ 219. The king and queen are dead.

Rex et regina mortui sunt.

Fire, water, and iron are very useful.

Ignis, aqua, ferrum sunt utilissima.

Rule. If the *Genders* in a Composite Subject are different, the rules for Adjective in Agreement are as follows:—

(1) If the Nouns are names of *living things*, the Adjective is put in the Plural and *follows the worthier Gender;* the Masculine being considered *worthier* than the Feminine, and the Feminine worthier than the Neuter.

(2) If the Nouns are names of *things not living*, the Adjective is put in the Neuter Plural.

Note. Here again, however, is to be noticed the tendency to *attract* the Adjective into agreement with the *nearest* Noun, as, animus et consilium et sententia civitatis *posita* est in legibus, *the spirit and purpose and feeling of a nation is expressed in its laws.*

§ 220. The chiefs of the conspiracy were whipped and beheaded.

Capita conjurationis virgis caesi ac securi percussi sunt.

Note. A *constructio ad sensum* (§ 183), caesi and percussi agreeing with the notion of *men* implied in capita.

§ 221. The quarrels of lovers are the renewal of love.   Amantium irae amoris integratio est.

Note. Est is here *attracted* to the Number of the nearest Noun. Cf. 'Words to the heat of deeds too cold breath *gives*.' Macbeth, act ii. sc. 1. (See § 95, *c.*)

§ 222. They cut down the tree which grew in our garden.   Arbŏrem, quae in horto nostro crescebat, succīdĕrunt.

The tree which I loved so much has been cut down.   Arbor, quam tantopere diligebam, succisa est.

The army which Hannibal brought with him was small.   Exercĭtus, quem Hannibal secum duxit, exiguus erat.

Rule. The Preposition cum, when used with the Personal Pronouns, and sometimes when used with the Relative, is enclitic (§ 179), as, mecum, tecum, secum, nobiscum, vobiscum, quocum, quibuscum.

It is said that Scipio commanded the army which overcame Hannibal.   Exercitui, qui Hannibălem superavit, Scipio praefuisse dicitur (§ 231).

We, who are in the country, send these presents to you, who are in the city.   Nos, qui ruri sumus, haec munera ad vos, qui in urbe estis, mittimus.

You and I, who have so long been enemies, have at length laid aside our enmity.   Ego et tu, qui tamdiu inimici fuimus, inimicitias tandem deposuimus.

§ 223. I will punish him who does this.   Qui hoc fecerit, in eum animadvertam (§ 298).

Rule. Avoid ille qui. When *is* is antecedent to qui, it is often either omitted altogether, or placed in the *following* clause, as above.

§ 224. Here am I who did it.   Adsum qui feci.
Here am I whom ye seek.   Adsum quem quaerĭtis.

In these examples the antecedent ego is contained in the Verb adsum. This constantly happens.

§ 225. All men praised my good fortune in having such a son.   Omnes laudare fortunas meas qui talem natum haberem.

Here the Antecedent is contained in the Possessive Pronoun meas, which = mei, *of me*. For the Historic Infinitive laudare see § 275.

§ 226. I came in time, which is the most important of all things.   In tempore veni, quod rerum omnium est primum.

Here the Antecedent is the sentence 'in tempore veni.'

§ 227. Thebes, which is the capital of Boeotia.   Thebae, quod Boeotiae caput est.

The Relative here is *attracted* into agreement in Number and Gender with the Appositional Noun in its clause. Sometimes, though rarely, the Relative is attracted into the Case of its Antecedent, in imitation of the Greek, as, *judice, quo nôsti, populo*, and, *rebus, quibus quisque poterat, elatis*. *Inverse Attraction*, confined chiefly to poetry, is where the Antecedent is attracted into the Case of the Relative, as, *urbem, quam statuo, vestra est, the city which I am founding is yours*.

§ 228. A boy whose name was Servius Tullius.   Puer cui Servio Tullio nomen fuit.

Here Servio Tullio, which should be Nominative in Apposition to nomen, is *attracted* into the Case of cui.

§ 229. Osiris was the first who made ploughs.   Osiris primus aratra fecit.

It is uncertain whether Osiris or Triptolemus was the first who made ploughs.   Osirisne an Triptŏlĕmus primus aratra fecerit incertum est.

He gave me the most beautiful flowers he had.   Flores, quos habuit pulcherrimos, mihi dedit.

Lucullus was the richest person who was then living at Rome.   Eorum qui tum Romae habitabant Lucullus ditissimus erat.

Note. Neither Ordinal Numerals nor Superlatives contain the Antecedent to the Relative in Latin, as they appear to do in English. 'Osiris primus erat qui aratra fecit' would mean, *Osiris, who made ploughs, was the first man*, without denoting in what respect he was 'first,' and by no means implying that it was in the making of ploughs. After Superlatives, some rendering similar to that given in the last two of the above examples must be adopted. 'Flores pulcherrimos, quos habuit' would simply mean, *very beautiful flowers, which he had;* and 'Lucullus ditissimus erat qui tum Romae habitabat' would mean, *Lucullus, who was then living at Rome. was a very rich person*. (For 'he sent back *all* the books he had' say 'libros, quos habuit, remisit omnes,' rather than 'omnes libros, quos habuit, remisit.')

Copulative Verbs and Apposition.

(See §§ 96-100.)

§ 230. Hector was son of Priam, the Trojan king.   Priămi, regis Trojāni, Hector filius fuit.

The poets say that Hector was son of Priam, the Trojan king.   Priămi, regis Trojani, Hectŏrem filium fuisse tradunt poetae.

§ 231. It is said that Galba was learned.   Galba doctus fuisse dicitur.

It has been related that Galba was learned.   Galbam doctum fuisse tradĭtum est.

Note. Do not say Galbam doctum fuisse *dicitur*. The Copulative Verbs (§ 96) prefer a Personal to an Impersonal construcion, except in the Tenses compounded with the Perfect Participle. See Madvig, § 400.

§ 232. The town was called Corioli.
They called the town Corioli.
He marched towards Capua, a city which had lately revolted.

Oppĭdum Coriŏli vocatum est (*or* vocati sunt, *by attraction*).
Oppĭdum Coriŏlos vocârunt.
Ad Capuam flexit iter, quae urbs (*not* urbem quae) nuper defecerat.

Rule. An Appositive Noun having a Relative Clause immediately dependent on it, as in the last of the above examples, is sometimes *attracted* into the Case of the Relative. So, the phrase 'a thing which' is always quae res, quam rem, etc.

§ 233. I wish to be made consul.
It is a glorious thing to be made consul.

Consul fieri cupio.
Consŭl*em* fieri magnĭfĭcum est.

Note. In the last example consulem, being a mere complement of fieri, follows the Case of the unexpressed Subject of that Verb, viz. the Accusative (§ 89, *footnote* 2).

§ 234. I am not permitted to be neglectful.

Mihi non licet esse negligenti.

Note. Mihi non licet esse negligent*em* is also correct Latin, negligentem agreeing with 'me' understood. If no Dative after licet is expressed, the Accusative is generally used, as, medios esse non licebit. Madvig. 393, *c. Obs.* 3.

Time, Place, and Measure.

(See §§ 101-107.)

§ 235. Priam reigned many years.
A report *was spread* that Priam had now reigned many years.

Priămus multos annos regnavit.
Pervulgatum est Priămum multos jam annos regnâsse.

Per multos annos is also good Latin.

He is twenty years old.

Viginti annos natus est.

§ 236. Caesar was killed on the Ides of March *in the year* 44 *before Christ*.
We have heard that Caesar was killed on the Ides of March.

Caesar Idibus Martiis, anno ante Christum natum quadragesimo quarto, interfectus est.
Caesărem Idibus Martiis interfectum esse accepimus.

Note. This Ablative is used to express (1) *at what time*, as above, (2) *within what time*, as, paucis diebus proficiscar, *I shall set out in a few days*, (3) *how long ago*, as tribus abhinc annis mortuus est, *he died three years ago*.

§ 237. Having sailed thence to Greece I returned to Rome and Italy in twenty days.

Inde ad Graeciam advectus viginti diebus Romam et in Italiam redii.

Note. Ad with the Accusative of towns and small islands means *towards*, *in the direction of*, as, ad Brundisium flexit iter.

§ 238. Dionysius *when* expelled from Syracuse taught boys at Corinth.
Dionysius Syracusis expulsus pueros Corinthi docuit.

It is *on record* that Dionysius when expelled from Syracuse taught boys at Corinth.
Memoriae traditum est Dionysium Syracusis expulsum pueros Corinthi docuisse.

The ambassadors returned *from* Carthage and Africa.
Legati Carthagine et ex Africā redierunt.

Note. Ab or ex with towns or small islands denotes either *from the interior of* or *from the neighbourhood of*, as, ex Cypro discessit; Caesar a Gergovia discessit. Ab is used with expressions of *measure*, as, tria millia passuum a Roma abesse.

§ 239. *When* at Rome I love Tibur, *when* at Tibur Rome.
Romae Tibur, Tibure Romam amo.

Horatius said that when at Rome he loved Tibur, when at Tibur Rome.
Horatius dixit se Romae Tibur, Tibure Romam amare.

Accusative Case.

(See § 110, *a, b.*)

§ 240. To play an insolent game.
Ludum insolentem ludere.

Note. Pure Cognate Accusatives as ludĕre ludum, ridēre risum, etc., are rare. It is more common to find an Accusative added to Intransitive Verbs to denote some *special part* of the whole action of the Verb, as, ludĕre aleam, *to play hazard*, i.e. ludĕre ludum aleae. So, pluĕre sanguinem, *to rain blood;* lampădem olēre, *to smell of the lamp;* mella sapĕre, *to have the taste of honey,* etc.

§ 241. The Suevi do not subsist much upon corn, but chiefly upon milk and cattle.
Suevi non multum frumento sed maximam partem lacte atque pecŏre vivunt.

Note. The Accusative of Limitation, as, maximam partem in the above example, is allied to the Cognate usage. It is immaterial whether we call multum here an Accusative of Limitation or a Neuter Adjective used Adverbially.

(See § 110, *c.*)

§ 242. Like unto a God in countenance and shoulders.
Os humerosque deo similis.

§ 243. Having his temples crowned with bay.
Redimītus tempora lauro.

Note. The Accusatives here and in similar instances, many of which occur in Virgil, as, perque pedes trajectus lora tumentes, *having thongs passed through his swelling feet,* inutile ferrum cingitur. *he girds on his useless sword,* etc., are not Accusatives of Respect, but are the Direct Object of the Verb or Participle, which is to be regarded either as retaining its Transitive force in the Passive Voice, or as being Reflexive. (See § 114.)

§ 244. Ask favour of the gods. Posce deos veniam.

Note. The Verbs of *asking* that take a double Accusative are posco, flagito, oro, rogo, interrogo. Peto, precor, postŭlo, quaero, sciscitor, prefer an Ablative of the *person* with ab or ex.

§ 245. My mother taught me my letters.   Mater mea me literas docuit.

I remember that my mother taught me my letters.   Matrem meam me literas docēre memĭni.

Note. The construction of memini with Present instead of Perfect Infinitive is to be noticed.

§ 246. Do not conceal these things from your father.   Haec nē patrem tuum celaveris.

Or, haec patrem tuum celare noli. But do not, in writing Prose, put nē celes, or nē cela. See § 378.

Dative Case.

(See §§ 116 and 117, a.)

§ 247. He owed his life to me.   Vitam mihi acceptam rētulit.

Do not ask, my countrymen, why he was indebted for his life to me.   Nolīte sciscitari, cives, cur vitam mihi acceptam retulerit.

They appoint a day for the trial of Titus Menenius.   T. Menenio diem dicunt.

To be angry *with* anyone.   Irasci (*or* succensēre) alicui.

If you *consult me* I will *consult your interests*.   Si me consuluĕris, ego tibi consŭlam (§ 298).

What have I to do with you?   Quid mihi tecum?

A shout ascends to heaven.   It clamor caelo.

Note. Caelo is Dative of *motion to*, for ad caelum; a poetical usage.

§ 248. This is common to me and you.   Hoc mihi tecum commune est.

This is common to all living creatures.   Commune animantium omnium hoc est.

That was peculiar to Tiberius.   Id Tiberio proprium fuit.

This is a vice peculiar to old age.   Hoc proprium senectutis vitium est.

He is like his father.   Patri suo similis est.

Do you think you are like me?   An tu mei similem esse putas?

Rule. Communis, proprius, and similis may take either a Dative or a Genitive. So also affinis and par.

§ 249. He took the young man *from* confinement and set him as leader over the people. — Extractum custodiae juvenem ducem populo imposuit. [See § 315, *b*.].

Note on custodiae. Many Verbs compounded with ab, ad, de, ex, and signifying *removal from* or *taking from*, are followed by a Dative of the Indirect Object (translated by *from*), where we should have expected an Ablative of Separation, or Ablative with Preposition. So, adimam cantare severis; paullum sepultae distat inertiae celata virtus, etc. The poets extend the usage to other Verbs, as, huic atro liquuntur sanguine guttae, *from it there flow drops of black blood*.

§ 250. He threw himself at Caesar's feet. — Caesari ad pedes se projecit.

(See § 117, *e*, *f*.)

§ 251. To be able to pay one's debts. — Solvendo esse.
To be able to bear the burden. — Oneri ferendo esse.
To sound a retreat. — Receptui canere.

§ 252. These things are a subject of anxiety to us. — Haec curae sunt nobis.
He is sent to the assistance of the army. — Exercitui auxilio mittitur.

Note. The Predicative Dative may take a Dative of the Indirect Object after it, as nobis and exercitui in the above examples.

§ 253. Whom did it benefit? — Cui bono fuit?

Note. Only Adjectives of *quantity*, as magnus, quantus, tantus, etc., are used with the Predicative Dative. Hence cui in the above example is an Indirect Object, not an Adjective in agreement with bono.

§ 254. Cassandra the prophetess was never believed. — Cassandrae vati nunquam creditum est (§ 119).
It is well known that Cassandra the prophetess was never believed. — Cassandrae vati nunquam creditum esse constat.

Ablative Case.

(See §§ 120, 121).

§ 255. He joined battle with the enemy in a favourable position. — Proelium cum hostibus loco opportuno commisit.

Note. Except in the case of towns and small islands, almost the only Ablatives of *Place where* used in Prose are loco, locis, dextrā, laevā, medio, terrā marique, and Nouns in the Ablative having totus or medius in agreement (Roby's Lat. Gr. § 1170). Hence the English *in* when used of *place* should usually be expressed in Latin by the Preposition **in** with Ablative. In Poetry this Ablative is very frequent with all sorts of Nouns.

§ 256. Sulla resigned the dictatorship.
Somebody said that Sulla had resigned the dictatorship.
Perhaps you may ask why Sulla resigned the dictatorship.

Sullă dictaturā se abdicavit. (See § 121, a.)
Dixit nescio quis Sullam dictaturā se abdicâsse.
Fortasse roges cur Sullă dictaturā se abdicaverit.

§ 257. Caesar was more fortunate than Crassus.
There *are* some who believe that Caesar *was* more fortunate than Crassus.
There *were* some who doubted whether Caesar *was* more fortunate than Crassus.
I think death easier than disgrace.
They live more on corn than on meat.

Caesar felicior Crasso erat. (See § 121, c.)
Sunt qui credant Caesarem feliciorem Crasso *fuisse*.
Erant qui dubitarent an Caesar felicior Crasso *esset*.
Puto mortem dedecore leviorem.
Frumento magis quam carne vivunt (§ 121, b).

Rule. The Ablative of Comparison is used (1) for quam with Nominative, as felicior Crasso for felicior quam Crassus, (2) for quam with Accusative, as feliciorem Crasso for feliciorem quam Crassum, *but not for quam with any other Case.* Thus we could not say 'frumento magis carne vivunt' for *they live more on corn than on meat.*

§ 258. You will be of as much value to others as you *are* to yourself.

Tanti eris aliis quanti tibi fuĕris (§ 298).

Note. The forms usually called Genitives of Value are tanti, quanti, magni, parvi, (with their Comparative Degrees and Compounds, as maximi, quanticumque, &c.), nihili, flocci, nauci, pili, terunci, assis, hujus, pluris, minoris. Mr. Roby (Lat. Gr. §§ 1186, 1187) calls them Locatives, and thinks the forms assis, pluris, &c., are due to false analogy. The phrase boni consulĕre, *to make the best of,* belongs probably to this usage.

§ 259. Why should I not exchange toil for rest?

Cur non laborem otio permutem? (§ 121, d).

Rule. Mutare and its compounds signify (1) to give in exchange, (2) to take in exchange. The thing given or taken is in the Accusative, and the thing for which it is exchanged is in the Ablative. Hence the above example *might* mean, 'Why should I not take toil in exchange for rest?' i.e. change rest for toil. The meaning to be assigned in any particular passage can only be determined by the context.

§. 260. *The* richer he is, *the* more covetous he becomes.
The more he studies *the* more he learns.

Quo divitior eo cupidior fit. (See § 121, g, and also § 373.)
Quo magis literis studet, eo plus discit.

He says that the more *he* studies the more he learns.	Ait se, quo magis literis studeat, eo plus discĕre.
They say that the more *he* studied the more he learnt.	Ferunt eum, quo magis literis studeret, eo plus didicisse.

Note 1. The quo Clause is subordinate to the eo Clause, and its Verb therefore takes its time from the Aorist didicisse. Studuisset for studeret would not be inadmissible (§ 206, *c*). For se and eum see § 291.

Note 2. Magis, *more in degree*; plus, *more in quantity*.

§ 261. The sun is many times greater than the earth.	Sol multis partibus major est quam terra (§ 121, *g*).
The city was *the* more easily taken because, &c.	Eo facilius capta est urbs, quod, &c.
Half as big again.	Dimidio major.

(See § 123.)

§ 262. *Having taken the city* Caesar departed from Gaul.	Urbe captā, Caesar ex Galliā discessit.
Christ was born *when Augustus was Emperor*.	Imperante Augusto natus est Christus.
I did this *because my father and mother ordered me*.	Haec, patre et matre jubentibus, feci.
If you appease the gods, you will escape the danger.	Dis placatis, pericŭlum vitabis.
He *left home and* set out for Italy.	Domo relictā in Italiam profectus est.
In the consulship of Gnaeus Pompeius, and Marcus Crassus.	Gn. Pompeio M. Crasso consulibus.

Notice the above varieties in the translation of the Ablative Absolute.

(See § 126.)

§ 263. Now is there need of courage, O Aeneas; now is there demand for strength.	Nunc animis opus, Aenea, nunc viribus usus.
Aeneas perceived that now there was need of courage, now a demand for strength.	Nunc animis opus esse nunc viribus usum sensit Aeneas.
There is need of haste.	Properato opus est.
'Why is there need of haste?' said he.	'Cur,' inquit, 'properato opus est?'
He asked why there was need of haste.	Cur properato esset opus quaesivit.

Rule. Opus, *need*, is used (1) with Ablative of a Substantive, as animis, (2) with a Perf. Pass. Part. used Substantively, as properato, (3) in Apposition to a Noun in the Nominative, as dux nobis opus est, *we have need of a leader*, (4) with an Infinitive Clause, as, non opus est id scire *or* id sciri, *it is not needful to know that*, or *that that should be known*. Usus is constructed similarly, but is less often found.

Genitive Case.
(See §§ 127-131).

§ 264. My care for you.   Mea cura tui.
Your care for me.   Tua cura mei.

Rule. Meus, tuus, suus, noster, vester, nostrum (Gen. Pl.), and vestrum (Gen. Pl.) are used Subjectively; mei, tui, sui, nostri (Gen. Pl.), and vestri (Gen. Pl.) Objectively.

§ 265. He was eager for praise.   Avĭdus erat laudis.
He *said* he *was* eager for praise.   Se laudis avidum *esse* dixit.
He *said* he *was not* eager for praise.   Negavit se laudis avidum esse.
They *say* he *was* eager for money.   Avidum pecuniae cum *fuisse* ferunt.
It *is* uncertain whether he *was* eager for praise or money.   Incertum est utrum laudis an pecuniae avidus *fuerit*.
It *was* uncertain whether he *was* eager for praise or money.   Incertum fuit utrum laudis an pecuniae avidus *esset*.

Note. The Adjectives that take an Objective Genitive, are (1) those denoting some active state of the feelings or mind, as avĭdus, cupidus, memor, peritus, &c., (2) Verbals in -ax, as Tempus edax rerum, (3) Adjectives denoting *fulness* or *want*, as dives, plenus, expers, pauper. The last two usages belong chiefly to poetry.

§ 266. The kingly government was designed for the preservation of liberty.   Regium imperium conservandae libertatis fuit.

This rare form may perhaps be a Genitive of Definition. Madvig (417, *obs.* 4) calls it a Genitive of Purpose.

§ 267. Where in the world?   Ubi gentium?
He arrived at such a pitch of folly that, &c.   Eo stultitiae venit, ut &c.

Note. Genitives dependent on Adverbs of Place, as quo, eo, ubi, &c., or of time, as, nunc, tunc, &c., are best referred to the head of Partition.

§ 268. Desist from wrath.   Abstineto irarum.

So, desine querelarum, and laborum decipitur, occurring in Horace. These are mere Graecisms, and must not be imitated in Prose.

The Impersonal Verbs.
(See §§ 132, 133).

§ 269. I ought to set out.   Me proficisci oportet.
I ought to have set out.   Me proficisci oportuit.
I almost think I ought to set out.   Haud scio an me proficisci oporteat.
'Do you think,' replied the general, 'that I ought to have done this?'   'Putasnĕ,' inquit imperator 'me hoc facere oportuisse?'

APPENDIX.

§ 270. I pity your folly. — Me stultitiae tuae miseret.
You repent of your faults. — Te culparum paenitet.
He was ashamed of his poverty. — Paupertatis eum pudebat.
We are ashamed to do this. — Nos hoc facere pudet.
They repent of having done this. — Eos hoc fecisse paenitet.
How happens it that no one lives contented with his lot? — Quî fit ut nemo contentus sorte vivat?

§ 271. It is your interest that there should be peace; it is his that there should be war. — Tuā interest pacem, illius bellum esse, (*or* ut pax, ut bellum sit).

Note. Meā, tuā, &c., are explained (1) as remains of an Acc. Fem. Sing., the original expression being inter meam rem est, tuam rem fert, &c., (2) as Abl. Fem. Sing. with ellipse of re. See also Roby's Lat. Gr. § 1285.

§ 272. This is of little consequence to Caesar. — Hoc Caesăris parvi rēfert.
This is of great consequence to me. — Hoc meā magni rēfert.

Note. The Genitive (or Locative) of Value, as magni, parvi, &c., (§ 120, *b*, *note* 2), is often found with interest and rēfert.

Infinitive Mood.

§ 273. I wish to go away. — Abire cupio.

Note. The Infinitive added to complete the sense after such Verbs as *wish, begin, be able*, &c. (Madvig, § 389), may be called the *Complementary Infinitive*. It is also known as *Prolative* (Pub. Sch. Lat. Gr. § 180).

§ 274. I am glad that you are well. — Gaudeo te valere, *or* gaudeo quod vales.

Note. Quod with Indicative is used instead of Accusative and Infinitive (1) with Verbs expressing some emotion of the mind, as gaudeo, doleo, &c., (2) with certain Impersonals. See Madvig, § 398, *b*.

§ 275. Then the plebeians began to look round about on the faces of the patricians. — Circumspectare tum patriciorum vultus plebeii.

Note. The *Historic Infinitive* is used (1) of sudden events, (2) of simultaneous events, (3) of events following in rapid succession.

§ 276. What! am I to shrink from my settled purpose? — Me-nĕ incepto desistĕre!

Note. The *Exclamatory Infinitive* is used both in Prose and Poetry, with or without -nĕ, to denote surprise or indignation. Compare the use of the English Infinitive in such phases as '*to think* of your doing this,' &c.

§ 277. Bold to endure all things. — Audax omnia perpeti.

Note. Perpeti is poetical for ad perpetiendum. For Infinitive used instead of Gerund with or without a Preposition see Madvig, § 419.

Gerund and Gerundive.

(See §§ 138-142.)

§ 278. I am desirous of satisfying the people.
Cupĭdus sum satisfaciendi populo.

Rule. The Gerund of a Verb governing the Genitive, Dative, or Ablative takes its case after it.

§ 279. For the sake of seeing something.
Aliquid videndi causā (*not* alicujus videndi causā).

For the sake of seeing the city.
Urbem videndi causā, *or* urbis videndae causā.

With a view to protecting the city.
Ad urbem tuendam (*never* ad urbem tuend*um*).

Rule. With Transitive Verbs (*a*) the Genitive Gerund often takes an Object in the Accusative, especially when ambiguity, (as noticed in § 138, *footnote*), or awkwardness of sound, as magn*arum* statu*arum* vidend*arum*, is to be avoided, (*b*) the Dative and Ablative less frequently have an Object, and (*c*) the Accusative with Preposition *never* has one. In these latter cases the Gerundive construction, as explained in § 138, is used.

§ 280. We must speak.
Dicendum est nobis.
We had to speak.
Dicendum erat nobis.
We must speak these things.
Haec nobis dicenda sunt, (*not* haec nobis dicend*um* est).

Note. Lucretius has 'Aeternas quoniam *poenas* in morte *timendum est*,' but among the classical writers such a phrase is not found (§ 141).

§ 281. He gave up Eumenes to his relatives to be buried.
Eumĕnem propinquis sepeliendum tradidit.
He caused a bridge to be made *over* the Arar.
Pontem *in* Arăre faciendum curavit.

Qui, Quum, and Ut.

(See § 143).

** For instances of the simple use of Qui see §§ 222-229.

§ 282. I pity you for having made this man your enemy.
Miseret tui me, qui hunc homĭnem inimīcum fecĕris.

The Relative thus used is known as 'Qui Caúsal.' It is often strengthened by the use of utpŏte or quippe.

§ 283. He will send ambassadors to beg for peace.
Legatos, qui pacem petant, mittet.
He sent ambassadors to beg for peace.
Legatos qui pacem petĕrent, misit.

The Relative thus used is equivalent to a clause introduced by ut, *in order that*, and is known as 'Qui Final.'

§ 284. You are not such a man as not to know what you are. — Non tu is es qui, quid sis, nescias.

The Relative thus used is equivalent to a Clause introduced by ut after talis, &c., and is known as 'Qui Consecutive.' It is found (1) after talis, tantus, and all other words implying *such*, (2) after dignus, indignus, idoneus, aptus, &c., as, dignus est qui imperet, *he is worthy to rule*, (3) after Comparatives with quam, as, aetate provectior est quam qui diu vivat, *he is too old to live long*, (4) after Interrogative, Indefinite and other Pronouns and Adjectives, as, quis, quidam, nemo, multi, &c., either expressed, as, quis est qui te timeat, *who is there who fears you?* or understood, as, sunt qui credant, *there are some who believe.* Almost all the uses of quin in Subordinate clauses are to be referred to this head.

§ 285. There is no one *but* can do this. — Nemo est quin hoc facĕre possit.
Who is there *that* does *not* see? — Quis est quin vĭdĕat?
Nothing is so difficult *that* it can*not* be accomplished. — Nihil tam diffĭcĭle est quin perfĭci possit.
It cannot be *that* the soul is *not* immortal. — Fĭĕri non potest quin ănĭmus immortālis sit.
There is no doubt *that* the case is so. — Non dŭbĭum est quin res ita se hăbĕat.
Nothing prevents our doing this. — Nihil obstat quin (*or* quominus) hoc faciamus.

Note 1. Quin stands (1) for the Nominative, qui non, quae non, quod non, as in the first three of the above examples, (2) for the Ablative quî non, *how not* or *in such a manner as not*, as in the last three examples.

Note 2. Quin in Principal clauses means '*why not?*' as, quin expergiscimini, *why don't you wake up?* and sometimes '*but*,' '*in truth*,' &c.

(See § 144.)

§ 286. Such being the case, I wish to consult you. — Quae quum ita sint, te consulĕre volo.
Such being the case, I wished to consult your interests. — Quae quum ita essent, tibi consulĕre volui.
§ 287. When summer returns we will go home. — Quum redierit aestas domum ibimus (§ 298).
§ 288. Caesar *seeing* the enemy off their guard suddenly attacked them. — Caesar, quum hostes incautos videret, eos subito adortus est.

Note. Quum meaning *at the time when* is occasionally found with an Imperfect Indicative. See Madvig § 358.

§ 289. Caesar *having returned* from Gaul entered the city without delay. — Caesar, quum ex Galliā redisset, urbem sine morā intravit.

(See § 145.)

§ 290. As you sow, so shall you reap.
Ut sementem feceris, ita metes (§ 298).

We asked them how they were.
Ut valerent interrogavimus.

Se and Suus.

§ 291. Fabius said that if Brutus would restore to him *his* property, he in turn would restore *his* to Brutus.
Fabius dixit, si suas res Brutus sibi redderet, se invĭcem ei res ejus redditurum (§ 298).

Cato is here with *his* son.
Cato cum filio *suo* hic est.

They have seen neither Cato nor *his* son.
Nec Catonem nec filium *ejus* aspexerunt.

Rule. Se and Suus refer to the Subject of the Principal Verb of the Sentence, if it be of the Third Person.

Note. Sui may however be used as Objective Genitive, e. g. conservatio sui, *self-preservation*, without necessarily referring to the Subject of the sentence. Suus may also be used without such reference, when the translation *his own*, *her own*, &c., is implied, as, Hannibalem sui cives e civitate ejecerunt, *his own countrymen expelled Hannibal from the state.* See Madvig, § 490.

Utrum, Num, -Ne, An.

§ 292. Is this yours or mine?
Scire { Utrum meum / Meumne / Num meum } an tuum est hoc?

I wish to know whether this is yours or mine.
Scire volo { utrum meum / meumne / num meum } an tuum hoc sit.

Notes. Num followed by an is rare. Utrum, -ne, num, are sometimes omitted in these double questions, as, eloquar an sileam, *shall I speak or be silent?* -Nĕ is sometimes used for an, as, albus aterne fueris ignorans, *not knowing whether you were white or black.*

§ 293. Can he do this or not?
Utrum hoc facĕre potest annon?

I wished to know whether he could do this or not.
Scire volui utrum hoc facĕre necnĕ posset.

Rule. For *or not* use an non in *Oratio Recta*, necnĕ in *Oratio Obliqua*.

§ 294. It is uncertain whether he will do this without compulsion.
Incertum est an sine vi hoc facturus sit.

Rule. After Verbs of *doubt* or *uncertainty*, the first clause of a double question is often omitted, and **an** is translated *whether.* In the above example supply utrum vi coactus after incertum est to complete the sense. See article on **an** in Andrews' Dictionary.

'Would,' the sign of the Future Tense in Oblique Sentences.

§ 295. ACTIVE VOICE.

(*a*) He would love. — Amāret.
He said that he would love. — Dixit se amātūrum esse.

With Verbs that have no Supine and consequently no Future Infinitive [which is formed from the Supine] the phrase, 'fore ut' *or* 'futurum esse ut,' with Imperf. Subjunctive is used, as, 'I hoped the boys would learn,' 'Speravi fore [*or* futurum esse] ut pueri discerent.'

It was uncertain whether he would love. — Amaturusnĕ esset incertum erat.

(*b*) He would have loved. — Amāvisset.
He said that he would have loved. — Dixit se amaturum fuisse.

With Verbs having no Supine, 'futurum fuisse ut,' with Imperfect Subjunctive would be used.

It is doubtful whether he would have loved. — An amaturus fuerit in dubio est.

§ 296. PASSIVE VOICE.

(*a*) He would be loved. — Amārētur.
He said that he would be loved. — Dixit se amātum iri.

With Verbs having no Supine, 'fore ut' *or* 'futurum esse ut,' with Subjunctive, would be used.

It was uncertain whether he would be loved. — Incertum erat an amārētur.

The Passive has no Special form for the Future Subjunctive. 'Incertum erat an amaretur' therefore may mean, 'It was uncertain whether he *would be* loved,' or, 'It was uncertain whether he *was* loved.' Such a form as 'futurum esset ut amaretur' is not found. But a Latin writer would probably resort to some contrivance for avoiding this ambiguity, such as changing the construction from a Passive to an Active form, &c.

(*b*) He would have been loved. — Amatus esset.
He said that he would have been loved. — Dixit futūrum fŭisse ut amāretur.

Quod.

§ 297. They accused Socrates, on the ground of his corrupting the youth, but in reality because he had become suspected by those in power. — Socratem accusârunt, quod juventutem corrumperet, re tamen ipsā quia in suspicionem magistratibus venerat.

They condemned Marcus to death on the charge of killing his father. — Marcum capĭtis damnârunt quod patrem occīdisset.

| The general refused to fight, not *because* he feared, but *because* he wished to delay. | Dux pugnam detrectāvit, non quod timēret, sed quia cunctāri vŏlŭit. |

Rule. Quod, *because*, takes an Indicative, except when it expresses (1) an *alleged* reason, as in the first two of the above examples, (2) after the Negative Adverb, a *supposed* or *possible* reason, a reason which *might* be the true one, but is not necessarily so, as in the last example. The *true* reason in such cases is usually expressed by quia or quod with Indicative.

Future Time.

§ 298. I will do it if I *am* able.	Faciam, si potero.
He said he would do it if he were able.	Dixit se, si posset, facturum.
When I *return* I will speak of these things.	Quum rediero, de his rebus dicam.
He said that when he returned he would speak of those things.	Dixit se, quum rediisset, de iis rebus dicturum.

Rule. When the Principal Verb of an *Oratio Recta* is in the Future, Subordinate Verbs, especially when introduced by Temporal or Conditional Conjunctions, must, as a rule, be in the Future also; in the Future Simple Tense, if the action be contemporaneous with that of the Principal Verb, in the Future Perfect if it be anterior. But in *Oratio Obliqua* such Subordinate Verbs are put in the Present, Perfect, Imperfect, or Pluperfect Subjunctive. See Madvig, §§ 339, *Obs.* 1., 340, and 378 (4). In the English idiom the futurity of the Subordinate Clause is lost sight of.

Construction of summus, medius, &c.

§ 299. He was standing on the top of a tower.	In summā turre stābat.
He said he was standing on the top of a tower.	Se in summā turre stare dixit.
They *said he was not* standing on the top of a tower.	Eum in summā turre stāre negārunt.
The captives will be led through the midst of the city.	Captīvi per mĕdĭam urbem dūcentur.
It is announced that the captives will be led through the midst of the city.	Captīvos per mĕdĭam urbem ductum iri nuntiātur.

Rule. Summus, the Superlative of superus, *high*, is not to be translated *highest* when used of *place*. Summus mons does not mean *the highest mountain* (of several), but *the mountain where it is highest*, i. e. the *top of* the mountain. So, medius mons does not mean *the middle mountain* (of several), but *the mountain where it is midmost*, i. e. the *middle of* the mountain. In the same way extremus and imus in agreement with a Noun must often be translated *end of* and *bottom of*.

To.

§ 300. Rule. *To* with Nouns is nearly always the sign of the Dative, except when it implies *motion to;* with Verbs it is usually the sign of the Infinitive, except when it means *in order to*.

This will be useful *to* me.	Hoc *mihi* utile erit.
He will send presents *to* me.	Munera *ad me* mittet.
He wished *to* kill Marcus.	Marcum occīdĕre voluit.
He sent men *to* kill Marcus.	1. Misit homines ut Marcum occīdĕrent.
	2. Misit homines qui Marcum occiderent (§ 283).
	3. Misit homines Marcum occīsuros (*very rare*).
	4. Misit homines ad Marcum occidendum (§ 279).
	5. Misit homines Marcum occidendi causā (§ 279).
	6. Misit homines Marci occidendi causā (§ 138).
	7. Misit homines Marcum occīsum (§ 136).

Note. An English Infinitive, e. g. *to kill*, may be (1) a Verb-Noun meaning *the act of killing*, or (2) an Adverbial phrase meaning *in order to kill*. But in Latin the Infinitive is *only* a Verb-Noun, and is *never* used Adverbially except by the poets. Such a sentence, therefore, as 'misit homines Marcum *occidere*' could only mean ' he sent men *the act of killing* Marcus,' which is absurd. Remember then that ' *the Infinitive should never be used to express a purpose in Latin.*'

§ 301. I command you *to* do this.	Impĕro tibi ut hoc facias.
I advise you *not to* do this.	Suadeo tibi ne hoc facias.
They allowed him *to* go.	Permiserunt ei ut iret.
He was allowed *to* go.	Permissum (*or* concessum) ei est ut iret.
We asked him *to* go down with us to the Forum.	Oravimus ut nobiscum in Forum descenderet.

Rule. By ut translate Infinitive
With *ask* and *wish, command, contrive,*
Allow, forbid, advise and *strive*:
But never be this rule forgot,
Put **ne** for **ut** when there's a '*not*.'

Exceptions. Volo, jubeo, veto, conor, sino, almost always take an Infinitive rather than an ut Clause. After Verbs of *forbidding* (except veto) always use nē, as the sense is ' to order *not* to do something.'

Having.

§ 302. The Perfect Participle Active, *having loved*, *having advised*, etc., is wanting in all Latin Verbs, except the Deponents and Semi-deponents. In translating into Latin an English Perfect Participle Active we must, therefore, remember the following

Rules. (*a*) If a Deponent can be found to suit the sense, it should be used, as,

Having thus spoken the general sat down.   Dux ita locūtus consēdit.

(*b*) If an Active Verb is employed, we must use quum with Pluperfect Subjunctive if the Principal Verb is a Historic Tense, as,

Having thus spoken the general sat down.   Dux, quum ita dixisset, consedit.

But with Perfect Subjunctive if the Principal Verb is a Primary Tense, as,

Having lived honourably so many years he is worthy of the utmost praise.   Quum tot annos honestè vixerit, summā laude dignus est. [Quum here = *since*, § 144].

(*c*) If the Verb is Transitive and has an Object, an elegant rendering can be made by means of the Ablative Absolute, as,

Fabius having conquered the enemy returned (will return) to Rome.   Fabius, hostibus victis, Romam rediit (redibit).

Note 1. Hostibus victis does not necessarily imply that Fabius was the person who conquered the enemy, which quum vicisset (*or* vicerit) *would*.

Note 2. Ceno, juro, nubo, poto, prandeo, have Perfect Participles Active, cenatus, *having supped*, juratus, *having sworn*, nupta (of a woman), *having wedded*, potus, *having drunk*, pransus, *having dined*.

§ 303. Caesar having exhorted his men sat down.   Caesar suos hortatus consedit.
Caesar having exhorted his men, a shout arose.   Caesare suos hortato, clamor exortus est.

Note. Beware of regarding as *absolute* a Substantive, with Participle in agreement, which forms the Subject of a Verb. In the first of the above examples the words 'Caesar having exhorted his men' are not *absolute* (i. e. *independent* of the rest of the sentence), but form an integral part of it.

Of.

§ 304. He will sail to the island *of* Cyprus.   Ad insulam Cyprum navigabit.
I almost think he will sail to the island of Cyprus.   Haud scio an ad insulam Cyprum navigaturus sit.

In these and similar expressions, as, 'the city *of* Rome,' &c., *of* is merely a sign of Apposition. Here are to be noticed the English expressions 'all *of*,' 'whole *of*,' where *of* cannot be expressed by a Partitive Genitive (§ 129, *b*), since the words *all, whole,* are from their meaning not partitive. For 'all *of* whom' say qui omnes (Nom.), quos omnes (Acc.); 'all *of* you,' vos omnes. Also 'three hundred *of* us were present,' trecenti adfuimus, if *of* is not used partitively; but trecenti nostrum, *or* ex numero nostro, adfuerunt, if it is used partitively.

§ 305. The barbarians use swords *of* wood. Barbări ligneis ensibus utuntur.

Of here denotes *quality* or *material*.

§ 306. He talks *of* battles, and makes light *of* danger. De pugnis loquitur, et periculum parvi facit.

Of in the first case = *concerning*; in the second it forms part of the Verb.

§ 307. To rob a temple *of* its gold. Templum auro spoliare.

Of after *rob, defraud, deprive,* Is but a sign of Ablative.

The.

§ 308. *The* soldiers on the wall perceived me. Qui (*or* quot) in moenibus erant milites me aspexērunt.

Note. There is no Definite Article in Latin, and care is required in translation in order to bring out the English meaning where necessary. Milites in moenibus me aspexerunt *might* mean *Soldiers on the wall perceived me* or even *soldiers perceived me on the wall*. For 'the' with Comparatives see §§ 260, 261. See also Dr. Abbott's Latin Prose, §§ 20, 21.

He is not *the* man to do this. Non est is qui hoc faciat.
The noble and eloquent Cicero. Cicero, vir nobilissimus atque facundissimus; *or,* Cicero ille nobilis ac facundus.
The fight at Cannae. Proelium ad Cannas commissum; *or,* Proelium Cannense.
I remember *the* bravery he shewed. Quantam (*or* quam) virtutem praestiterit memini.
He sent *the* trustiest slave he had. Servum misit, quem habuit fidelissimum.
The remarkable reputation which he enjoyed. Existimatio, quam insignem habuit.

Without.

§ 309. He *is without* wisdom. Săpĭentĭā căret.

Note. 'Without' before a Substantive is usually expressed by *sine* with Ablative, except when it means 'outside of' which is extra. 'To be without' is carēre or egēre: 'without the knowledge of' is clam, see § 353. The chief difficulty in the translation of 'without' is when it precedes the Gerund in -*ing*, as in the following examples.

§ 310. I never saw him *without* laughing.
Nunquam eum vidi quin riderem.

The town was taken *without* a single man *being killed*.
Ne ūno quidem interfecto, urbs capta est.

They set out *without delaying* any longer.
Non amplius morati proficiscuntur.

He made a long speech *without persuading* any one.
Orationem longam habuit, nec tamen ulli persuasit.

He was condemned *without being punished*.
Damnatus quidem sed non supplicio affectus est.

You cannot learn *without studying*.
Discĕre non pŏtes nĭsĭ literis stŭdueris.

You cannot study *without learning*.
Literis studēre non pŏtes quin discas.

Note. Nisi here implies 'without *previously* studying'; quin 'without *subsequently* learning.'

Instead of.

§ 311. I go *instead of* you.
Pro te eo.

Hannibal, *instead of* retiring to Capua, ought to have attacked Rome.
Hannĭbal non Capŭam recēdere sed Romam oppugnare dēbŭit.

Hannibal retired to Capua *instead of* attacking Rome.
Hannĭbal Capŭam rĕcessit, quum Romam oppugnare dēbŭisset (*or* neque Romam oppugnavit).

Instead of desiring the honour, he refuses it when offered him.
Tantum abest ut hŏnōrem cŭpĭat (*or*, adeo non honōrem cupit), ut oblātum rejĭcĭat.

Too.

§ 312. The way is *too* narrow.
Via nĭmis angusta est; *or*, Via angustior est.

The shoe is *too* large for the foot.
Calcĕus major est quam pro pede.

Marcus was much *too* old to have the command of armies.
Marcus multo provectior aetate fŭit quam ut [*or*, quam qui] exercĭtĭbus praeesset.

Nothing was *too* arduous for him to undertake.
Nihil tam ardŭum fuit quin is suscĭpĕret.

So, Such, As.

§ 313. *As* many men, *so* many opinions.
Quot hŏmĭnes, tot sententiae.

He is *such as* he has ever been.
Talis est quālis semper fuit.

He is not *so* mad *as* you.	Non tam āmens est quam tu.
Such as remained in the city he rewarded.	Eos, qui in urbe manebant, praemĭis affēcit.
He is not *such* a man *as* to do that.	Non is est qui id făcĭat.
Cato, *such* was his sagacity, found out this.	Cato, quae erat ejus săgācĭtas (*or* quā erat sagacitate), hoc deprehendit.
Such is your temperance.	Quae tua est temperantia.
As far *as* you are concerned, *or, as* regards you.	Quod ad te attinet.
As far *as* I know.	Quod sciam.
He raises *as* great forces *as* possible.	Quam maxĭmas potest copĭas compărat; *or,* copias quam maximas compărat.
As soon *as*. The *same as*.	Simul atque. Idem qui.
Such was the valour of the soldiers that they fought the whole day long.	Ea erat milĭtum virtus, ut totum diem pugnārent.

Some, Any.

§ 314. Some one may ask.	Quaerat quispiam (*or* aliquis).
Some one may say.	Dixerit (*or* dicat) aliquis.
Some said that Croesus, *others* that Cyrus would conquer.	Ălĭi Croesum, ălĭi Cyrum victūrum dicēbant.
Some fly in one direction *some* in another.	Ălĭi ălĭam in partem (*or* ălĭas in partes) fŭgĭunt.
Let no one say this.	Ne quis hoc dicat.
If I have any ability.	Si quid ingenii in me est.
There are some who think.	Sunt qui putent.
There were some who thought.	Erant qui putarent.
Does anyone think so?	Ecquis ita putat?

Rules. (*a*). *Some,* meaning 'some one or other,' whom we do not know, is aliquis or nescio quis; meaning 'a certain person,' whom we know but do not think it necessary to name, it is quidam.

(*b*) *Some,* meaning 'a few' or 'several' is nonnulli or aliquot; meaning 'a little' it is nonnihil, and, when used of quantity, aliquantum.

(*c*) *Any* is quispiam and sometimes aliquis; *any* in a question is ecquis or num quis; *any you please* is quivis, quilibet; *any at all* quisquam (Subst.), ullus (Adj.); after 'if' or 'lest,' *any* is usually quis.

(*d*) *Nobody, no one,* [i.e. not *any* body, not *any* one] is nemo; but instead of 'that nobody,' in Final Clauses, the Latins said 'lest anybody,' nē quis. But in *Consecutive* Clauses 'that nobody' is ut nemo. In Commands, for 'let nobody' they said 'let not anybody,' nē quis. For 'and no one' they said 'nor any one,' nec quisquam, nec ullus, and in Commands neu quis, neve quis.

English use of the Demonstrative.

§ 315. In Co-ordinate Sentences (§ 84, *note*) we often employ Demonstrative (or Personal) Pronouns in English to avoid the repetition of a Substantive, as 'we found some mushrooms and ate *them*.' The Demonstrative is seldom so used in Latin, the repetition of the Substantive being avoided
(*a*) by making it the Object of both Verbs, as,

Some covet riches, others despise *them*.	Divitias alii cupiunt, alii spernunt.

Note. This cannot be done if the Verbs take different Cases, as,

Some blamed the general, others congratulated *him* on his victory.	Alii ducem culpare, alii victoriam ei gratulari (§ 275).

(*b*) by making a Participle do duty for one of the co-ordinate sentences, as,

He summoned the soldiers, and thus addressed *them*.	Milites convocatos ita allocutus est.

§ 316. In particular be careful *never* to translate *literally* the expressions *that of, those of.* Either
(*a*) repeat the Substantive, as,

The fleet of the Romans joined *that of* the allies.	Sociorum classi classis Romanorum conjuncta est.

or (*b*) introduce an Adjective with which the second Substantive can be understood in agreement, as,

The fleet of the Romans joined *that of* the allies.	Sociorum classi Romana conjuncta est.

Here classi coming immediately before Romana shews that classis is to be understood with the latter word.
or (*c*) omit the second Substantive altogether, as,

The keels are much flatter than *those of* our ships.	Carinae aliquanto planiores quam nostrarum navium sunt.

Ways of translating by a Latin Participle.

§ 317.

He *attacked and* routed the enemy.	Hostes adortus profligāvit.
He *burnt and* destroyed the bridge.	Pontem incensum delevit.
This accident impedes his right hand *as he is endeavouring* to draw his sword.	Hic casus gladium edūcĕre cōnanti dextram morātur manum.
Leonidas, *though* overpowered, would not yield.	Leŏnĭdas sŭpĕrātus cēdĕrĕ tamen nōlŭit.

Xerxes, *when* conquered by the Greeks, fled back to Asia.	Xerxes a Graecis victus in Asiam refūgit.
If expelled from Rome, he will go to Athens.	Româ expulsus Athēnas ibit.
I did this *because* Caesar advised me.	Haec Caesăre mŏnente fēci.
Much like *one who fears*.	Multum similis metuenti.

Uses of the Prepositions.

** These Prepositions are arranged in the order given in §§ 111, 122. Only the commoner uses are here given. For a further account consult any good Dictionary, Roby's Lat. Gr. §§ 1800-2192, or the Publ. Sch. Lat. Gr. §§ 70-72.

(See § 111.)

§ 318. **Ante**, *before*, as, ante muros, *before the walls*, ante lucem, *before dawn*. Often used as an Adverb, *previously*.

§ 319. **Apud**, *at*, *near*, and—when used of an author—*in*.

To sup *at* a friend's house.	Apud amicum cenare.
They waited *near* the town.	Apud oppĭdum morati sunt.

Note. Apud denotes *rest* at or near, ad denotes direction, motion, etc. Originally also apud was used only of nearness of *persons*, ad only of nearness of *places*.

We find this *in* Plato.	Apud Platonem hoc invenimus.
He is not in his senses.	Non apud se est. (*Poet.*)

§ 320. **Ad**, *to*, *towards*, *at*, *about* or *almost* (of number).

I wrote a letter *to* him.	Litteras ad eum dedi (scripsi).
From this point the country stretches *towards* the North.	Inde ad Septentriones regio vergit.
The defeat *at* Cannae.	Clades ad Cannas accepta.
About (almost) 40 years old.	Annos ad quadraginta natus.

Note. Other phrases are, ad extremum, *finally*; ad hoc, *in addition to this*; ad verbum, *word for word*; servi ad remum = remiges, *rowers*; nihil ad me (sc. attinet), *this is no concern of mine*.

§ 321. **Adversum, Adversus**, *toward* or *to* (in a friendly sense), *against* (in a hostile sense).

How shall I conduct myself *towards* Caesar.	Quonam modo adversus Caesarem me geram?
To these things he replied.	Adversus ea respondit.
I will strive *against* you.	Adversus te contendam.

§ 322. **Circa, Circiter, Circum**, *around*, *about*.

Around the city walls.	Circum (circa) muros urbis.
About the eighth hour.	Octavam circiter horam.

§ 323. **Cis, Citra,** *on this side,* as Belgae cis Rhenum incolunt, *the Belgae dwell on this side the Rhenus.*

§ 324. **Contra,** *opposite, against.* Often used as Adverb, *on the opposite side, on the other hand, on the contrary.*

One side of this island is *opposite* Gaul.
To conspire *against* a king.

Hujus insulae unum latus est contra Galliam.
Contra regem conjurare.

§ 325. **Erga,** *towards* (almost always in a friendly sense, amongst the Classical writers), as, benevolentia amicorum erga nos, *the kind feeling of our friends towards us.*

§ 326. **Extra,** *outside, beyond,* as, extra muros, *outside the walls,* extra modum, *beyond measure.*

§ 327. **Infra,** *below, beneath,* as, terra infra caelum est, *earth is below the heaven,* id infra grammatici officium est, *That is beneath the business of a grammarian.*

§ 328. **Inter,** *between, among, during.*

Mount Jura is *between* the Sequani and Helvetii.
He is *amongst* the wounded.
All the iniquitous and disgraceful deeds that have been committed *during* ten years.

Mons Jura inter Sequănos et Helvetios est.
Inter saucios est.
Omnia quae inter decem annos nefarie flagitioseque facta sunt.

Note. Inter sicarios damnari, *to be condemned on a charge of assassination,* inter falcarios venire, *to visit the scythe-makers' street.* The Reciprocal Pronoun *one another* is rendered by inter, as, colloquimur inter nos, *we converse with one another;* pueri inter se amant, *the boys love one another.*

§ 329. **Intra,** *within,* as, intra urbem, *within the city.*

§ 330. **Juxta,** *near, next to.* Often used as Adverb, *near, equally,* or *in like manner.*

Near the temple of Castor.
Next to the worship of the Gods let faith between man and man be cultivated.

Juxta aedem Castŏris.
Juxta divinas religiones fides humana colatur.

§ 331. **Ob,** (rarely) *before,* (much more commonly) *on account of.*

Death often passed *before* his eyes.
On account of the mindful wrath of Juno.

Mors ob oculos saepe versata est.
Memŏrem Junonis ob iram.

§ 332. **Penes,** *in the power of,* as, me penes est custodia mundi, *the guardianship of the world is in my power.*

§ 333. **Pone,** *behind* (rare), as, pone aedem Castoris, *behind Castor's temple.* Used rarely as Adverb, *behind, after.*

APPENDIX.

§ 334. Post, *behind, after.* Often used as Adverb, *behind, afterwards.*

You were hiding *behind* the bed of sedge.	Tu post carecta latebas.
Six years *after* the capture of Veii.	Sexennio post Veios captos.

§ 335. Praeter, *beside* or *past, beyond, contrary to, in addition to, except.* Also used as Adverb, *besides.*

Next day he led out his forces *past* the camp of Caesar.	Postridie ejus diei (*see also* § 372, *note*) praeter castra Caesaris suas copias produxit.
Many things happened to me *beyond* my hopes.	Multa praeter spem mihi evenerunt.
He arrived *contrary to* everyone's expectation.	Praeter opinionem omnium pervenit.
They brought ten men each *besides* themselves to the conference.	Denos praeter se ad colloquium adduxerunt.
They have no clothing *except* skins.	Vestītus, praeter pelles, non habent.

§ 336. Prope, *near,* as prope Caesaris hortos, *near the gardens of Caesar.* Often used as Adverb, *near, nearly,* the Comparative and Superlative of which, propius, proxime, are often used as Prepositions with an Accusative.

§ 337. Propter, *beside* or *near* (rare), *on account of.*

We sat down *near* Plato's statue.	Propter statuam Platonis consedimus.
On account of the cold the corn was not ripe.	Propter frigus frumenta matura non erant.

§ 338. Per, *through, during, by* = by means of.

Through the waves.	Per undas.
During many years.	Per multos annos.
He who acts *by* another acts *by* himself.	Qui facit per alium facit per se.

§ 339. Secundum, *along, next to, according to.*

Along the river.	Secundum flumen.
Next to you I have no greater friend than solitude.	Secundum te nihil est mihi amicius solitudine.
To live *according to* nature.	Secundum naturam vivere.

§ 340. Supra, *above, beyond.* Used also as Adverb, *above, previously, more.*

Atticus was sitting *above* me at table, Verrius below.	Supra me Atticus, infra Verrius accumbebat.
Beyond one's powers.	Supra (*also* ultra) vires.

§ 341. Versus, *towards,* as, Brundisium versus, *towards Brundisium.*

§ 342. **Ultra,** *beyond,* as, ultra cum locum, *beyond that place.*

§ 343. **Trans,** *across,* as, trans mare, *across the sea.*

§ 344. **In** with Accusative, *into, to, for* (of time), *according to, against.*

They make an incursion *into* the territories of the Remi.	In fines Remorum incursionem faciunt.
He puts the enemy *to* flight.	Hostes in fugam dat.
Peace was made *for* two years.	Pax in biennium facta.
After the manner of slaves.	Servilem in modum.
Turn your swords *against* me.	In me convertite ferrum.

Note. Other phrases are, in multam noctem, *deep into the night;* in horas, *from hour to hour;* in posterum, *for the future;* treceni nummi in capita, 300 *sesterces for each person.*

§ 345. **Sub** with Accusative, (motion) *under, up to, about* (of time), *just before* or *just after* (of time).

To send an army *under* the yoke.	Exercitum sub jugum mittere.
They come *up to* the wall.	Sub murum succedunt.
About nightfall.	Sub noctem.
Just after cockcrow.	Sub galli cantum.

§ 346. **Super** with Accusative, *above,* as, Nomentanus erat super ipsum, Porcius infra, *Nomentanus was above the host at table, Porcius below him.*

§ 347. **Subter** with Accusative, *beneath,* as, subter fastigia tecti, *beneath the roof of the house.*

(See § 122.)

§ 348. **A, Ab, Abs,** *from, by* = by agency of, *on the side of.*

How changed *from* the mighty Hector!	Quantum mutatus ab illo Hectore!
He was slain *by* his own men.	A suis interfectus est.
Gaul touches the Rhine *on the side of* the Sequani.	Gallia ab Sequanis Rhenum attingit.

Note. So, ab aliquo stare, facere, sentire, *or* esse, *to be on one's side;* hoc est a me *or* a me facit, *this is in my favour.* Other phrases are, a summo bibere, *to drink in succession beginning from the head of the table;* (servus) a manu, *a secretary;* a fronte, *in the van;* a latere, *in the flank;* a tergo, *in the rear.*

§ 349. **Absque,** *without,* rare except among the comic writers in phrases like absque te foret, *if it were not for you.*

§ 350. **Coram,** *in the presence of,* as, coram populo loqui, *to speak in presence of the people.*

§ 351. **De,** *from, down from, of, concerning.*

They set forth *from* their territories.	De finibus suis exierunt.

He threw himself *down from* the wall.	De muro se projecit.
The other instances *of* this kind.	Cetera de hoc genere.
A temple built *of* snow-white marble.	Templum niveo de marmore factum.
They treat *concerning* peace.	De pace agunt.

Note. Other phrases are, de nocte, *by night;* de tertia vigilia, *at the third watch;* de more, *according to custom;* de integro, *afresh;* de improviso, *unexpectedly;* de industria, *on purpose.*

§ 352. **Palam,** *in the presence of,* as, palam Caesare, *in the presence of Caesar.* More commonly used as Adverb, *openly.*

§ 353. **Clam,** *without the knowledge of,* as, clam patre (*also* clam patrem), *without my father's knowledge.* Often used as Adverb, *secretly.*

§ 354. **Cum,** *with,* (1) in the sense of *together with,* as, vagamur egentes cum conjugibus et liberis, *we are wandering in poverty with our wives and children;* Romani cum Gallis contendunt, *the Romans contend with the Gauls;* (2) denoting *manner,* as, cum celeritate venit, *he came with speed.*

§ 355. **Ex, E,** *out of, from, after, of, on account of, in accordance with.*

He runs *out of* the house.	Ex aedibus currit.
He returned *from* Asia.	Ex Asia rediit.
After his consulship Cotta set out for Gaul.	Cotta ex consulatu est profectus in Galliam.

Note 1. So aliud ex alio, *one thing after another;* diem ex die expectare, *to wait one day after another, from day to day.*

A statue made *of* bronze.	Statua ex aere facta.
When the state had grown alarmed *on account of* the debt.	Quum esset ex aere alieno commota civitas.
In accordance with a decree of the Senate.	Ex senatusconsulto.

Note 2. Other phrases are, e re, *for the advantage of;* ex injuria, *for the injury of;* e regione, *opposite;* e vestigio, *instantly;* ex improviso, *unexpectedly;* ex aequo, ex commodo, etc., *for* aeque, commode, etc.; heres ex asse, *heir to the whole estate.*

§ 356. **Sine,** *without,* as, sine ulla dubitatione, *without any doubt.*

§ 357. **Tenus,** *as far as,* is placed after its Case, and takes Gen. or Abl., as, urbium Corcyrae tenus, *as far as the cities of Corcyra;* Arimino tenus, *as far as Ariminum.*

§ 358. **Pro,** *before, in the front part of, for* = in behalf of, *instead of,* as, *in proportion to* or *according to.*

The camp is pitched *before* the walls.	Castra pro moenibus locantur.

Having announced this matter on (*i.e.* standing on the front part of) the platform.	Hac re pro suggestu pronuntiata.
To fight *for* altars and hearths.	Pro aris et focis pugnare.
I will go *instead of* you.	Ego ibo pro te.
I have brought him up *as* my own son.	Hunc pro meo filio eduxi.
According to one's ability.	Pro virili parte.

§ 359. **Prae**, *before, compared with, owing to.*

He carried a dagger *before* him.	Prae se pugionem tulit.
They are thought little of *in comparison with* him.	Prae illo parvi habentur.
Owing to the multitude of darts we shall not see the sun.	Solem prae jaculorum multitudine non videbimus.

Notice also the phrase prae se ferre, *to shew, exhibit.*

§ 360. **In** with Ablative, *in, on, during, in the case of.*

He is *in* the city.	In urbe est.
He has a crown *on* his head.	Coronam in capite habet.
During my youth.	In adolescentia mea.
This happens most fortunately *in the case of* Crassus.	Hoc in Crasso percommode accidit.

Note. Other phrases are, in aere alieno esse, *to be in debt;* pons in flumine, *a bridge over a river.*

§ 361. **Sub** with Abl., *under,* (of time) *at,* as, sub divo, *under the open sky,* sub adventu Caesaris, *at the arrival of Caesar.*

§ 362. **Super** with Abl., *upon* (rare), *concerning,* as, multa super Priamo rogitans, *asking many things about Priam.*

§ 363. **Subter** with Abl., *under,* as, subter densa testudine, *under a thick testudo.*

Miscellaneous.

§ 364. Whilst humouring the young men I forgot that I was old.	Dum obsĕquor adolescentibus me senem esse oblītus sum.

Rule. Dum, in the sense of *whilst,* is usually found with the Present rather than the Imperfect Indicative in describing past events. Madv. 336, Obs. 2.

§ 365. He causes engines to be constructed *in order that* he may *more* easily storm the city.	Machĭnas exstruendas curat quo facilius urbem expugnet.

Rule. Quo is used for ut final with comparative Adjectives and Adverbs.

§ 366. How much strength still remains to you!	Quantum robŏris adhuc tibi supĕrest!

He had eloquence enough but too little wisdom.   Satis eloquentiae, sapientiae parum habuit.

Rule. The Neuters of Adjectives denoting *quantity* are frequently used as Substantives, and take a dependent Genitive of Definition, e. g. quantum, tantum, aliquantum, quid, nonnihil *or* aliquid, plus, plurimum, minus. (To these must be added the Adverbs, parum, *too little*, satis, *enough*, nimis, *too much*, and abunde, *abundance of*.) The poets extend this usage to other Adjectives besides those of quantity, as, amara curarum, *the bitterness of cares*.

§ 367. He departed from Rome unwillingly.   Romā invitus discessit.

Note. It is constantly necessary, particularly in poetry, to translate a Latin Adjective by an English Adverb. The use of matutinus, vespertinus, nocturnus, for *in the morning, in the evening, at night*, etc., is especially frequent.

§ 368. Not even a king may kill men uncondemned.   Indemnātos occidere ne rēgi quidem licet.

Rule. The words ne quidem, *not even*, are never written together but always have the word or words *emphasized* by quidem written *between them*.

§ 369. He has accurately described *not only* the earth *but also* the stars.   Non sōlum terras sed ĕtĭam stellas accurātē descripsit.

He *not only* did *not* spare foreign troops, but *not even* his own.   Non mŏdŏ ălĭēnis sed ne suis quidem mīlĭtĭbus pĕpercit.

Rule. Non modo, *not only*, when followed by nē quidem is used for non modo *non*. Madvig, 461, b (*b*).

§ 370. *It was owing to* Cato that I was not condemned to death.   Per Catōnem stetit quōmĭnus căpĭtis damnārer.

That victory *cost* the Carthaginians much blood.   Multo sanguĭne ea Poenis victōrĭa stetit.

Literally, *stood to* (*the credit of*) *the Carthaginians at the price of much blood*. Poenis is Dat., and sanguine Abl. of Price.

§ 371. The Romans were superior *not only* in forces *but more especially* in money.   Romāni quum copiis tum argento superiōres erant.

Caesar, Pompey, *and* Crassus.   Caesar, Pompeius, Crassus; *or*, Caesar, et Pompeius, et Crassus.

§ 372. Publius Crassus with the 7th legion was wintering very near the Ocean.   P. Crassus cum legione septima proximus Oceanum hiemabat.

Note. An Accusative is sometimes found after the Adjectives propior, proximus; also after the adverbs pridie, postridie, as postridie pugnam, *on the day after the battle*.

§ 373. He is more prudent than wise. — Prudentior quam sapientior est.

The wiser a man is the happier he is. — Quo quis sapientior eo beatior; *or* Ut quisque sapientissimus ita beatissimus.

More than six hundred fell. — Plus sexcenti cecĭdērunt.

Note. Quam is often omitted after plus, amplius, minus.

§ 374. I entrust you *with* the command. — Impĕrĭum tĭbi committo [*or* permitto].

I threaten you *with* death. — Mortem tĭbi minor.

This happened to me *when* a boy. — Hoc mihi puero accidit.

§ 375. They were delighted with your letter. — Eos epistolā tuā summo gaudio affecit.

Note. It is often advisable to throw an English Passive into the equivalent Active form, in translating into Latin.

§ 376. He is dead. — Mortuus est.

Note. The English Present, especially in the Passive Voice, as, 'the trees are cut down,' often implies a *completed* action, and in such case must always be rendered by the Latin Perfect. So 'the trees *were* cut down' if *were* = *had been*, must be Pluperfect in Latin.

§ 377. I begin to love. — Amare coepi.
I begin to repent of the deed. — Paenitēre me facti coepit.
I ceased to love. — Amare desii.
I ceased to be ashamed of my poverty. — Paupertatis me pudēre desiit.

Note. Certain Verbs, as possum, coepi, debeo, desino, soleo, are used Personally or Impersonally according to the nature of their Complementary Verbs (§ 273). Coepi and desino sometimes take a Passive form when their Complementary Verb is Passive (Madvig, § 161), as,

The city began to be besieged. — Urbs obsidēri coepta est.

§ 378. Be sure you return. — Fac redeas.
Don't speak. — Ne locutus sis.

Note on the Imperative. The Latins employ many circumlocutions to avoid a direct Imperative. Thus (*a*) for Affirmative Imperatives we find fac intelligam, fac valeas, velim abeas, etc., (*b*) for Negative Imperatives we find cave credas, nolo dicas, noli contendere, ne credideris. Nē with 2nd Pers. Present Subjunctive, as ne credas, is seldom used, and nē with 2nd Pers. Imperative, as ne crede, *hardly ever* except in Poetry. The poets also use the forms fuge suspicari, mitte sectari, parce timere, omitte mirari, absiste moveri, desine sperare, and the like, for *suspect not, follow not,* etc.

§ 379. These things are difficult to do (*or* to be done). — Haec factu difficilia sunt.

It is difficult to tame a lion. — Leonem domare difficile est.

Note. The Supine in -u is Passive in its signification, and does not govern a Case. As a rule, avoid using it unless it can be rendered in English by a Present Infinitive Passive. See also Madvig, § 412.

§ 380.   Lo, Priam!   En Priamus!
         Lo, four altars!   En quattuor aras!

Note. Most Interjections may be followed by a Nominative or Vocative Case; some, as en, ecce, by an Accusative also. Hei and vae prefer a Dative, as, hei mihi, vae victis.

§ 381.   He hopes to come.   Sperat se venturum esse.
         He promises to come.   Promittit se venturum esse.

Rule. After *hope* and *promise* use the Future Infinitive in Latin.

§ 382.   He promised to come.   Promisit se venturum.

Note. Venturum for venturum *esse*. The omission of esse generally, and of est, sunt, in Principal (rarely in Subordinate) Clauses is common in all Latin authors.

§ 383.   It is necessary that you should do this.   Necesse est hoc făcĭas [*for* ut hoc facias].
         Take care you do not waste your time.   Cave tempus absūmas [*for* ne absumas].

Rule. When licet, necesse est, and oportet take the Subjunctive, they usually omit ut. Ne is sometimes omitted after certain Verbs, as caveo.

§ 384.   He pities no one.   Nullius misereatur.

Rule.   From nemo let me never see
                                   Neminis or nemine.

Use nullius, nullo, instead of neminis, nemine.

§ 385.   Many great disadvantages.   Multa et magna incommŏda.

Rule. Two Adjectives cannot be joined to the same Noun in Latin without a connecting particle in the same way as they are in such English phrases as 'a *bold bad* man,' 'a *cold wet* day,' &c. Say homo audacissimus ac sceleratissimus, &c.

§ 386.   They returned each man to his own city.   In suam quisque urbem redierunt.
         He has leisure for studying philosophy.   Philosophiae vacat.
         It is all over with the state.   Actum est de republica.
         For four years I have been the pupil of Socrates.   Quartum jam annum Socratem audio.

§ 387.   I fear he *will* come.   Vereor ne veniat.
         I fear he will *not* come.   Vereor ut (*or* ne non) veniat.
         I feared he *would* come.   Verebar ne veniret.
         I feared he would *not* come.   Verebar ut (*or* ne non) veniret.

§ 388. I have no reason to find fault with old age.
I have no reason to fear you.

Nihil habeo quod incūsem senectutem.
Non est cur te timeam.

§ 389. Whether this news is true or false, I shall set out at dawn.
Whether this news is true or false is uncertain.
I wish to ascertain whether we are conquerors or conquered.
I wish to act honourably, whether we are conquerors or conquered.

Sive verā sive falsā haec sunt, primā luce proficiscar.
Utrum vera an falsa haec sint incertum est.
Utrum victōres an victi simus cognoscere volo.
Honeste agere volo, sive victores sive victi sumus.

Note. 'Whether' introducing a *supposition* is sive; when Interrogative it is utrum.

§ 390. He is the best poet in all the world.
All the best citizens are accused of theft.
The pleasantest days are *always* the shortest.

Poeta est qualis in toto orbe terrarum nemo.
Optĭmus quisque cīvis furti accusātur.
Jucundissimus quisque dies brevissimus est.

§ 391. (*Latin Letter.*) Cambridge, October 18.

My dear Marcus,

I am writing in great haste, as the post is just going out. I arrived here yesterday, and have visited most places of interest in the town; but it would be impossible in this hurried letter to do justice to its numerous and splendid buildings, and indeed it is not worth while attempting to do so, as you will, I expect, be here yourself in a few days, which I am very glad of. I am quite well and hope to have an equally good account of you. Give my love to all at home, and
            Believe me, Your affectionate brother,
                    Quintus.

Quintus Marco S. D. P.

S. V. B. E. E. V. Summa festinatione scribebam, carissime frater, quod in eo erat ut tabellarius proficisceretur. Huc heri perveni, et quae in oppido digna visu sunt pleraque inspexi, sed neque raptim scribenti tot tantaque aedificia satis describere licet, neque enim operae pretium est id facere conari, quod te ipsum intra paucos dies adfore arbitror, quae res me vehementer delectat. Te tuosque multum amamus. Vale.

Data (*or* dabam) a. d. xv. Kal. Nov. Cantabrigiae.

CONDITIONAL OR HYPOTHETICAL SENTENCES.

§ 392. Sentences containing a Conditional clause (§ 199 e) may be divided into three classes.

(a) Where the condition is *assumed to be a fact*, and we wish to state what the consequence is. The usual formula is

> Si haec facis, peccas.
> (Greek. εἰ ταῦτα δρᾷς, ἁμαρτάνεις.)
> *If you do this, you sin.*

(b) Where the condition is assumed, as (1) *likely*, (2) *possible*, and we wish to state what the consequences (1) *will be*, (2) *would be*, respectively. The formulas are

> 1. Si haec facies, peccabis.
> (εἰ ταῦτα δράσεις, ἁμαρτήσει.)
> Si haec feceris, peccabis.
> (ἐὰν ταῦτα δράσῃς, ἁμαρτήσει.)
> *If you do this, you will sin.* (See § 298.)
> 2. Si haec facias, pecces.
> (εἰ ταῦτα δρῴης, ἁμαρτάνοις ἄν.)
> *If you were to do this* (at any time), *you would sin.*

(c) Where the condition is assumed as (1) *not taking place now*, (2) *not having taken place previously*, and we wish to state what the consequences (1) *would be*, (2) *would have been*, respectively. The formulas are

> 1. Si haec faceres, peccares.
> (εἰ ταῦτα ἔδρας, ἡμάρτανες ἄν.)
> *If you were doing this* (now), *you would sin* (or *be sinning*)[1].
> 2. Si haec fecisses, peccasses.
> (εἰ ταῦτα ἔδρασας, ἥμαρτες ἄν.)
> *If you had done this, you would have sinned.*

§ 393. In Oratio Obliqua these forms are

> (a) Ait te, si haec facias, peccare.
> (b) Ait te, si haec { facias / feceris } peccaturum esse.
> (c) 1. Aiebat te, si haec faceres, peccaturum esse.
> 2. Aiebat te, si haec fecisses, peccaturum fuisse.

---

[1] Si with Imperfect Subjunctive denotes *continuous* action, and *as a rule* refers to present time. But sometimes it refers to past time, and then (in default of an exact English equivalent) we must translate 'If he had done (or been doing) this, he would have sinned.'

PRONUNCIATION OF LATIN[1].

§ 394. **Latin was probably pronounced as follows:—**

(1) Vowels.

ā like the *a* in *father*; ă like the *a* in *along*.
ē like the *a* in *pane*; ĕ like the *e* in *men*.
ī like the *i* in *machine*; ĭ like the *i* in *pity*.
i preceded by a vowel was probably pronounced like *y*: thus *maior, eius, Troia, cuius* [often written *major, ejus, Troja, cujus*] are pronounced *mā-yor, ē-yus, Trō-ya, cū-yus*.
ō like the *oa* in *moat*; ŏ like the *o* in *cot*.
ū like the *u* in *rule*, not with a y-sound prefixed as in *mule*; ŭ like the *u* in *put*, not as in *cut*.
y as German ü, the sound inclining to *i*.

(2) Diphthongs. The rule is to pronounce each constituent vowel as rapidly as possible. This will give—
ae as the *ai* in *bail*.
au as the *ow* in *power*.
oe as the *oy* in *boy*, the *o* being more distinct than the *e*.
ui (in *huic, cui*) as French *oui*.

(3) Consonants.

c was always pronounced as *k*; *g* as *g* in *get*.
ng as *ng + g*, as in *anger*, not as in *hanger*.
r was always trilled; thus *per* is sounded as in *perry*, not as in *pert*.
s was almost always sharp [as the *s* of *sin*]; in a few words where the *s* comes between two vowels, as *rosa, musa, miser*, it had a soft sound like *z*.
t was pronounced as it is in English, except that it never had the sound of *sh* when followed by *io*.
ch was sounded as *k* followed by *h*.
bs, bt were sounded as *ps, pt*, and were often so written, as *aps, supter*.
v perhaps as *w*. *qu* as in English.

---

[1] Originally these rules were founded on the Syllabus of Latin pronunciation (Deighton and Bell, Cambridge; Parker, Oxford), drawn up in 1873 at the request of Head Masters of Schools. They have now been altered in order to admit some of the views propounded in Roby's Latin Grammar, §§ 29 82. The question is still open to so much doubt and uncertainty that the reader who desires detailed information must consult the works above mentioned, and other treatises on the subject.

Clarendon Press Series

OF

School Classics.

I. LATIN CLASSICS.

Author.	Work.	Editor.	Price.
Caesar	Gallic War, Books I, II	Moberly	2s.
,,	,, Books III-V	,,	2s. 6d.
,,	,, Books VI-VIII	,,	3s. 6d.
,,	Civil War	,,	3s. 6d.
,,	,, Book I	,,	2s.
Catullus	Carmina Selecta text only	Ellis	3s. 6d.
Cicero	Selections, 3 Parts	Walford	Each 1s. 6d.
,,	Selected Letters	Prichard & Bernard	3s.
,,	Select Letters (text only)	Watson	4s.
,,	De Senectute	Huxley	2s.
,,	Pro Cluentio	Ramsay	3s. 6d.
,,	Pro Milone	Poynton	2s. 6d.
,,	Pro Roscio	Stock	3s. 6d.
,,	Select Orations	King	2s. 6d.
,,	In Q. Caec. Div. and In Verrem I.	,,	1s. 6d.
,,	Catilinarian Orations	Upcott	2s. 6d.
Cornelius Nepos	Lives	Browning & Inge	3s.
Horace	Odes, Carm. Saec., Epodes	Wickham	6s.
,,	Odes, Book I	,,	2s.
,,	Selected Odes	,,	2s.
Juvenal	XIII Satires	Pearson & Strong	6s.
Livy	Selections, 3 Parts	Lee-Warner	Each 1s. 6d.
,,	Books V-VII	Cluer & Matheson	5s.

I. LATIN CLASSICS.

Author	Work	Editor	Price
Livy	Book V	Cluer & Matheson	2s. 6d.
,,	Book VII	,, ,,	2s.
,,	Books XXI–XXIII	Tatham	5s.
,,	Book XXI	,,	2s. 6d.
,,	Book XXII	,,	2s. 6d.
Ovid	Selections	Ramsay	5s. 6d.
,,	Tristia, Book I	Owen	3s. 6d.
,,	,, Book III	,,	2s.
Plautus	Captivi	Lindsay	2s. 6d.
,,	Trinummus	Freeman & Sloman	3s.
Pliny	Selected Letters	Prichard & Bernard	3s.
Quintilian	Institutionis Oratoriae, Liber X.	Peterson	3s. 6d.
Sallust	Bellum Cat. & Jugurth.	Capes	4s. 6d.
Tacitus	Annals I–IV	Furneaux	5s.
,,	Annals I	,,	2s.
Terence	Adelphi	Sloman	3s.
,,	Andria	Freeman & Sloman	3s.
,,	Phormio	Sloman	3s.
Tibullus and Propertius	Selections	Ramsay	6s.
Virgil	With an Introduction and Notes	Papillon & Haigh	12s.
,,	Bucolics and Georgics	,, ,,	3s. 6d.
,,	Aeneid I–III	,, ,,	3s.
,,	,, IV–VI	,, ,,	3s.
,,	,, VII–IX	,, ,,	3s.
,,	,, X–XII	,, ,,	3s.
,,	Bucolics	Jerram	2s. 6d.
,,	Georgics, I, II	,,	2s. 6d.
,,	,, III, IV	,,	2s. 6d.
,,	Aeneid I	,,	1s. 6d.
,,	,, IX	Haigh	2s.
Introduction to Latin Syntax		Gibson	2s.

II. GREEK CLASSICS.

Author.	Work.	Editor.	Price.
Aeschylus	Agamemnon	Sidgwick	3s.
,,	Choephoroi	,,	3s.
,,	Eumenides	,,	3s.
,,	Prometheus Bound	Prickard	2s.
Aristophanes	Acharnians	Merry	3s.
,,	Birds	,,	3s. 6d.
,,	Clouds	,,	3s.
,,	Frogs	,,	3s.
,,	Knights	,,	3s.
Cebes	Tabula	Jerram	2s. 6d.
Demosthenes	Orations against Philip, Vol. I, Philippic I, Olynthiacs I-III	Abbott & Matheson	3s.
,,	Vol. II, De Pace, Philippic II, De Chersoneso, Philippic III	,, ,,	4s. 6d.
Euripides	Alcestis	Jerram	2s. 6d.
,,	Cyclops	Long	2s. 6d.
,,	Hecuba	Russell	2s. 6d.
,,	Helena	Jerram	3s.
,,	Heraclidae	,,	3s.
,,	Iphigenia in Tauris	,,	3s.
,,	Medea	Heberden	2s.
Herodotus	Selections	Merry	2s. 6d.
,,	Book IX	Abbott	3s.
Homer	Iliad I-XII	Monro	6s.
,,	,, I	,,	2s.
,,	,, III	Tatham	1s. 6d.
,,	,, XIII-XXIV	Monro	6s.
,,	Odyssey I-XII	Merry	5s.
,,	,, I	,,	1s. 6d.
,,	,, II	,,	1s. 6d.
,,	,, VII-XII	,,	3s.
,,	,, XIII-XXIV	,,	5s.

II. GREEK CLASSICS.

Author.	Work.	Editor.	Price.
Lucian	Vera Historia	Jerram	1s. 6d.
Lysias	Epitaphius	Snell	2s.
Plato	Apology	Stock	2s. 6d.
,,	Meno	,,	2s. 6d.
,,	Crito	,,	2s.
,,	Selections	Purves	5s.
Plutarch	Lives of the Gracchi	Underhill	5s.
Sophocles	(Complete)	Campbell & Abbott	10s. 6d.
,,	Ajax	,, ,,	2s.
,,	Antigone	,, ,,	1s. 9d.
,,	Electra	,, ,,	2s.
,,	Oedipus Coloneus	,, ,,	1s. 9d.
,,	Oedipus Tyrannus	,, ,,	2s.
,,	Philoctetes	,, ,,	2s.
,,	Trachiniae	,, ,,	2s.
Theocritus	Idylls, &c.	Kynaston	4s. 6d.
Xenophon	Easy Selections	Phillpotts & Jerram	3s. 6d.
,,	Selections	Phillpotts	3s. 6d.
,,	Anabasis I	Marshall	2s. 6d.
,,	,, II	Jerram	2s.
,,	,, III	Marshall	2s. 6d.
,,	,, IV	,,	2s.
,,	,, Vocabulary	,,	1s. 6d.
,,	Cyropaedia I	Bigg	2s.
,,	Cyropaedia IV, V	,,	2s. 6d.
,,	Hellenica I, II	Underhill	3s.
,,	Memorabilia	Marshall	4s. 6d.

Easy Greek Reader	Abbott		3s.
First Greek Reader	Rushbrooke		2s. 6d.
A Greek Testament Primer	Miller		3s. 6d.

Oxford: CLARENDON PRESS.
London: HENRY FROWDE,
Oxford University Press Warehouse, Amen Corner, E.C.

www.ingramcontent.com/pod-product-compliance
Lightning Source LLC
Chambersburg PA
CBHW020918230426
43666CB00008B/1487